BITTER CHOCOLATE

ALSO BY CAROL OFF

The Lion, The Fox and The Eagle
The Ghosts of Medak Pocket

BITTER CHOCOLATE

ANATOMY OF AN INDUSTRY

CAROL OFF

THE NEW PRESS

NEW YORK
LONDON

Requests for permission to reproduce selections from this book should be mailed to: Permissions Department, The New Press, 120 Wall Street, 31st floor, New York, NY 10005.

First published in Canada by Random House Canada, Toronto, 2006
First published in the United States by The New Press, New York, 2008
This paperback edition published by The New Press, 2014
Distributed by Perseus Distribution

ISBN 978-1-59558-980-4 (paperback)
ISBN 978-1-59558-984-2 (e-book)

The Library of Congress has cataloged the hardcover edition as follows:

Off, Carol.
Bitter chocolate : the dark side of the world's most seductive sweet / Carol Off.
    p. cm.
  "First published by Random House Canada, Toronto, c2006."
  Includes bibliographical references and index.
  ISBN 978-1-59558-330-7 (hbk.)
  1. Chocolate industry. 2. Cocoa trade. 3. Chocolate industry–History. 4. Cocoa trade–Social aspects. 5. Chocolate industry–Moral and ethical aspects.   I. Title.
HD9200.A2O34 2008
338.1'7374–dc22

                                                                    2007043501

The New Press publishes books that promote and enrich public discussion and understanding of the issues vital to our democracy and to a more equitable world. These books are made possible by the enthusiasm of our readers; the support of a committed group of donors, large and small; the collaboration of our many partners in the independent media and the not-for-profit sector; booksellers, who often hand-sell New Press books; librarians; and above all by our authors.

www.thenewpress.com

TEXT DESIGN BY CS RICHARDSON

Printed in the United States

10 9 8 7 6 5 4 3 2 1

TO THE CHILDREN OF SINIKOSSON AND TO
GUY-ANDRÉ KIEFFER, WHO GAVE HIS LIFE IN THE
PURSUIT OF THE TRUTH ABOUT THEIR WORLD

CONTENTS

IN THE GARDEN OF **GOOD AND EVIL**

"In my dreams I gorge on chocolates, I roll in chocolates, and
their texture is not brittle but soft as flesh, like a thousand little
mouths on my body, devouring me in fluttering small bites. To
die beneath their tender gluttony is the culmination of every
temptation I have known."

—JOANNE HARRIS, *Chocolat*

THE BROAD HIGHWAY LEADING OUT OF THE CITY OF
Abidjan is marked on the map of Côte d'Ivoire as a principal two-
lane thoroughfare, but with the city behind us, it narrows quickly
and degenerates into a potholed road no wider than a driveway.
Tangled vines and shrubbery encroach on both sides of our vehicle while we push through what resembles a dark, leafy tunnel.
Constant precipitation—a perpetual cycle from warm mist to
torrential thundershowers to steam—seems to stimulate new jungle growth before my eyes.

Koffi Benoît is at the wheel on this excursion into the unknown.
He's an unflappable Ivorian, and I would trust him in any situation. Ange Aboa is our principal guide into *la brousse*, as he calls
it—the bush. Ange is a reporter for the Reuters news agency and
spends much of his time in Côte d'Ivoire's backcountry trying to
make some sense of the murky, muddled world of African business. Together, we travel west out of Abidjan, deep into the tropical forests and remote farm country that stretches for hundreds of
kilometres towards the Liberian border. Our mission is to seek

out the truth about Côte d'Ivoire's most precious commodity, cocoa.

My two companions know the bush country well, but they are perpetual strangers here where people trust only their own clans. We need help from local residents if we are to penetrate the walls of history and vegetation and probe the mysteries within. In a small village, we meet up with Noël Kabora, a seasoned *pisteur* who travels the tiny *pistes*, or back trails, every day as he makes his rounds of farms, gathering sacks of cocoa beans from the farmers. Abandoning the relative comfort of Benoît's Renault for Noël's dilapidated truck, we turn off the highway and head deep into the bush. Ange has moved to the back of the truck to chat with some local people while I sit in the cab with Noël. Benoît decides to stay behind and have tea with some newfound friends.

Nearly half of all the cocoa in the world comes out of this humid West African jungle and eventually finds its way into the confections that enrich the diets and the moods of chocolate lovers around the world. The bonbons, truffles, hot chocolate, cookies, cakes, ice cream sundaes and the ubiquitous chocolate bars; the sweet morsels that ostensibly say, "I love you" on Valentine's Day, "Merry Christmas," "Happy Birthday," the Halloween treats; the Easter eggs—they started the long journey into our stomachs and our ceremonies here in this tropical hothouse. Yet I could not be farther away from those cherished ceremonies of life, the pageants of celebration and happiness in the developed world, than I am driving along these rutted paths through the jade-coloured forests of Côte d'Ivoire.

Noël points out the cocoa groves tucked in among the tall banana trees, the mangoes and the palms. Exotic green, yellow and red cocoa pods, the size of butternut squash, cling precariously to the smooth trunks of the trees called, in Latin, *Theobroma cacao*—"food of the gods." Farmers lop the ripe pods from the bark with machetes and split them open to harvest the riches within: dozens of grey-purple seeds the size of almonds embedded in pale tan-coloured pulp. Through the bushes, we can see the racks and mats where the contents of the pods are piled up to ferment for days in the humid heat, producing a marvellous alchemy in which the seeds steep in the sweet, sticky juice from the pulp while sweltering in the hot tropical sun.

Micro-organisms in the fetid pile go to work, stirring into action about four hundred different chemicals and organic substances that magically transform a bland bean into the raw material that is the essence of the world's most seductive sweet. After five or six days of malodorous mulling, the beans are then laid out on racks to dry. This delicate series of operations, augmented by manufacturing techniques, has made chocolate addicts out of millions of people around the world throughout history. Children invest meagre allowances for just a bite of it; some women say they prefer fine chocolate to sex; and modern science claims for chocolate myriad potential health benefits, from reducing cholesterol to boosting libido. Chocolate is the embodiment of temptation. It creates a mysterious addiction, which, in turn, sustains a vast international trade and an industry with a seemingly insatiable appetite for raw product. For their survival, the captains of the chocolate industry depend on these remote farms and the *pisteurs* who make daily excursions into the bush, gathering sacks of carefully fermented and dried cocoa beans.

Noël expertly navigates a mind-boggling road that seems at times to disappear completely. He points towards the tops of hills where groves of cocoa trees grope for sunlight and comments knowingly on the quality of each farmer's produce, noting the ones who have perfected drying and fermenting and castigaing those whose beans are always dirty. From time to time, we can see a little one-room schoolhouse or tiny chapel surrounded by the poor mud houses of the people who cultivate "the food of the gods."

Farmers in this region have been growing the world's cocoa for a relatively short time—since the 1970s and '80s, when Côte d'Ivoire's benevolent dictator and founding father, Félix

Houphouët-Boigny, realized that this fecund farmland could grow a botanical equivalent of gold. He wanted to transform his post-colonial country, just reclaimed from France, into the economic engine of West Africa. In the 1960s Houphouët-Boigny announced that he would turn the jungle into Eden and everyone who lived here would enjoy the fruits of their own labour. The creationist vision worked and, for a time, Côte d'Ivoire became arguably the most profitable and stable country on the continent, mostly through providing the world with cocoa. All that has changed.

Le Vieux, as Ivorians affectionately called Houphouët-Boigny, was the nation's strongman, and when he died in 1993 the mantle of power passed to men of much lesser vision and much greater avarice. Côte d'Ivoire has been sliding into chaos and violence ever since, particularly in the coveted cocoa groves, where a low-grade war continues, despite ceasefires, to reduce this paradise to purgatory—and sometimes hell. Much of the fighting is over ownership of cocoa-producing land, as conflicting armies and paramilitaries vie for control of Côte d'Ivoire's immense agricultural wealth. All of those involved in cocoa production are under constant threat of attack.

Noël Kabora is wary as he makes his rounds, gathering jute bags full of cocoa for shipment out of the great ports of the Gulf of Guinea to factories and, ultimately, the candy counters of North America and Europe. At regular intervals along the trail I see the sacks stacked hopefully, despite the menace. Ultimately, war doesn't interrupt a commercial venture that seems to be the economic salvation of everyone around here. Soldiers are paid with cocoa profits, and they know enough not to impede its movement. But that doesn't prevent the armed militiamen— who are everywhere—from augmenting their incomes through extortion. We encounter numerous roadblocks with demands for "special" fees. We hand over money to armed thugs who reek of cheap palm wine and do nothing to conceal their contempt for a foreigner such as myself, though Noël says he faces their loathing every day. He too is a foreigner, from the neighbouring country of Burkina Faso, and as such he is often the subject of both racism and robbery by armed forces.

Our old cocoa truck coughs and wheezes up a steep hill, spinning its bald tires in the slick red mud for the final climb. We arrive at a collective farm run by people who are also originally from Burkina Faso. The village is called Sinikosson, which in the official French language of Côte d'Ivoire translates into "*Faite pour Demain*" and in English means "Made for Tomorrow." In fact, the villagers seem to make everything for today, living hand to mouth with little remaining for tomorrow. They grow some corn and cassava and cultivate bananas for food, but their primary activity here is to produce cocoa for the international market. As such, they earn just enough money from cocoa sales to pay for rice and cooking oil. There's usually nothing left over.

As remote as the community is, it is also the poorest I have seen in the region. Everyone looks tired and hungry, but at least for the time being the village has escaped the violence in the surrounding countryside. The drunken Ivorian soldiers we met at the last roadblock couldn't exert themselves to come all the way up here to either conquer or extort.

The arrival of a visitor from a faraway country is an extraordinary event in Sinikosson. Within minutes, the covered verandah of the central house in the village is crowded with people—all of them men and boys. The few women and girls who are visible remain a discreet distance away, preparing a meagre meal of rice and maize. But it is obvious that they are trying to hear what is going on.

The village elders want an exchange of news. What is happening with the war? Will there be more French peacekeepers? The ones already in the region, brought in to protect villages from attack, don't seem to be much help. Will there be elections, as the government has pledged?

They tell me their village has been here since 1980, when they first came to work for local landowners and then to grow their own cocoa under a crop-sharing arrangement. There was a lot of fertile virgin territory then but very few workers, and Le Vieux lured thousands of poor farmers away from the depleted lands of neighbouring Burkina Faso and Mali to settle here and drive his economic miracle. At the time they were happy to do so but their existence here is now tenuous. No one has ever given these Burkinabè farmers any legal title to the land they have been cultivating now for decades. They have no deeds or documents to support their claims to ownership yet they believe that the land is theirs. And, morally, it is. But their future here is based on vague memories of handshakes and promises made while Houphouët-Boigny was still alive. Nobody has yet seriously challenged their claim, though it's only a matter of time.

The community's livelihood comes from growing "the food of the gods," but this is a long way from paradise. None of the children here go to school, and there are no services—no electricity, no phones, no clinics or hospitals. The farmers eke out an existence here in the hills, in a land infested by volatile gunmen. Yet they seem satisfied. Even in the midst of all the trouble around them, they say they are better off than they would be in their drought-stricken home country, where people are chronically hungry.

I explain to them that I am writing a book about cocoa. They all nod. Cocoa is something about which they have immense knowledge. The quality of beans, the capricious rains, the unpredictable harvests, the cost of pesticides, the threat of witch's broom (a disease of the _Theobroma_ tree), the see-saw prices and the exorbitant government taxes. These farmers know everything about the difficulties of growing cocoa in this region.

"What would you do if you couldn't grow cocoa anymore?" we ask.

"A catastrophe," one man answers, and they all look very grim.

"This is our life," declares the chief, Mahamad Sawadago. He tells me he is fifty-four, but he looks many years older. Three of the women here are his wives; he has eleven children.

"Where does the cocoa go after it leaves here?" Ange asks the villagers. There is a confused silence, and everyone turns to Mahamad.

"It goes to the great port of San Pedro," the chief explains with authority, "and then on to people in Europe and America." They all nod.

"What do those people do with the cocoa beans?"

Silence again, and everyone looks to the chief. But this time, he too seems puzzled.

"I don't know," he answers honestly.

He's certain they make something with it, for sure, but he doesn't know what.

They make chocolate, I explain. Has anyone ever tasted chocolate? One man says he tried it once when he was away from the village and thought it tasted good. No one else even knows what it is.

Even Ange Aboa, who reports on the Ivorian cocoa industry, is surprised by how little these people know about the commodity they harvest. Ange tears a sheet of paper from his notebook and rolls it up into an oval tube. He explains that people in the West grind up the cocoa and add lots of sugar to make little bars this size. The bars are quite sweet and delicious. Sometimes milk and even peanuts are added. Children in Europe and America often get such things as treats.

Ange goes on to explain that one of these bars costs about 500 West African francs (roughly equivalent to a Canadian dollar). Their eyes widen in disbelief. The sum strikes them as staggering for such a small treat—almost enough to buy a good-sized chicken or an entire bag of rice. It represents more than the value of one boy's work for three days, if they are being paid at all, which I'm sure they are not. I explain that a child in my country will consume such a chocolate bar within minutes. The boys look awed. Days of their effort consumed in a heartbeat on the other side of the world. And yet they don't begrudge North American children such pleasure. West Africans rarely express envy.

As I look at the young faces, the questions in their eyes are the measure of a vast gulf between the children who eat chocolate on their way to school in North American and those who have no school at all, who must, from childhood, work to survive. And I feel the profound irony before me: the children who struggle to produce the small delights of life in the world I come from have never known such pleasure, and most likely, they never will.

It's a measure of the separation in our worlds, a distance now so staggeringly vast . . . the distance between the hand that picks the cocoa and the hand that reaches for the chocolate bar.

I tell the boys of Sinikosson who do not know what chocolate is that most people in my country who eat chocolate don't know where it comes from. The people in my country have no idea who picks the cocoa beans or how those people live. The boys of Sinikosson think it would be a good idea if I told them.

Chapter One

DEATH BY CHOCOLATE

"The main benefit of this cacao is a beverage which they make called chocolate, which is a crazy valued thing in that country. It disgusts those who are not used to it, for it has a foam on top, or a scum-like bubbling . . . It is a valued drink which the Indians offer to the lords who come to pass through their land. And the Spanish men—and even more the Spanish women—are addicted to this black chocolate."

—José de Acosta, *National and Moral History of the Indies, 1590*

THE STORY BEGINS IN THE PREDAWN OF HUMAN HISTORY, more than three thousand years ago. At least, that's the beginning we can glean from the scant records of Meso-American people, about whom we know only fragments: the Olmec. And it probably begins with women, harvesting the colourful gourds from the dappled limbs of wild cocoa trees then liberating beans from the pulpy interior; mashing them to a fatty, viscous goo mixed with water and starch and then dispensed among the more elevated classes of their people.

The staple of the Olmec diet was maize, which sat overnight in tall urns filled with water and wood ash, or sometimes lime and the pulverized shells of snails. In the thin light of the early day, the women scooped out the dissolved mixture and washed away the transparent hulls. They'd beat the grain into a doughy mass, then serve it to the masters often fortified by the dark,

9

magical substance they'd extracted from the bean called *kakawa*, or, as we know it, cocoa.

It was a perfect gastronomical marriage. The starchy maize absorbed much of the heavy, fatty cocoa butter and made it more digestible, while the rich flavours of the bean gave the mixture zest. The Olmec women served it as thick, bitter-tasting drink, stimulating, nourishing and—they believed—healing as well. The wisest among the Olmec would have been hard pressed to explain the origins or the mysterious chemistry of this dark and bitter additive. Why it seemed to restore the weak and add vigour to even the strongest among them; why adversity seemed more manageable and pleasures more enjoyable under its benevolent influence; how it helped them through their daily challenges—fatigue, despair and even, among their warriors, fear. But time and custom had evolved a deep, unshakeable faith in the beneficial properties of cocoa. The purity and potency of an Olmec chocolate cocktail is impossible to come by nowadays—the mass-produced and processed product we know as chocolate is a pale substitute. But one thing is consistent: then and now, chocolate is a luxury consumed by the privileged at the cost of those much less so. For thousands of years, the chocolate cravings of an elite have been satisfied by the hard labour of an underclass.

~

Theobroma grows in a band around the world, hugging the equator, and thriving only where there are perfect temperatures and plentiful moisture. But three thousand years ago, when the Olmec first harvested its riches, cocoa could be found only in the dense tropical rain forests of Central America and southern Mexico. According to American anthropologists Sophie and Michael Coe, the same fecund climate that allows cocoa to thrive also provided the perfect conditions for destroying written records about its cultivation, as well as many of the Olmec's more fragile artifacts. What did survive were some of the most renowned and recognizable Meso-American relics: giant stone heads with smooth faces as inscrutable as the history that time erased.

According to the Coes, the Olmec were probably the first people in the Americas to form a class-based society in which a select few were able to live comfortably off the toil of those less fortunate. Olmec clans established permanent villages and relied on agriculture for their economic well-being. Making use of a servant class, they developed sophisticated methods for preparing food, not least among them the first known recipes for cocoa.

Archaeologists have never settled the dispute over the relationship between the Olmec and the Maya—whether they were descendants, trading partners or simply neighbours. Olmec civilization mysteriously disappeared around the same time as the Maya rose to dominate the region, in the first or second century AD. But it's clear that the Maya built upon the centuries of wisdom and know-how of their predecessors, including the fine art of making cocoa concoctions.

Over many centuries, the Maya came to occupy parts of the countries now known as Belize, Honduras and Guatemala, as well as the Yucatán peninsula of Mexico. These fertile, humid lands supported the highest-quality cocoa beans ever to be found, in particular the bean known as the Criollo, a variety as coveted by today's chocolate-makers as Cabernet Sauvignon grapes are by wine snobs. For over two thousand years, Mayan civilization rivalled or surpassed anything found in Classical Greece and Rome, while Mayan pottery, ceramics, painting and textiles dazzled all who saw them. The Maya built pyramids, stone houses, parks and gardens in their stately cities. And the culinary delights they made from cocoa would confound even the most advanced modern-day chocolatier.

We know something of how the Maya prepared their chocolate drinks from surviving manuscripts and also from the detailed scenes of court life depicted on pottery and frescoes. For *cacahuatl,* literally "cocoa water," the beans were soaked, aerated, ground and then mixed with a wide range of spices and flavours, including chili pepper, flowers, vanilla and herbs, along with edible dyes. Occasionally, Mayan aristocrats took their chocolate sweet, with honey added to it; but it was always mixed with ground corn, making the beverage a kind of thin gruel. Key to the enjoyment of chocolate was a topping of frothy bubbles. Cocoa liquid was poured from one vessel to another—splashed, really—to beat air into the mixture. The cook would stand holding a pitcher of *cacahuatl* and transfer the contents into a second jug placed on the floor—the extra height presumably increased the bubble content—as lords, high-ranking warriors and honoured dinner guests looked on raptly. The cocoa would then be served in cups of calabash or clay, depending on the status of the guest. The foam (some Europeans called it scum) was consumed first, as a special treat.

As befits a food of divine provenance, cocoa was also associated with religious rituals and the worship of various deities. In the Dresden Codex, one of the few surviving texts of this age, gods are depicted seated on thrones holding cocoa pods and dishes heaped with cocoa beans. Another image, of the New Year ceremonies, shows the opossum god holding the rain god on his back and providing cocoa for his food. A drawing in the Madrid Codex shows gods piercing their ears and sprinkling their blood over the cocoa harvest, indicating a strong association between blood and cocoa in Meso-American tradition. Humans were often sacrificed to guarantee a good cocoa harvest. First, the prisoner was forced to drink a cup of chocolate—sometimes spiked with blood—as the Maya believed it would convert the victim's heart into a cocoa pod. Temple priests devised many elaborate means of slaughter: beheading, throat slitting, crushing, hurling from towers or extracting the still-beating heart. After the poor wretch had expired, the presumably transubstantiated organ was offered to the gods.

The Popol Vuh, a manuscript believed to originate with the Izapan (who were closely associated with the Olmec and likely passed on the secrets of chocolate to the Maya), shows cocoa as a divine product, awarded to human beings from the mythical Mountain of Sustenance. In a particularly vivid story, one of the so-called hero twins—the children of the man and woman who created the universe—is decapitated. His head is then posted on a cocoa tree, where it manages to impregnate the ruler's daughter, who gives birth to other hero twins. These offspring subsequently save humankind from the evil denizens of the underworld.

By the ninth century, Mayan territory was vast and its culture well developed. But as often happens when great cultures turn imperial, Mayan generals became belligerent. As the empire expanded, the Maya were obliged to wage frequent wars to defend their holdings from a host of enemies. The conquered tribes of the Mayan empire rarely added up to a coherent society, though Mayan cities were as densely overpopulated as some of the large urban centres of the world today. The aristocracy grew decadent and wasteful as the Maya denuded their forests and depleted their farmlands.

Anthropologists call it the "Classic Maya Collapse," the time when Mayan civilization seems to have caved under its own weight. Environmental degradation, chronic warfare, natural disasters and, finally, a revolt by people in the working class against the elites all contributed to the downfall, though it's not clear why the disintegration was so sudden and so complete. While a modest population of Maya survives to this day, by the end of the tenth century, the grand Mayan empire was gone.

~

Christopher Columbus met Maya, or a part of their diminished numbers, on his last trip to the New World in 1502. Off the coast of what we now call Honduras, the famed explorer and his men spotted boats as awesome to the Europeans as their own caravels must have appeared to the natives. They saw two enormous dugout canoes—each about fifteen metres long, propelled by slaves and navigated by people wearing elaborate garb—more ornate than anything Columbus had found in all of his travels to the Americas.

Columbus was looking for land and wealth, though, not cultural experiences. He didn't have the time or energy to explore the Honduran coast or to learn more about its people. Nonetheless, the admiral did order the mysterious boats seized, and from this encounter Columbus acquired some fleeting knowledge of the Maya while they still had a glimmer of their former glory. The canoes were filled with consumer goods, mostly food but also cloth and objects of admirable craftsmanship.

The most curious discovery was of some strange brown almond-shaped beans. Columbus's son, Ferdinand, recorded what he saw in this way: "They seemed to hold these almonds at a great price; for when they were brought on board [Columbus's ship] together with their goods, I observed that when any of these almonds fell, they all stooped to pick it up, as though an eye had fallen." This was the outside world's first encounter with cocoa, a substance later destined to be transformed into the international capstone of confections and laid as the foundation of a multi-billion-dollar industry. But beyond Ferdinand's amused recollections, Columbus had nothing more to do with the beans or the Maya. He went on his way and eventually returned to Spain, disappointed and frustrated that he was unable to find a passage to Asia.

The Maya did tell Columbus something of great interest to him, news he passed on to others: Deeper into the continent and well into the mountain plateaus of the interior, there was an even grander and more commanding civilization than anything the Europeans had yet encountered in the New World. This was the land of the Aztecs, fierce warriors who had not only conquered the former Mayan territory but also built upon the knowledge and craftsmanship of all the other Meso-American people.

If the Europeans thought the Maya appeared stunning, they would be unprepared for the opulence and grandeur of the Aztecs. Their monarch was a man feared and loathed by all tribes throughout the New World, a man whose cruelty and rapaciousness was exceeded only by his depravity and decadence. Among his excesses was one that would later earn him the moniker of The Chocolate King.

Motecuhzoma Xocoyotzin, ninth emperor of the Aztecs, known in popular history as Montezuma II, was undoubtedly one of the wealthiest and most powerful men in the world when he took the Aztec throne in 1502, the same year Columbus made his final voyage, though at the time Montezuma knew nothing of the universe beyond his own vast domain. And the outside world knew of him only as a rumour.

Montezuma's great capital, Tenochtitlán, undoubtedly the biggest city anywhere in the world at that time, was built on an island in the salt lake of Texcoco—where Mexico City is today—while the territory under his control stretched to both the Pacific Coast and the Gulf of Mexico and extended south for about two hundred kilometres to present-day Nicaragua. The population of Montezuma's empire is estimated to have been between six and seven million people of different tribes, including the Maya.

Historians describe Montezuma as a ruthless and despotic leader who was obsessed with conquering territory and who murdered thousands of his subjects in ritual sacrifices. The fact remains, however, that under Montezuma, the Aztecs also developed a sophisticated and advanced society. Splendid houses for generals and noblemen lined the wide avenues stretching through Tenochtitlán. State-financed canal systems and aqueducts fashioned from bricks and mortar provided both a source of fresh water and transportation for the capital. Engineering, architecture, mathematics and music flourished. The Aztecs

loved books—specifically those about themselves—and they created an extensive record of their existence. Traders with goods
from across the empire and even beyond its borders came to the
bustling markets of Tenochtitlán, and as many as sixty thousand
people could swell the central squares on any given day. This was
a civilization to rival anything in Europe at the time, an Emerald
City in an uncharted continent.

Great banquets and feasts were routine in Montezuma's court,
where several hundred different dishes might grace his tables,
even though the emperor was said to be a spare eater. He shared
these feasts with his noblemen, his warriors and the long-
distance traders whose job it was to bring the vast stores of wealth
back to Tenochtitlán from all of the Aztec-controlled provinces.

No matter what else was on the menu, the highlight was one
of the most coveted foodstuffs in all the Meso-American culture:
cacahuatl. Vessels of liquid cocoa concluded meals, though
Montezuma refreshed himself with cups between courses. In
fact, he consumed vast quantities of cocoa daily, taking his frothy
beverage in mugs of painted calabash and never drinking twice
from the same cup.

As it was for the Maya, the preparation and consumption of
cacahuatl was an entirely elitist pursuit, far out of the reach of
the common folk and a luxury even for those who harvested the
beans. Cocoa was such a valued commodity that it was beans,
not bullion, that served as the coins of the realm in Montezuma's
treasury and the empire's official currency. At the height of his
power, the emperor had a stash of nearly a billion cocoa beans,
all extracted begrudgingly from the hard labour of his empire.

Montezuma's warriors were treated as nobles, and as such
they consumed cocoa as well, but they also took *cacahuatl* on
their conquests. The Aztecs had developed the first solid chocolate bars or tablets, portable nourishment that was later dissolved in water to make a drink. A chunk of rehydrated cocoa
could sustain a man over a long day of trekking and provide

sustenance to soldiers while they put down insurrections and sacked villages. Montezuma's uncompromising warriors helped make Tenochtitlán the superpower of Central America. No army could stand up to them.

As with so many other luxury goods in the Aztec capital, cocoa didn't come from the lands around Tenochtitlán, where the soil and climate was inhospitable to such tropical plants, but from the farthest reaches of the empire, particularly the highly fertile cocoa-producing region of Xoconocho, where the prized Criollo beans flourished. This coveted and prolific parcel of land on the Pacific Coast is now the Chiapas region of Mexico, but Xoconocho also included a part of what is now Guatemala. A twice-yearly supply of two hundred loads of the precious beans (the fruit of about 160,000 pods) had to be delivered from Xoconocho to Tenochtitlán, but even this was not enough to satisfy the capital. Other beans came from the conquered Tabasco region of the Maya and from the area around what the Spanish would later call Vera Cruz, the original source of Olmec chocolate production. Cocoa bean consumption in the capital was insatiable, and the demand on farmers and serfs was crippling.

Montezuma had been an impressive leader when he first came to power in 1502. He had the unusual distinction of being trained as both a soldier and a priest—considered stabilizing professions, and ideal preparation for a future Aztec ruler. As a young emperor, he often led his armies on their warring expeditions, while on the domestic front, his public aqueducts and canal systems rivalled anything to be found in civilization.

But it was all too good to last. After only two decades, the reign of Montezuma changed fundamentally, setting in motion forces that would, over time, destroy his empire. He suddenly stopped appearing in public and cut off contact with all but select members of his inner circle. Soon half of the people under his dominion were employed in the business of suppressing insurrections by the other half. Montezuma's taxes, necessary to pay for the lavish excesses at his court, had become exorbitant. Eventually, the gluttonous, drunken banquets became too much for a people who were, at heart, a pious and puritanical lot. The decadent, pleasure-driven Aztec court, of which the arrogant Montezuma was both symbol and a centrepiece, turned even his most loyal subjects against him.

Montezuma had enemies everywhere, yet he believed his large and ruthless army, energized by loyalty and cocoa, was more than enough to keep his poor and disorganized enemies at bay. But there was one thing Montezuma's sublime confidence and military muscle couldn't handle: the intangible power of a prophecy.

Aztecs believed their culture to be superior and their mastery over others to be a God-given right. They believed their society came about through divine intervention, that they were directed to their island stronghold capital by the god Quetzalcoatl, ruler of civilization and lord of the forces of good and light. But Aztec religious belief held that Quetzalcoatl would return one day with a host of white-skinned gods sporting long beards, and that these strangers would claim their rightful ownership of the Aztec throne. The predicted time for the arrival of these strange creatures was upon them. And according to the prophecy, the emperor would be unable to resist their power.

~

Charles V, a Hapsburg and the Holy Roman Emperor, was also the King of Spain (in his role as the Spanish monarch, he was also Charles I). In 1519, while Montezuma presided over a vast but uncertain empire, Charles enjoyed authority over a newly united and emboldened Spain, finally liberated from eight centuries of domination by the Islamic Moors. Not only was Charles the sovereign of a strong and expansive Spanish dominion, but he also had a large and growing collection of colonies around the globe. Spain was rapidly becoming the biggest and most influential imperial power in Europe. But Charles wanted to expand his wealth and control over even more of the world. Fantastic rumours of rich societies in yet-undiscovered places beyond the western sea persuaded him to secure more territory for the greater good of Spain by financing a band of avaricious and uncompromising mariners and soldiers to pursue his interests. They would come to be known collectively as the conquistadors.

Hernán Cortés was one of them. He was an artillery officer based in Cuba, already in his thirties, facing a limited future with few opportunities for advancement and little hope of ever getting rich. Cortés was young and quite handsome, a broad-shouldered lady's man who had abandoned his law studies and fled to the Caribbean at the age of nineteen to escape the jealous husband of his lover. Though he had grown up in privilege, he was a relative nobody in the overcrowded colony of Cuba, Spain's base in the New World and holding bay for its treasure fleet.

In 1519, Cortés was competing with too many others for promotion. The young officer had none of the experience of the soldiers under his command, men who had honed their military skills in the barbaric battles of the Moorish wars. But while Cortés may not have been as skilled or as bloodthirsty as the older men, he was certainly as acquisitive.

Diego Velasquez, the governor of Cuba, was anxious to invade the coastal areas of the Gulf of Mexico before others did, chasing rumours of gold and silver. He didn't entirely trust Cortés, but Velasquez had been impressed with the charismatic captain's abilities. The governor chose him to lead an important expedition into the heart of Mexico, promoting him to the rank of captain-general.

Cortés set sail for the Yucatán Peninsula on February 18, 1519, arriving on the mainland in early spring. He immediately renounced his prior loyalty to the governor in Cuba and founded his own capital: Villa Rica de la Vera Cruz (the "Rich Town of the True Cross"). So his men couldn't leave him, Cortés had all but one of his ships scuttled—filled with water and sunk up to their masts. Almost immediately Velasquez had lost control over Cortés's expedition. Though he betrayed his immediate sponsor, the newly minted captain-general knew enough to keep in the good books of the Spanish king.

Cortés understood that Charles was primarily interested in wealth and territory. But the monarch was also anxious to appear to be more than just another greedy acquisitor and he wanted his conquistadors to be more than just murderous, rapacious thugs. Charles instructed his officers to serve God as well as himself by converting to Christianity any Indians they encountered in the New World. Such a command gave the expeditions a veneer of noble purpose. No matter how savage the conquest, Spaniards— and their sovereign—could sleep at night in the knowledge that they were killing and conquering in the name of the Almighty. Cortés used his one remaining ship to dispatch letters to the royal palace in Spain, promising that he would give the poor wretches of the New World the Good News of Christianity and kindle a light in their pagan darkness while he conquered Mexico. King Charles replied that he heartily approved.

Along with his dubious piety, Charles also possessed a redeeming curiosity. He demanded more from his explorers than gold and territory. Because the native people in the new lands were to be his subjects, he wanted to know as much as possible about their customs and indigenous products. If not for this interest, Europe might never have learned about cocoa—or would have discovered it long after the extermination of any native who might have been able to explain the mysteries of its goodness and how it could be liberated from the unlovely cocoa bean.

There wasn't much interest in anthropology amongst the conquistadors. They were ravenous tourists, looking to see what they could cart away from the New World. But Cortés had also brought with him men of the cloth, whose job it was to convert the Indians. The priests also served as record-keepers, methodically investigating and describing the customs and habits of the native people. Among their most enduring discoveries would be the processing of cocoa beans, first into an edible paste, then into the various potions that were so popular in Meso-America.

The new Spanish settlement of Vera Cruz was in the middle of the former heartland of the Olmec and was one of the chief cocoa-producing regions of Mexico. Written records indicate that Cortés was obliged by native customs to drink *cacahualtl*. Though he never developed a taste for the New World beverage, he did start to understand its worth.

Cocoa as legal tender dated back to the Maya and was so entrenched in the monetary system of the Americas that counterfeiting cocoa beans out of painted clay or stone had become a thriving industry. Goods could be priced in units of cocoa: a slave cost 100 beans; the services of a prostitute, 10 beans; a turkey, a whopping 200 beans; the daily wage of a porter, 100 beans. Cortés quickly realized that the ugly cocoa bean had the economic clout of gold.

As he learned the customs of the region, Cortés also discovered that, far from being in a savage wilderness, he was on the edge of a vast empire that included millions of people from many tribes, each with its own language and customs. The centrepiece of this empire was the capital city on a mountain plateau located more than two hundred kilometres from Vera Cruz. The land between was hostile to foreigners, and the aggressive Indian warriors had fighting skills and tactics that were unfamiliar even to veterans of the dirty wars with the Muslim Moors. But the local people were also traders with a high level of political sophistication. They were formidable warriors who were also peacemakers amenable to treaties and arrangements that would advance mutual interests. Cortés soon learned from the natives that there was tremendous discontent with Montezuma and that many of the regions were anxious to be liberated from the grip of Tenochtitlán. Cortés said he could oblige them. And he sent word that he wanted to meet the great emperor.

~

Reports of the arrival of extraordinary-looking white men reached Tenochtitlán quickly. It wasn't long before Montezuma's agents were in Vera Cruz to investigate the strangers and the ships that looked like floating houses with wings. Ever mindful of the prophecy, the emperor wanted to know what these strangers looked like. He instructed his agents to produce drawings of Cortés and his men, their horses and their heavy weapons. When Montezuma's royal court saw the images, they were impressed by the cannon, but were staggered by the drawings of the Spaniards' sixteen horses—creatures they had never before seen.

Cortés had only about a thousand men, so the pictures exaggerated his power. But the ultimate impact of the drawings had little to do with conventional military assets. The images set before the great Montezuma played perfectly into the Quetzalcoatl prediction—that white men with beards would come to take their rightful place on the throne. For the Aztecs, the superstition was in the order of the second coming of the Messiah in Christian doctrine.

There had been disturbing portents that the fulfillment of the prophecy was near at hand. The new deities were expected to arrive at the end of a fifty-two-year cycle. The year 1519 marked the end of such a period. A series of natural disasters, coupled with repeated apparitions—the most frightening were reports of a faceless woman who had begun to appear at water wells—added to the foreboding. Montezuma and his court advisors were almost paralyzed by news of the visitors. After much consultation with his priests and his generals, the emperor concluded that it was pointless to resist. The newcomers were supernatural beings. To fight them would be futile. Yet even gods are vulnerable to flattery and gifts, and Montezuma dispatched an entourage that included one hundred slaves to carry the gifts he hoped would appease the aliens and send them home happy.

In his better days, Montezuma might have been less vulnerable, less likely to fold before the imaginary menace of an exposed and relatively weak intruder. But the increasingly arrogant and reclusive Aztec king was out of touch with both his empire and reality. Hernán Cortés, for his part, was a cunning and conniving manipulator. Back at his base camp in Vera Cruz, he accepted the gifts and listened patiently as Montezuma's emissaries explained that there could be no audience. Cortés then told them to return to the great man and convey the message that he had no intention of leaving without personally paying his respects and those of the king of Spain, whom he represented. With or without a formal invitation, he was going to drop in on Montezuma.

By Easter week of 1519, the conquistadors were ready to set off on their long trek to Tenochtitlán. Cortés delivered a pep talk calculated to inspire his men, whose basic instincts he well understood: "I hold out to you a glorious prize, but it is to be won by incessant toil. Great things are achieved only by great exertions and glory was never the reward of sloth. If I have laboured hard and staked my all on this undertaking, it is for the love of that renown, which is the noblest recompense of man. But, if any among you covet riches more, be but true to me, as I will be true to you and to the occasion, and I will make you masters of such as our countrymen have never dreamed of!"

For many months after they set off, the conquistadors were obliged to fight their way past Aztec loyalists, and by the time they had reached the Mexican plateau, almost every conquistador had been wounded at least twice. Even with the support of Montezuma's enemies, Cortés lost many of his soldiers in the fighting and also to the rigours of the debilitating tropical climate. The rainforests of Mexico and Central America are hospitable to poisonous snakes and reptiles as well as disease-bearing insects. There were several near-mutinies. These were soldiers of fortune, not disciplined fighters, here for plunder not for military valour, and so far they had nothing to show for their risks and exertions.

Luckily for Cortés, the army also included veterans of the fierce campaigns against the Moors, who had an uncompromising sense of warfare, none more so than Cortés's sadistic chief lieutenant, Pedro de Alvarado. He had, among other soldierly assets, a keen appreciation of the usefulness of torture. Intransigent groups of natives soon yielded to his skills, and the conquistadors slowly advanced towards the capital. Few native populations blocked the army's way for long, wilting before the cruelty of the Spaniards. But also, as Cortés had suspected, many of the tribes willingly joined his campaign, assuming that the contest was already decided in favour of the Spaniards.

For all their skills at warfare and their mastery of terrorism, the Spaniards were awestruck when they first set eyes on Tenochtitlán, shimmering in the distance. Could heathens have really built a city of such splendour? Cortés, and what was left of his forces, finally arrived at the Aztec capital on November 19, 1519. The achievement of simply getting there seemed sufficient to persuade Montezuma that, indeed, these Spaniards were possessed of godly power. He couldn't have been more mistaken about this motley crew of self-interested mercenaries.

Cortés, as the first European to stride into the heart of the Aztec empire, was at once both awed and alarmed by what he encountered inside its gates. He found a city of over 300,000 people, rivalling anything in Europe at the time. The island plateau habitat rose like an apparition before them, magnificent beyond compare. As Cortés describes it in colourful letters back to King Charles, he was met at the gates of the fortification by a thousand men, "all dressed richly after their own fashion." After he crossed the main bridge, "Montezuma came to greet us and with him were some two hundred lords, all barefoot and dressed in different costumes." Montezuma was the only noble wearing sandals.

Cortés was on horseback, which obviously enhanced the power of his presence. Since no one had never seen a horse before, the more impressionable might have thought at first glance that horse and rider were one. Cortés dismounted, walked towards Montezuma and, to the astonishment of all around, embraced the emperor though he'd been told it was strictly forbidden to touch him. Protocol required that he kneel before Montezuma and kiss the earth at his feet. Cortés, from the beginning, would make it clear that the world of the Aztec people was about to change dramatically.

The conquistadors could see from the size of the population and the potential fighting power of the throng surrounding Montezuma that, with or without horsemen, they were no match for the Aztecs. But to their surprise and obvious relief, Montezuma invited Cortés to enter his palace. There he pledged homage to Spain, declaring that his kingdom properly belonged to the white men. Cortés took Montezuma at his word and promptly placed him under house arrest.

Such an act of breathtaking arrogance was made possible by a convergence of tragically mistaken assumptions: that it was the destiny of the Aztecs to be ruled by godlike white men; and that it was the divine mission of the Spaniards to conquer and convert as much of the world as they could lay their hands on. Montezuma and his people were doomed by the emperor's pessimistic piety. And so, with the backing of fewer than a thousand men, the renegade Cortés defeated an indigenous nation of millions led by the most feared and ruthless figure in the Americas. Montezuma quickly submitted, converted to Christianity and deferred decision-making to his captors. The Spaniards decided to keep him nearby as a figurehead and to maintain the illusion that he was really still in charge. But not for long.

Cortés continued to send back glowing tributes to the king of Spain and to inform him of all his wonderful accomplishments, including his control over cocoa production. Cortés saw cocoa not as the essence of a dubiously scummy beverage, but as currency, reserving any gold he obtained for the king and, of course, for himself.

Metals such as gold and silver were so plentiful in Mexico that they were used by the Aztecs for decoration, not for money. The conquistadors, for their part, told the Indians that they suffered from an illness that required large amounts of gold to heal, and went so far as to claim that they ate gold. Here was the supreme irony: the conquistadors hoarded what they considered of value—gold—while the Aztecs hoarded cocoa. Montezuma's beans were crammed into vast storehouses, secured in a kind of chocolate Fort Knox.

The city of Tenochtitlán genuinely fascinated Cortés: "I cannot describe one hundredth part of all the things which could be mentioned," he wrote to King Charles, before going on to paint a picture of a truly great habitation. He described markets piled high with exotic goods, food stalls, barber shops, herbalists, couturiers and weavers. There was even an organized and publicly supported market police force whose job it was to make sure all transactions were conducted according to the law. Cortés wrote of temples, palaces and grand houses, all built with stone and fine woodwork: "Yet so as not to tire Your Highness with the description of this city . . . I will say only that these people live almost like those of Spain, and in much harmony and order as there, and considering that they are barbarous and so far from the knowledge of God and cut off from all civilized nations, it is truly remarkable to see what they have achieved in all things."

The Spaniards would soon help put an end to all that.

~

Cortés's betrayal of his former boss, Velasquez, came back to haunt him. The governor sent out a party to arrest the wayward conquistadors, compelling Cortés to return to Vera Cruz and confront the soldiers dispatched from Cuba. By the time Cortés had defeated Velasquez's force—or co-opted them by offering to share the gold—and returned to Tenochtitlán, he had lost control of the Aztec capital.

Pedro de Alvarado had been left in charge, and his innate ruthlessness had quickly provoked an insurrection. After mistaking a religious ceremony for rebellion, Alvarado ordered the slaughter of several thousand Indians. As a result, Cortés found himself in the middle of a full-fledged uprising, which he tried to get Montezuma to quell. When the emperor attempted to address the mob they jeered and stoned him.

Cortés and his men were compelled to flee Tenochtitlán and plan their return attack. The bloody battle that ensued is known in history as *la noche triste* (the sad night) for its bloodshed. Cortés then razed the city. Montezuma was killed—whether at the hands of the conquistadors or his own people is unclear. The once-dazzling Aztec empire was no more. Only a few items of value survived the sacking of Tenochtitlán, among them cocoa beans. But not because Cortés had any foresight that the intoxicating substance made from *Theobroma* fruit would have a future in Europe or would one day be the continent's favourite confection. Cocoa production survived because it was—literally—money growing on trees.

Chapter Two

LIQUID **GOLD**

"It seemed more a drink for pigs than a drink for humanity. I was in the country for more than a year and never wanted to taste [chocolate], and whenever I passed a settlement, and some Indian would offer me a drink of it, and would be amazed when I would not accept, going away laughing. But then, as there was a shortage of wine, so as not always to be drinking water, I did like the others."

—GIROLAMO BENZONI, *La Historia del Mondo*, 1565

CAPTAIN-GENERAL HERNÁN CORTÉS WAS QUICK TO PUT his conquered colony to work, using Indian labourers to mine gold and Indian farmers to supply food. They reconfigured Tenochtitlán as a European city, erecting a cathedral in honour of St. Francis on the site of an Aztec temple that Cortés's soldiers had destroyed. They laid the foundations for a new colony that would appeal to Spaniards living in the Caribbean and abroad, inducing them to settle and build grand estates. Over time colonists did just that, and the old Aztec stronghold became a modern urban capital: Mexico City.

The transformation from conquistador to colonist didn't lighten the heavy hand of the Spanish. The native people were obliged to be baptized before being able even to grind corn for their masters. But living together did require the Spaniards in the New World to accept some of the ways of the Indians, who were now their servants, slaves and, in many cases, brides and concubines. Gradually the two worlds fused—cultures, languages and cuisine.

Chocolate became a sensual bridge between the world of Montezuma and the triumphal Spaniard settlers, a perpetual reminder of an ancient, mysterious and lost civilization.

To suit cocoa to their own palates, the colonists modified the taste of native *cacahuatl* by adding large amounts of Caribbean sugar to the cocoa liquid. Some historians suggest it was Cortés himself who first added sweeteners, but it's more likely that the innovation came from Spanish priests and monks. Aztecs and Maya were known to have occasionally made chocolate more delectable with honey, and this probably inspired the clergy to experiment further.

Tinkering with ancient cocoa recipes was just a start. Familiarity with native customs bred, in some of the Spanish clergy, a certain admiration for the aboriginals, their culture and their history, in addition to their food. Saving the pagans from damnation required a certain social intimacy. And studying these savages up close gradually revealed unexpected depths of wisdom and sophistication. While they were preaching salvation, the Spanish priests were learning old secrets for surviving and thriving in the mysterious and dangerous New World.

The Franciscan monk Fray Bernardino de Sahagún was probably the most dedicated scholar in Meso-America, learning native languages and recording much of the lore that he acquired in a twelve-volume text: *General History of the Things of New Spain*. In his dissertation on food, Sahagún describes how an Indian chief would settle down contentedly after a long meal: "Then, by himself in his house, his chocolate was served: green cacao-pods, honeyed chocolate, flowered chocolate flavoured with green vanilla, bright red chocolate, *huitzecolli*-flower chocolate, flower-coloured chocolate, black chocolate, white chocolate."

Sahagún was also fascinated by Aztec and Mayan religion and went so far as to raise the scandalous idea that the Indians might not have been fallen beings after all. What if they were merely different manifestations of the Holy Spirit? It was the time of the

Inquisition, a period of systemic terror. People in Spain were facing rack and bonfire for such radical ideas. But the reality of experience in the New World had watered down many of the European certainties about the natural supremacy of Christianity. The missionaries were impressed by the civility and, indeed, morality they found among the natives.

Dominican missionaries were among the first to learn the detailed secrets of the Indian diet and to understand the central role of cocoa in native life. They learned to modify the native food to suit Spanish taste buds and developed a unique recipe for hot chocolate, a kind of trans-colonial brew. Meso-American cocoa was spiced with cinnamon and black pepper from Asia, sweetened with sugar from Cuba, coloured with achiote (a red-coloured dye) from the West Indies and spiked with almonds and hazelnuts from Spain. The concoction was served heated—one of the earliest forms of hot chocolate.

Cocoa underwent an etymological transformation as well. The word *cacahuatl*—cocoa water—became *chocolatl*, the root of the term used universally today. The anthropologist and chocolate historian Michael Coe speculates that the change could have been contrived to distance the product from the root of the word *kaka*. Europeans simply couldn't bear the association of excrement with the thick brown liquid to which they were becoming addicted. But the word *chocolatl* may have been simply another term, roughly translating as "bubbly water," that the Aztecs used for cocoa. In any event, *chocolatl* became the name of choice for the drink. The beans remained cacao or, after entering English usage and cuisine, cocoa.

~

Chocolate quickly became a mainstay of the hybrid Spanish-American diet as a beverage but also as a flavour to spike savoury gravies and stews. It took many more years, however, before cocoa crossed the ocean to fuse with Spanish culture on the European continent, though there's no evidence to credit Cortés with the auspicious introduction.

Cortés went to see King Charles shortly after the conquest of Mexico and brought along an extraordinary collection of wild animals, beautiful crafts and even people, including one of Montezuma's sons. But if cocoa beans were among the curiosities presented to the court, there is no mention of it in written records of the occasion. Cortés had certainly mentioned cocoa in his letters to the king—in 1520, he described a "divine drink, which builds up resistance & fights fatigue" and "permits man to walk for a whole day without food."

For men engaged in exploring and subduing an entire new continent, the value of such a potion hardly needed much elaboration. Yet Cortés's main source of fascination with the bean continued to be cocoa's monetary value in the New World. He was able to report to the king that, "they value [the bean] so highly that it is treated like currency throughout their land and they buy with it everything they need, in the markets and elsewhere."

The Spanish could use cocoa to pay for goods and services in their colony—even to pay the meagre wages of the miners and porters who dug gold and silver and dragged it to the waiting transport vessels; even for the land they grabbed for the estates of the nobility; even for the purchase of slaves and prostitutes.

While the soldiers and the nobles knew the monetary value of cocoa, it was the clergy who understood its worth as nourishment. For this reason, it is most likely that priests and monks introduced chocolate to Europe.

~

These were chaotic times in continental Europe. As Holy Roman Emperor, Spain's King Charles spent a lot of time away from home defending the realm from upstart dynasties in France and the far-flung Hapsburg empire. Imperialism is expensive, and Spaniards were struggling under the growing burden of war-driven taxation. To find himself master of new dominions rich with conventional resources and a local currency that grew on trees seemed to Charles like a gift from the Almighty.

By 1543, Charles, almost overwhelmed by imperial responsibilities, put his young son in charge of Spain. He saw to it that Philip, then just sixteen, was first well married and properly instructed in the affairs of state and then, despite his tender years, handed him the reins.

Philip was actually among the first European monarchs to seriously consider the effect Spain was having on those remote and difficult new territories and he disapproved of what he had heard about the abuse of Indians by the conquistadors. Philip's main source of information was an extraordinary priest—a Dominican named Bartolomé de Las Casas.

Throughout history, in the midst of all the crimes and errors of Christian zealotry committed against aboriginals in the Americas, individuals like Las Casas emerged who seemed genuinely committed to human rights and justice. The priest warned the political and religious hierarchy back home that Spain was embarked on a project that would be its ruin; the abuse of the natives was mortal sin on a massive scale, and it would bring the wrath of God upon his country. Las Casas's message was also pragmatic: the success of the New World project required the cooperation of the natives. Kindness and respect were more effective than coercion in winning the hearts and minds of those they needed as their willing partners. And he was shrewd enough to know that such a radical departure in colonial policy was going to need sympathetic support at the very top of the political system. From everything Las Casas had heard, Philip might be prepared to listen.

In 1544, a delegation of Dominicans, probably appointed by Las Casas, escorted a group of Kekchi Maya Indians to the

Spanish court. They were from Guatemala, a place of fertile valleys tucked among tall cloud-clad mountains, where the forests of Xoconocho yielded some of the finest cocoa in the New World. Though their empire was crushed and their numbers diminished, the Maya could still be as dazzling as they'd been nearly half a century before when first presented to Columbus on the shores of Honduras and also, as Las Casas had learned, just as defiant.

The Maya brought many gifts for Philip, all of them associated with their own ancient deities and monarchs: thousands of rare and valuable feathers from the colourful quetzal bird, traditionally used to adorn the headdress of their leaders; sacred copa, a tree resin used to make incense, lacquered gourds—and jars of prepared liquid chocolate.

Records of the encounter are silent on whether the teenaged monarch actually sampled the mysterious brown broth, full of froth and bubbles. But it was the first known formal introduction in Europe of what was destined to become the continent's most cherished treat. We can easily imagine the dramatic scene: a pale, curious teenaged prince surrounded by hooded monks and scantily clad copper-skinned Indians bedecked in feathers and beads, transfixed by a dark mélange in an ornate pot. It is less easy to imagine that any of them understood the social destiny of this vaguely noxious mixture.

The priests, inspired by the compassion of Las Casas, were thinking about human rights, not commerce, when they arranged the historic meeting between the young regent and his new subjects. Judged in that light, the visit was probably a failure. But it had the unanticipated effect of identifying the Dominicans as the proprietors of cocoa's mysteries, and it wouldn't be long before the friars were introducing their own recipes for cocoa treats to the Iberian court.

By the end of the century, cocoa was a crucial component of the trans-Atlantic trade. And soon the monks of Spain were busy turning out the new commodity. Monasteries had been involved in food production (and consumption) since the Middle Ages. Popular images of fat, waddling friars were inspired by their long association with wine and beer, cheese and butter, and now chocolate. As with many of their other products, they kept their new recipes a secret. They were so successful that Spain had a virtual monopoly over cocoa until well into the seventeenth century.

Spain also controlled what, for decades, was the only known source of cocoa beans. In fact, other Europeans didn't even know of cocoa's existence until long after it had become a luxury item at the Spanish court. In 1579, when English pirates boarded a Spanish vessel laden with cocoa, they mistook the dried brown beans for sheep manure. The disgusted buccaneers set the ship alight and sent the precious cargo to the bottom of the sea.

The conquistadors quickly expanded from Mexico City and soon controlled almost the entirety of what was once the Aztec Empire, including the fertile valleys of Central America, all the way to Guatemala. With an expanding market in Spain, the cocoa farms became more lucrative, and the pressure to produce more beans intensified. As the flow of New World silver and gold bullion forced down the value of precious metals in European markets, cocoa became a kind of liquid asset and a new source of economic stability.

The pressure intensified on Maya and other natives labouring in the expanding cocoa groves of what are now Belize and Guatemala. There was an insatiable demand for beans for the confectioners in Spanish monasteries and for the custodians of the Mexican and Spanish treasuries. Spanish colonists grabbed up the land, flattening large sections of the rainforest for new and expanded cocoa plantations. Cocoa's inherent elitism played out again with the Spanish, as the "food of the gods" became a luxury for the upper classes, produced by the down-trodden.

In spite of the good intentions of the monks and young Philip back in Spain, working conditions on the cocoa plantations became even more horrendous. A medieval system called *encomienda* gave Spanish colonists the right to demand the services of local workers on their lands. The doctrine, as it was practised in Europe, required that landowners release their serfs for a few days a week to look after their own crops. But in the distant colonies it was easy to ignore this crucial aspect of the contract, and *encomienda* gradually became a sanctioned form of slavery.

Officially, Spain condemned the practice, especially for those natives who had converted to Christianity and, somehow, became more entitled to the rights of "humans." Bartolomé de Las Casas had persuaded the Spanish monarch to pass new laws that were designed to protect the Indians from abuse, but Cortés successfully made the case that the colonists could not survive without this involuntary native labour pool. And the Spanish colonists believed that, when it came to work, the only incentive the natives understood was brute force.

~

The growing popularity of chocolate in Spain and later throughout Europe was associated, at least in part, with a widespread belief in its pharmaceutical benefits. Certainly the Indians of the Americas had long recognized the medicinal properties of cocoa and had prescribed it for many minor ailments. Cocoa butter helped heal burns. Spaniards in the New World believed that cocoa was a drug, while some accounts from the monks and conquistadors even suggest that it was a hallucinogen or even an aphrodisiac. King Philip's personal physician thought cocoa had a calming effect and helped relieve a fever, while other doctors claimed it was a pick-me-up.

To this day, chemists debate chocolate's pharmaceutical properties. Cocoa contains theobromine and caffeine, alkaloids that excite the central nervous system and dilate blood vessels. A morsel of good-quality chocolate can also contain serotonin—a mind-altering chemical believed to alleviate depression. And there's also phenylethylamine in cocoa, often called the love drug because it's believed to be a sexual stimulant. Other scientists (often funded by chocolate companies) claim that a piece of dark chocolate delivers as much antioxidant as a glass of red wine and might even contain epicatechin, thought to inhibit chemically induced cancers such as those caused by tobacco.

Sixteenth-century pharmacists prescribed chocolate to help emaciated patients gain weight, to stimulate digestion and elimination, to revive lethargic people from their sluggishness and to remedy bowel dysfunction. A cup of cocoa before bed was sure to rouse even the most flaccid libido.

Whether cocoa was a panacea or a placebo, whether food or drink or medicine, the market for cocoa beans was growing in Spain, and consequently so was the demand for cheap labour in the New World. The Spanish monarchy mildly protested the abusive labour practices to their governors and agents in the New World, but their sentiments were easily ignored in the distant colonies. Over time, all the good intentions in the world would melt like chocolate before the overarching economic imperatives of the day: Spain needed all the wealth it could generate in the New World to maintain its imperial position in the old one.

~

Prince Philip became King Philip II after his father stepped aside in 1556, and the high ideals of his teenage years began to fade in the harsh light of necessity. The wars continued, as did the taxes. The wealth generated in the New World served to fuel inflation, and the king didn't have a clue what to do about it—except to crank out more wealth from the colonies in America and now, just across the Straits of Gibraltar, in Africa. Sugar, spice and cocoa were too important to the imperial economy to be compromised by naive principles.

It is difficult to estimate the death rate of the aboriginal population in the Americas at the time. There was no census taken before contact with the Europeans, but some statistics estimate that, by the seventeenth century, as much as ninety per cent of the population in parts of Mexico and the Americas may have been wiped out. Hundreds of thousands, if not millions, succumbed to smallpox, measles and venereal diseases, while countless others perished from overwork, abuse and war.

Bartolomé de Las Casas wrote a book about the excesses of the colonial class, A *Short Account of the Destruction of the Indies* (which included the Caribbean, Central America and Mexico), based on his own observations in the New World. In it, he described acts of cruelty amounting to mass murder, and he warned that such atrocities as he had witnessed would not go unpunished by the God he believed to be defined by justice and compassion. Las Casas dedicated the manuscript to King Philip and petitioned the monarch to stop the barbarism.

Las Casas started a debate, if little else. Neither his monarch nor the princes in the Church he served were willing to take the kind of punitive action necessary to stop the colonial abuse. Neither Spain nor any other European country knew how to take advantage of the wealth of the New World without exploiting and trampling on the human rights of the native peoples. There was alarm at the evidence that those people were dying off in genocidal numbers—but mostly because of the obvious manpower shortage that would result. Luckily, there was a solution.

The traffic in African slaves to work in the Caribbean sugar plantations was already well established by the mid-sixteenth century. Now their labour was required to meet the growing shortages in Central America and Mexico. Hundreds of thousands of Africans were now diverted to the Spanish American cocoa plantations.

With a potentially unlimited labour pool assured and a seemingly infinite supply of sugar and cocoa, chocolate consumption expanded even further, crossing European borders and capturing the attention of markets throughout the continent. The privileged took their cocoa with them everywhere. It became a refreshment to enjoy during public spectacles, and it wasn't just for pleasure. The grim business of the Inquisition was lightened by the availability of cocoa for the clerics and aristocrats as they witnessed the agonies of suspected heretics.

Europe remained unstable throughout the century and into the next. Intermarriage between the various dynastic households became a contrivance to effect some kind of unity. There was no guarantee of success and, indeed, a high likelihood of even worse national hostility resulting from domestic discord in unsuccessful unions of convenience. But intermarriage was, if not a sure vehicle for peace, a medium for new ideas and shared discoveries. And when the granddaughter of King Philip II of Spain—Anne of Austria—married Louis XIII of France in 1615, chocolate was part of the marital package.

The French court was as skeptical of the strange brew as they were of Anne—France had been at war with Spain for decades. And whatever the supposed virtues of chocolate as an aphrodisiac, it's worth noting that Anne's new husband didn't consummate their marriage for years, preferring to spend his time in the company of young men (he was fourteen when they wed). But it was a new beachhead for chocolate, and Anne was not entirely alone in her affection for it. The king's powerful advisor, Cardinal Richelieu—who effectively ran France at the time—was a habitual cocoa drinker.

While chocolate caught on slowly in France, it gained quick acceptance on the Italian peninsula. The powerful Medicis were early aficionados, having been introduced to it by Spanish aristocrats in Tuscany. While Italy was an entanglement of feuding statelets in the seventeenth century, there did seem to be a nascent national consensus on the merits of chocolate. Cosimo de' Medici, fat and unhealthy from overconsumption of food, ran a corrupt and venal system that eventually fell into stagnation and ruin, but he was also a celebrated patron of the arts and science. Among his beneficiaries was a celebrated doctor and philologist, Francesco Redi.

We owe to Redi our modern understanding of how maggots materialize on rotting flesh—and, paradoxically, Redi was also responsible for many exotic innovations involving chocolate. With the maggot mystery solved (they are the larva of flies that are drawn to the decomposition), the food-infatuated Cosimo wanted some Italian refinements to the Spanish cocoa drinks. Cocoa was still classified as medicine, as was tobacco, and Cosimo saw chocolate's unlimited potential as a sensual experience. Redi cooked up batches of chocolate mixed not only with spices but also with perfumes, including ambergris, a rare and valuable musk oil derived from the excretions of sperm whales. He served up his concoctions to enthusiastic approval in the Medici court. In a flourish of artful chauvinism, Redi revised the history of chocolate to modestly include his own inventive role: "Chocolate was first introduced from America by the court of Spain, where it is made in all perfection. And yet to the Spanish perfection has been added, in our times, in the court of Tuscany, a certain I know not what of more exquisite gentility, owing to the novelty of divers European ingredients; a way having been found of introducing into the composition fresh peel of citron and lemons, and the very genteel odour of jasmine, which together with cinnamon, amber, musk and vanilla has a prodigious effect upon such as delight themselves in taking chocolate."

~

Cocoa made its inevitabe journey up the Thames, arriving in London almost simultaneously with tea and coffee—along with a new spirit of democracy coloured the erstwhile elitist beverage. England was giving birth to a "middle class," an extension of a merchant culture nurtured in the expanding world of trade and travel whose members enjoyed many of the privileges and pleasures once exclusively reserved for royalty. Unlike in France and Italy, where chocolate was principally served in snobby salons, English cities opened public coffee and chocolate houses, where the stimulating brew was more or less slopped together and served quickly while men gambled, bantered and debated the state of the economy and politics.

On the continent, chocolate would continue for a long time to be part of the royal prerogative. The son and successor to the sexually unsatisfied Louis XIII, the ultimately more famous Sun King, Louis XIV, didn't like chocolate, but his wife, the Spanish Maria Theresa, was, predictably, a cocoa addict. Under her influence, the elixir grew in popularity in the French court, especially among women. A typical cocoa drink usually included vanilla extract—which had to be very fresh and oily—cinnamon, cloves, pepper and, of course, sugar. French servants presented the hot drinks in delicately painted porcelain cups perched on recessed saucers that were designed and made exclusively for sipping chocolate. And while the ladies and gentlemen of the court quaffed their cocoa, they naturally talked and debated every issue of their time.

The emergence of chocolate as a bracing social beverage coincides with the birth of revolutionary theories about social structures, human rights and natural justice. The case could be made that chocolate was a major element in the movement we now know as the Enlightenment. The drink was on the table when eighteenth-century thinkers started questioning long-held verities: the supremacy of the Church; the rights of kings; the potential for improvement in the common man and woman. And along with the middle-merchant class in England, a new division of intellectuals, artisans and authors was emerging. Ordinary people in

Europe, Britain and the American colonies were abuzz with new ideas, exchanging them, writing them down and translating them into their various languages.

The arguments of Hume, Locke, Voltaire and Rousseau crossed national and linguistic borders freely. Following the example of the Spanish priest Las Casas, philosophers such as Montaigne challenged the morality of slavery. Knowledge, by the early eighteenth century, was available in books for anyone who could read; the written word was no longer exclusively for the priests and scholars, nor was it limited to Latin texts. Progress, once the prerogative of God, became a goal to be pursued by everyone, and a mandate for people in control of human institutions. A whole new class of public advocates emerged in France: the Philosophes, secular intellectuals and independent thinkers who were accountable only to their principles. And it was in the chocolate houses, the coffee houses and the salons where a cross-section of a newly awakened public could ponder ideas and events, and read and exchange journals, broadsheets and books fresh off the ever-improving printing presses. The Cocoa-Tree Chocolate House on St. James Street in London became a popular hangout for Voltaire when he visited. Alexander Pope's epic *The Dunciad* makes reference to White's Chocolate House, probably the most famous cocoa hangout of its time, even before Pope immortalized it.

But the eighteenth century was, in the words of the future social commentator Charles Dickens, "the best of times, and the worst of times." While the great thinkers debated equality, fraternity and liberty and championed the rights of man, they were sipping sugar-sweetened chocolate and coffee produced by the blood and sweat of slaves.

The native population in the Caribbean and on the mainland had been reduced to a fraction of what it had been when Cortés first arrived. And Africans, subjected to the most extreme abuse, struggled to survive the brutality of the Americas.

Cocoa production relied on a horrific system called triangular trade, a commercial arrangement of merchants and tycoons who plied the waters from Europe to Africa to the Americas. Ships would sail from European ports to the shores of West Africa bearing a variety of products, from salted cod to weapons. Once unloaded there, the ships would fill up with human cargo, bound for the Americas, where the slaves would be traded for agricultural products to be shipped back to Europe. The Africans would then be put to work raising more produce—sugar, rum, cocoa and raw cotton—for European factories and markets. It was a hugely successful system, made possible and vastly profitable by an incalculable cost in human lives and dignity.

Slave traders, with the help of Africans, who were recruited to do most of the dirty work, rounded up hundreds of thousands of men, women and children from their villages in Africa, marched them to collection centres with their necks in yokes, branded them with hot irons, manacled them together and stuffed them so tightly into the holds of ships that they sat between each other's knees for the voyage across the Atlantic. Tens of thousands died en route and were thrown overboard—sometimes cast into the ocean alive because they were too sick or too mutinous to be carried for the rest of the journey. Those who survived the crossing were delivered into conditions so arduous that their numbers had to be constantly replenished. Over the four hundred years in which the slave trade was active, an estimated twelve to fifteen million Africans became chattel in this highly lucrative, well-organized, church-sanctioned system.

There was a jarring disconnection between the reality of the slave ships furnishing the American plantations, and the elevated conversations in the salons and public houses of Europe. It was the age of enlightened speculation and idealistic schemes for the improvement of humankind, but it was also the age of mercantilism, a newly liberated business class with unfettered dreams of wealth and public influence. It was the beginning of a new age of dissent. Influential merchants felt free to protest any hindrance to the flow of capital and goods — taxes and regulations were tantamount to oppression. The market should be a self-regulating organism. A new doctrine, laissez-faire capitalism, took on respectability once reserved for theology. The Philosophes could argue and discuss human rights until they bored each other to distraction, but nothing was going to interfere with an inspired new economic system that was transforming the world, and delivering cheap pots of coffee and cocoa to the tables where all the thinkers sat and speculated.

The new merchant class had money and time for recreation. They were clearing away the cobwebs of the medieval ages: superstition, witchcraft and ignorance. They were conspicuous consumers of goods from around the world. Chocolate was a natural adjunct to this ferment of enthusiastic sentiment. Prepared in the silver pots of the new chocolatier in Paris or tossed together in the rowdy chocolate houses of London's St. James Street, from beans ground by the housewives of New Spain or by professional cocoa grinders who went door to door in the fashionable enclaves of Madrid, chocolate, in this age of enlightenment, became as much a fixture in the lives of the newly wealthy merchants and liberated intellectuals as it had been for the aristocracies of times gone by.

In France, Louis XV fed chocolate to his many mistresses, and the most noted, "Madame de Pompadour," became a famous addict, using cocoa as a treatment for her sexual dysfunctions. The Marquis de Sade, possibly the world's first serious sexologist, was hooked on chocolate. Doing hard time in prison for pornography and lewd offences, he ordered up copious supplies of chocolate: "boxes of ground chocolate and mocha coffee; cacao butter suppositories [a popular cure for constipation]; crème au chocolat; chocolate pastilles; large chocolate biscuits; chocolat en tablettes à l'ordinaire."

The European demand for chocolate gradually overwhelmed the capacity of the plantations in Mexico, Guatemala and Belize.

New cocoa groves appeared in Venezuela and Brazil, and eventually in the West Indies and Jamaica. Hardy new varieties of cocoa bean emerged as diseases caused by overproduction on plantations created havoc for the cultivation of old varieties.

Meanwhile, the exertions of the intellectuals of Europe would eventually bear fruit in violent assertions of democracy in France and the colonies of North America. Declarations affirming the essential dignity of man would inspire new constitutions that guaranteed government accountability and the protection of basic human rights. The pious sentiments applied to everyone, it seemed—except where, in the name of commerce, expedient exclusions were deemed sadly necessary. Among them were the millions of wretched human beings engaged in primary production in the colonies: the harvesters of cotton, hewers of sugar cane and handlers of cocoa.

From the elite world of Montezuma's court, with its human sacrifices and overwrought banquets, to the rarefied chambers of European aristocrats with their powdered wigs and foppish clothes, to the loud and smoky clubs of English gentlemen, to the perverted pleasure palaces of de Sade's imagination— chocolate had arrived as the world's most seductive sweet.

Chapter Three

COCOA ON TRIAL

"Daddy, I want a boat like this! I want you to buy me a big pink
boiled-sweet boat exactly like Mr. Wonka's! And I want lots of
Oompa-Loompas to row me about, and I want a chocolate river
and I want . . . I want . . ."

—Veruca Salt in Roald Dahl's *Charlie
and the Chocolate Factory*

The images are printed in the cultural memory,
thanks to Blake and Dickens: smoke and flame belching from
the stacks of giant factories and mills; the wretched working class
living in squalid hovels and teeming tenements; sprawling towns
and cities turning the green Elizabethan countryside into an
apocalypse of Victorian misery.

This is our emblem of the Industrial Revolution and the
nineteenth-century transformation of British, European and
American economics and society. It was, indeed, a time of massive dislocation, country people moving from small, marginal
farms and rustic villages into new factory towns, where sweat and
brawn and time had monetary value; where wages seduced peasants away from the unpredictable moods of the land and the
weather, and the need to grow or build or beg or steal the necessities for survival. Now they could buy the basics with their hard-
earned pay. And along with the necessities, the miracle of
mass-production also made available small gratifications, pleasures once exclusively for wealthy merchants and the ruling classes.

Chocolate was democratized. And the working class indulged with zeal.

~

In the early 1800s, people still bought their cocoa in the apothecary shops, where it was sold along with other New World stimulants, including tobacco. But cocoa was losing its cachet and its market as customers eschewed the greasy, gritty chocolate drink in favour of more refined—and more easily prepared—beverages like tea and coffee.

The problem, from the beginning, had been cocoa's fatty by-product, a kind of butter, valued by the Maya and the Aztecs for its caloric richness, but unpleasant to the modern British-European palate. They'd attempted boiling and skimming and beating to remove it, and sweetening it to moderate the taste. They had succeeded in producing a tolerable and stimulating drink. But it took a lot of effort and a lot of time and the end product was still fifty per cent fat! In the age of progress and rising expectations, chocolate and cocoa were becoming a bit too bothersome when there were other more accessible sources of sensory gratification. Cocoa, and chocolate with it, was on the way out, relegated to the status of breakfast food for children. But machinery and the rampant spirit of invention would intervene on chocolate's behalf as they had for so many other commodities.

Even as a teenager working in his father's factory in Amsterdam, a visionary Dutchman named Coenraad Van Houten had been obsessed with figuring out how to separate the fat from the cocoa bean. It would take the invention of the hydraulic press—a product of the explosive growth in knowledge of mechanics in the middle of the nineteenth century—to pull it off efficiently. Where the Olmec and Maya spent hours grinding up small batches of beans into a crude but digestible paste, Van Houten applied the full force of steel and fluid-driven piston to achieve what the Meso-Americans could never do by hand.

Van Houten's cocoa-pressing machine used six thousand pounds of pressure to squeeze the grease from the carefully roasted beans. The process left hard cakes of cocoa in one pan and a shimmering pool of coagulated yellow fat in another. It was the defatted cocoa Van Houten was after. The butter that gave generations in the New World energy to march for days through wilderness, conquering and pillaging as they went, was now mostly waste. The European housewife wanted a quick, easily prepared formula that would dissolve in hot water or milk, and Van Houten obliged. Through a careful alchemy, he determined the right amount of cocoa butter that should remain in the final product in order to impart a rich chocolatey flavour yet still create a compound that would emulsify. Van Houten ground the cocoa cakes up into powder, which he passed through a sieve, and then added quantities of alkaloids that improved the flavour and helped it blend with liquid. He gave cocoa a new lease on life: bottles of brown powder, labelled Van Houten's "Dutch" cocoa, soon filled the shelves of food shops all over Europe.

In 1828, Van Houten showed up at the patent office in Amsterdam, registered his revolutionary cocoa-processing method and took a well-deserved place in the history of chocolate. It was the first major improvement in the preparation of cocoa in nearly three thousand years, and it would soon take the little bean to the forefront of world confection. Van Houten also established the Netherlands as the leading cocoa powder producer in the world, aided by the fact that Holland possessed one of the best sources of raw material.

The Dutch were aggressive international traders: they had cornered the world's tea production through the East India Company; they controlled the Spice Islands; and now the West Indian subsidiary of their principal trading company monopolized the market for the high-quality Criollo beans coming out of their own New World colonies in Venezuela.

The Dutch had the same source of labour as all the other cocoa-growing settlements. Whether it was the British in the Caribbean, the Spanish in Guatemala or the Portuguese in Brazil, the common denominator in cocoa economics was slavery. And it would become an even more important factor as the demand for cocoa-based products caught on and spread throughout the vast and expanding working classes of Europe, Britain and North America. Slavery, as a moral issue, mattered only to a relatively small group of human rights activists. Ironically, some of the most influential people in this tiny movement were also building industries—and fortunes—based on slavery.

~

The Quakers had their own historical experience with persecution and discrimination. They'd been excluded from most of the privileges of British society since their sect was founded in the seventeenth century. First established as the Religious Society of Friends, they claimed to need no intermediary to witness their relationship with God but instead were guided by an "inward light" supplied by the Holy Spirit. They refused to attend the Church of England or to pledge oaths to the British Crown, and, as pacifists, they would not bear arms. Britain barred them from attending universities and owning land. In the seventeenth century, British monarchs imprisoned or banished thousands of them. Large numbers of Quakers fled England for the colonies, the most famous being the followers of William Penn, founder of Pennsylvania.

By the nineteenth century, Britain had finally relaxed its persecution of those who were not members of the official church. Quakers in England assimilated to some degree—though the society remained tightly knit—and they took an active interest in politics and social reform. Quakers were industrious and successful entrepreneurs. And they took a particular interest in chocolate.

Cocoa was regarded by nineenth-century society as an innocent pleasure, a non-alcoholic stimulant. While abstemious themselves, the Quakers hadn't entirely avoided the booze business. For generations, they had justified production of beer and ale on the grounds that these were acceptable alternatives to the potent rum and gin favoured by hard-drinking Brits in their raucous taverns. Like many moralists, the members were capable of pragmatic rationalizing, a trait that would serve some enterprising members well in the chocolate business.

When it first arrived in Europe, chocolate was considered a wholesome food with medicinal value, and so it was that a Quaker medical doctor in Bristol named Joseph Fry set up his own healthful chocolate-making company in the early 1700s. The doctor's grandson took the operation one step further, figuring out how to mass-produce cocoa powder by hitching together the Dutch invention of Coenraad Van Houten with the Englishman Thomas Watt's revolutionary innovation, the steam engine. The offspring was a steam-powered hydraulic press that revolutionized the business and turned the Fry family enterprise into a business empire. But that was only the start.

Van Houten's machine had been inspired by his determination to produce the finest possible form of dry chocolate powder. The residue—that unappetizing cocoa butter—became a useless by-product. But Fry and his family found a purpose for it. By blending small amounts of melted, clarified cocoa butter with cocoa solids—along with sugar and flavours—the company had a substance they could mould. Spanish monks had produced greasy little lumps of sweet chocolate to be eaten, while French shops turned out the dry, crumbly wafers and pastilles that the Marquis de Sade so piteously craved in his prison cell. This product of the Frys, however, was something new and different: a melt-in-your-mouth treat that could be mass-produced and sold at an affordable price. It was, for all intents and purposes, the modern chocolate bar.

By the 1840s, the Frys were producing their famous Chocolat Délicieux à Manger—chocolate you could eat off the shelf. It didn't take long for the business to take off and J.S. Fry & Sons became the world's pre-eminent chocolate producers. But they soon had stiff competition—from other Quakers.

John Cadbury had just finished apprenticing as a tea dealer in Leeds at the age of twenty-two when he decided to set up a store-front business selling tea, coffee and chocolate in Birmingham, right next to his father's drapery shop. With start-up capital from his Quaker circle and help from his brother and nephews, Cadbury began to manufacture his own products from imported beans. By 1860, he was selling dozens of varieties of chocolate and cocoa drinks.

About that time, John's son, George Cadbury, made a fortu-itous trip to Amsterdam, where he bought a Van Houten press. Soon after, the Cadburys were manufacturing their own high-quality Cocoa Essence powder, advertised as "Absolutely pure and therefore Best."

Crude though the boast may sound, the Cadburys had discov-ered something more important than machinery. They were among the first in the business to display a formidable talent in marketing. The Cadburys produced the first boxes of chocolate bonbons, which were similar to the chocolate bars the Frys had invented but fashioned into bite-sized pieces and presented in pretty little containers decorated with saccharine images of small children and fluffy kittens. The clever packaging caught the sen-timental fancy of Victorian consumers. The Cadburys also found a way to appeal to their ambiguous prudery, playing up the inno-cence of chocolate as a sensual indulgence. It was the firm's mar-keting genius that first made chocolate a part of Valentine's Day in Great Britian and a symbol of romantic love. In 1875, Cadbury

Brothers sold the first chocolate Easter egg. In one stroke, chocolate became an integral part of the most important celebration on the Christian calendar, a way to mark the end of Lenten sacrifice, a harbinger of spring.

For centuries, cocoa had been consumed to achieve a practical outcome: to increase energy, or to relieve constipation, or to stimulate sexual desire. Now it was pure pleasure, in and of itself. It just tasted good. It gratified the consumer. Naturally, other businessmen took note, and other companies provided competition. And they, like the Frys and Cadburys, were Quakers.

~

Joseph Rowntree grew up in the city of York, the son of a Quaker grocer with a strong social conscience. As a teenager studying in London, the young Rowntree became interested in politics and attended debates at the House of Commons. He returned to York to work with his father, but in 1869 he teamed up with his brother Henry at the family-run Cocoa, Chocolate and Chicory Works. It was still a small business when Henry died in 1883, but by the end of the nineteenth century—and with the new developments in chocolate candy-making—the factory employed four thousand people, manufacturing chocolate drops as well as Fruit Gums and Jelly Babies. But there was more to the Rowntree family than a business based on society's passion for sweets. They also had a passion for justice.

Joseph Rowntree was preoccupied for much of his life with trying to improve the lives of his employees. He provided a library in the factory and education for workers under the age of seventeen and also free medical and dentistry services and a pension fund—all unheard of in the England of sweatshops and indentured labour.

Joseph's son, Benjamin Seebohm Rowntree, went even further than his father. Not only was Seebohm working for the family business in York, he was also Britain's first labour director. Seebohm wrote a number of influential studies on the conditions of Britain's workforce, including *Poverty: A Study of Town Life*, in which he argued that Britain had two kinds of poor people: working folk who couldn't earn enough to make ends meet; and those who earned enough but wasted it on wicked pursuits such as liquor. Seebohm lobbied on behalf of both groups while he endeavoured to put his moral principles to work on behalf of his employees. The Rowntrees became leaders in a movement promoted by a few of the better proprietors of the day: "paternalistic capitalism."

Seebohm Rowntree and his fellow Quakers believed strongly in the Victorian notion that the road from poverty to wealth was open to anyone prepared to work hard and behave in a disciplined manner. Wealth was no longer strictly determined by bloodline. The market ruled, and the market was driven by unprecedented demand for a limitless range of goods at home and abroad. Capitalism and the social dislocations it engendered also bred overwhelming social problems. But the Rowntrees believed that the state had a moral obligation to intervene on behalf of those who would not —or could not—help themselves.

Seebohm Rowntree was among a group of moral businessmen who tried to lay the foundations for Britain's first welfare state. He lobbied government to establish a minimum wage and a system of family allowance payments for all British workers. He was active in the Liberal Party and argued that the appropriate seat of democratic power was the elected House of Commons and not the unelected House of Lords. And he went even further, creating a model community for his own workers at his chocolate factory in York, insisting on a clean, safe working environment. Seebohm believed the shop floor had greater impact on a person's life than the church. In the Chocolate Works, he established a democratic system for employees to choose their own managers and he insisted on rigorous timekeeping for shift workers and scheduled payment of salaries and benefits. The rights and responsibilities of workers and their managers were declared by the company in writing.

Seebohm Rowntree was not the only paternalistic capitalist in the chocolate industry who dabbled in social engineering. Appalled by the general state of working conditions in nineteenth-century British factories, the Cadburys decided to move their operations from Birmingham to a greenfield "Factory in a Garden." In 1878 the Cadburys bought four and a half acres of land in the countryside and began to build their community on the banks of the river Bourn, establishing a pretty little town they called Bournville.

The Cadburys' factory offered landscaped grounds with flowers and green spaces for relaxation, and a dining room with wholesome meals. The idyll on the banks of the Bourn was supposed to inspire employees and create a healthy atmosphere — notions that the Cadburys took from the "garden city" movement. According to the pioneering ideas of the nineteenth-century town planner Ebenezer Howard, the garden city was designed to bring together the best of urban and country life while offering employment to its citizens. While most so-called garden cities eventually became bedroom suburbs of larger urban centres, Bournville was considered a model of the concept, and is a tourist attraction to this day.

There was, of course, at the heart of all the idealism of Quaker cocoa barons, a heavy-handed moralism. Cadbury Brothers expected its workers to live by a strict moral code, to attend church and to conduct their lives properly. Couples received Bibles when they wed, and newly married women had to leave the factory so that they could raise their families. Pubs and drinking establishments were banned in Bournville.

The experiment seemed to work, at least from a commercial point of view. The Quakers came to dominate the chocolate industry, despite stiff competition from the rest of Europe. National policies helped. Great Britain encouraged trade by lowering taxes on imported cocoa beans, and soon England was on the cutting edge of international chocolate manufacturing. They were producing the first affordable chocolate—no longer something for the elite.

But for all the social justice in their words and factories, there was a disturbing blind spot in how these idealistic capitalists saw their businesses. They managed what was near at hand with impeccable regard for human dignity. But it was a different story beyond the horizon of their social conscience, in those dark and distant places where the raw material for their business came from. The humane working conditions enjoyed by their employees, the "Absolutely pure and therefore Best" products purchased by their customers, the consistent strength of their profit figures—all depended on the efforts of people who worked for next to nothing, had hardly any control over their destinies and lived and died as slaves.

Theoretically, the slave trade had ended by the middle of the nineteenth century. Laws outlawing slavery were in force all over industrialized Europe. Abolitionists from Washington to London had triumphed. But somehow, on the margins of civilized society, people still lived in slavery, the reality of their circumstances obscured by wilful blindness and by euphemism. All the good intentions of King Charles of Spain, and later Philip, couldn't save the Maya and the Aztecs from murderous exploitation. The extraordinary priest Bartolomé de Las Casas spent a lifetime trying to do something about it, and in the end he failed. But in the nineteenth century, the voice of moral outrage would come not from a priest but from an entirely new phenomenon: the crusading investigative reporter.

~

The Englishman Henry Woodd Nevinson was part of a new breed of journalist who emerged in the late nineteenth century, writers

who combined a moralistic zeal with a flare for storytelling. They
trekked around the world, exposing the sins of empire through
their reporting. Nevinson's parents were evangelical Christians,
but he was more inclined to conduct a secular battle for the rights
of the working class, here and now, than to await the promises of
heaven. He spent time with Henrietta and Samuel Barnett, the
celebrated poverty activists who had installed a university settlement in London's East End to provide education to the under-
privileged; he also joined Britain's first socialist party.

Nevinson was a scholar of Greek and Latin and taught history
in various schools throughout London while writing books about
the plight of the poor. He hiked and cycled all over England and
sometimes spent days walking while contemplating the human
condition. But Nevinson longed to travel in uncharted places, to
see the world and to write about it.

In the late 1890s, he got his chance. A liberal English newspaper called the *Daily Chronicle* dispatched Nevinson to cover
the Greek uprising against the Ottomans on the island of Crete.
He was hardly over the experience when, in 1899, he was off to
report on the Spanish-American war. Then it was the Boer War
in South Africa. Such events were of great interest to an intellec-
tual Anglo socialist who eschewed the imperial chauvinism of
his own native country. By the time he was covering events in
Macedonia, Nevinson had established himself as a formidable
journalist with a penchant for exposing the social injustices of a
rapidly changing world, a spokesman for the downtrodden. At
forty-eight, he was working for the *Daily Chronicle*, writing
books, hiking furiously and generally enjoying himself when he
got the most important assignment of his career.

The respected American magazine *Harper's Monthly*—which
over the years counted among its contributors Horatio Alger,
Mark Twain, Henry James and Jack London—was always on the
lookout for writers anywhere in the world willing to go to "adven-
turesome" places and bring back a piece of the action for its

readers. The editors at *Harper's* asked Nevinson to come up with a story proposal for them, and he did.

As with many social activists of the age, Nevinson was captivated by the reports then emerging from the Congo about a new manifestation of slavery that was on a scale to match the worst excesses of the eighteenth century. During triangular trade, European and British merchants regarded Africa as a massive labour pool for their colonies in the New World. But King Leopold II of Belgium saw the value of Africa to his Empire a bit differently. He laid claim to vast areas of the Congo, declaring it a free state but in reality, launching one of the most devious campaigns of wealth extraction in human history, as he enslaved native people to facilitate his ruthless harvest of ivory and rubber. Africans who refused to work for the Belgians were routinely beaten to death. Whole villages of people were murdered. To reluctant workers, Leopold's agents displayed buckets of the severed hands of others who had resisted. Despite widespread international laws against such exploitation, Leopold got away with murder on an epic scale. In fact, the world celebrated the Belgian king as a humanitarian, subscribing to Leopold's claims that he was introducing the savage natives of the Congo to the redeeming ways of European civilization. No one knew (or admitted to knowing) what the Belgian monarch was really up to until it was exposed by an enterprising writer.

Edmund Morel discovered the horrific abuse while working for a Liverpool shipping company, and he began to keep a detailed record of what he learned. Though it would destroy his career in shipping and eventually land him in prison, Morel painstakingly documented the Belgian atrocities in the Congo, many of them reported by Belgian bureaucrats. The Congo was a commercial success story in a place few people ever visited. With the king in charge, the likelihood of whistle-blowers seemed just as remote as the place itself. If not for the crusading journalism of Morel the world might never have discovered the full breadth of a scheme that claimed the lives of as many as ten million Africans.

Leopold, like many greedy potentates before him, had discovered the value of euphemism in obscuring the true nature of his imperial behaviour. To escape the legal implications of slavery, he simply called it something else. His involuntary workforce in the Congo was "indentured," and his colonial bureaucrats claimed that the African labourers worked willingly for wages — there was no coercion. Leopold had actually convinced other European governments that his mission in Africa was charitable and that he was providing job opportunities for the Congolese. The fact that the Africans arrived at work in chains at gunpoint somehow didn't register.

Nevinson was fascinated and appalled when he read Morel's exposés but he learned that Leopold was not alone in his clever deceit. Nevinson heard about particularly egregious practices on the coast of equatorial Africa, where there was a seemingly innocuous trade in a product the very name of which conjured up the best of human impulses. It seemed that cocoa, by now Britain's most cherished confection, the raw material for the high-minded Quaker industrialists, was produced by slaves. The story, like the product, was delicious. This investigation was one Nevinson could get his teeth into, following in the famous footsteps of Morel. But as was the case for Morel, the story would consume Nevinson for the rest of his life, and would never be completely resolved.

~

By the mid-1800s, the cocoa trees of the Caribbean and the Spanish Americas were depleted and disease ridden: colonists had destroyed the *Theobroma* stock through over-production and poor management, just as they had ravaged the populations that had taught Europe about cocoa. But cocoa traders had learned that the beans could grow anywhere within a twenty-kilometre belt north or south of the equator, provided the atmosphere was humid and the altitude was not excessive. The Dutch had already transplanted cocoa stock to their colonies in Indonesia. The Portuguese found the ideal terrain for their own plantations on two small islands under their control in the Gulf of Guinea, just off the coast of present-day Cameroon. For years they'd been transporting Africans to the Americas to work as slaves on cocoa farms. Now they'd take the cocoa trees to Africa. One thing wouldn't change: The Africans would continue to work the cocoa farms in appalling circumstances.

The islands of São Tomé and Príncipe had served as transfer stations for the earlier slave trade. Millions of hapless Africans had passed through warehouses on the tiny islands and had caught their last glimpses of their homeland from the gang-planks of ships in São Tomé's harbour. For a time, the islands had been cultivated for sugar, but that ended when the Caribbean plantations became the main source of the world's sweetener. The Portuguese continued to grow some coffee but had found no other purpose for the islands. As the world demand for cocoa increased and the plant stock in the New World diminished, the Portuguese finally realized they were in possession of a goldmine.

The first cocoa plants arrived on São Tomé in 1824, and within two decades, as Van Houten's machine revolutionized production — and boosted demand — the Portuguese expanded their plantations dramatically. Soon cocoa was flourishing on the island and then on neighbouring Príncipe. By the turn of the century, São Tomé was the leading producer of cocoa in the world, supplying the factories of Great Britain, the Netherlands and to a lesser extent the United States. There were few people native to the islands to perform the labour-intensive work of cocoa farming, but this was of little concern. The Portuguese had control of populous Angola.

Since the sixteenth century, the Portuguese had exported an estimated three million Angolans to the Americas. Now, with a huge international demand for chocolate candy, Angolans would serve Portuguese interests once more. Officially, the Angolans were being offered jobs and wages in the cocoa groves. They were told they were free to come and go and were promised proper compensation for their efforts. That was what it said on paper. São Tomé wasn't far away—not like the Americas. Presumably they'd work for a while, then return to where they came from. But, curiously, no one did.

Nevinson wanted to know why.

One of his best sources of information about Portuguese labour practices in Africa came from an enterprising newsletter put out by Britain's Anti-Slavery Society, called the *Reporter*. In its pages, Nevinson combed through myriad accounts of abuse dispatched by the field workers and missionaries who worked in Africa. What they described, in detailed letters and articles, was a systemic forced labour scheme supplying workers to the Portuguese coffee and cocoa plantations. Reports of appalling abuse begin to appear in the *Reporter* as early as the 1850s, and each decade the stories become more shocking.

In May 1883, a letter described "the shipments of Slaves" to the Portuguese islands where the author reports that three thousand workers had recently arrived. Technically, they were free to go home at any time, "however, as the offer is never made, nor the opportunity afforded," said the source, "they become permanent indentured labourers." More reports throughout 1885 contradicted claims by the Portuguese that the workers were treated humanely: "Why then torture them by squeezing their fingers in the copying press, cutting their parts and ears off, thrash them, men, women heavy in the course of nature, and children so unmercifully?" says the *Reporter's* dispatch. Other missionaries claimed the workers arrived on São Tomé with iron rings around their necks. How could the Africans be anything other than slaves?

What fascinated Nevinson more than the bulletins, which continued to pile up into the 1890s, was that the bland denials of the
Portuguese were accepted by British authorities or, at least,
regarded in the same light as the passionate accounts of missionaries to the Portuguese islands. These differing versions were
accepted simply as two sides of the story. Why had no one done a
proper investigation when the evidence was so thick and the
narratives—covering a period of five decades—so consistent?

Before departing for Africa in 1904, Nevinson contacted the
Cadburys. With their reputation as social activists, it would have
been reasonable to assume they'd be as curious as he was about
the disturbing reports from the islands off West Africa, where
Nevinson was certain most of their cocoa originated. Surely they
had heard and read the same disturbing accounts! Maybe they'd
help him by providing names of contacts there. But Nevison
found the Cadburys strangely coy about labour conditions on the
Portuguese islands. George Cadbury, the paterfamilias, told
Nevinson that the company had plans to do its own investigation
and was actively seeking someone suitable to send to the islands.
Nevinson was not their man.

Something about their unwillingness to talk made the
reporter suspicious. The Cadburys were well-known abolitionists, extremely active in the anti-slavery societies and were major
contributors in the campaign to expose the evils of the system
King Leopold had created in the Congo. William Cadbury, in
particular, was deeply involved in the movement and later
became not only Edmund Morel's benefactor but also his confi-
dant. Why wouldn't the Cadburys want to know everything they
could about alleged abuses on the African cocoa farms? As he
recorded in his diaries, it took Nevinson a long time to realize
that it was because they already knew a lot more than he or any
of his sources did. And they had no idea what to do about it.

In an archive at the library of the University of Birmingham
lie the Cadbury family's collected papers. The archive shows not

only that the company had a subscription to the Anti-Slavery Society's *Reporter*, but also that individual members of the family subscribed to it. If the Cadburys read the periodicals, they would have seen the same articles and anecdotes that Nevinson had, where contributors described conditions on the Portuguese islands to be as bad—or worse—than in Leopold's Congo.

The only conclusion Nevinson could make is that the Cadburys chose to turn a blind eye. Even though it was the Portuguese, not the English Quakers, who ran the wretched islands and the trade in cocoa beans, the manufacturers who bought the beans benefited from a system that kept the prices of their raw materials minimal through cruel exploitation. But the first record indicating that the Cadburys raised the issue with their board of directors was in 1901. In January of that year, the *Reporter* had published an account from a missionary that must have stunned all chocolate-making abolitionists: "I have never seen such slave gangs bound west as pass us day after day since crossing the Quanza, and the many dead bodies left on the side of the road tell the sad tale— knocked on the head to end their misery or hamstrung and left." The Cadburys would have known about the abuses for years before Nevinson came calling.

William Cadbury tried to downplay the reports when he wrote to another Quaker activist: "[One] looks at these matters in a different light when it affects one's own interests but I do feel there is a vast difference between the cultivation of cocoa and gold or diamond mining [in reference to reports of the time concerning British abuse in African mining]."

According to archival records, the Cadbury family was getting almost half of its cocoa from the islands, as were all the other Quaker cocoa companies, including Rowntree and Fry, with the remainder coming from British colonies in the Caribbean. The companies had numerous meetings among themselves at the turn of the century to discuss whether they should boycott the Portuguese islands. But they inevitably concluded that a boycott wouldn't have much effect on anything except their own bottom line.

True to their word, the Cadburys did find their own investigative researcher. Joseph Burtt was a businessman in his early forties, handsome, keen and dedicated to the principles of the anti-slavery movement. He might have been the right man, but in a colossal act of foot dragging, the Cadburys insisted that Burtt conduct his inquiries in Portuguese, a language he knew nothing of. So they sent him to Lisbon to learn it.

While there, he and the Cadburys held meetings with Portuguese officials, who attempted to reassure the chocolate-makers that reports of labour abuse were highly exaggerated. The Portuguese fell back on old arguments used by King Leopold to justify his own actions in the Congo. It wasn't really slavery, they said, but employment. The Africans were not captives but willing partners in what they called the *serviçal* system. They were engaged to work for some years as wage earners and then allowed to return home. If they stayed on the islands for the rest of their lives, well, that's because they were better off in São Tomé than in Angola, where there was nothing for them to do. One shouldn't judge labour conditions in Africa by European standards.

The Cadburys clearly wanted to believe such lies and Burtt, when he wasn't struggling with grammar lessons, was anxious to please his chocolate-making masters. The problem for all of them was that the evidence of slavery was stacked so high. The Anti-Slavery Society's *Reporter* documented over and over again that the Angolans wouldn't be in shackles if they were willing labourers; they wouldn't be dying at an appalling rate if they were part of any normal workforce. And the records show that no one ever returned home from the islands of São Tomé and Príncipe.

~

With his assignment from *Harper's Monthly Magazine* and some funds in his vest pocket, Nevinson arrived in Angola to launch his investigation in December 1904. He spent the next six months following the slave route from its source all the way to the island of São Tomé. He learned that the Portuguese had already sent tens of thousands of Africans to the Angolan ports of Luanda and Benguela, where they were bundled onto ships and brought to the islands to work. The road leading to the ports was littered with the bleached bones and corpses of those who never made it. Nevison came upon small groups of natives being transported by gun-toting guards, and he heard the crack of the whips and slap of the paddles used to punish those who attempted to escape.

Nevinson identified the sham of the *serviçal* tribunal system. The Angolans were required to swear before a judge that they were going to the islands of their own free will. Nevinson could see that the natives had no choice—their responses to questions weren't even recorded. Everyone Nevinson talked to made it clear that the passage to São Tomé was a one-way trip. He later wrote in *Harper's* of the sleight of hand that turned "slave" into "*serviçal*": "The climax of the farce has now been reached. The deed of pitiless hypocrisy has been consummated. The requirement of legalized slavery have been satisfied . . . They went into the tribunal as slaves, they have come out as 'contract labourers.'"

What disgusted Nevinson almost as much as the cruelty was the derision white people demonstrated towards the Africans. He watched an Angolan woman with a newborn baby attempt to mount an unsteady gangplank to a ship bound for São Tomé. She lost some of her belongings when they fell into the water, and stumbled several times before she finally struggled into her place with the other slaves. As pitiable as the scene was to Nevinson, he realized that the spectacle was merely amusing to other European passengers on board. The boat served as both a cargo vessel and a passenger ferry, so Nevinson was able to observe the scene from the upper deck, along with a large crowd of first-class passengers: "I have heard many terrible sounds," he later wrote, "but never anything so hellish as the outbursts of laughter with which the ladies and gentlemen of the first class watched the slave woman's struggle up the deck."

Nevinson eventually got to São Tomé, and it didn't take him long to learn why no African workers returned to Angola. Many died of disease and abuse. Doctors and missionaries on the island believed that vast numbers of them passed away from sheer despair.

Harper's published Nevinson's articles in a series that ran from August through February. In 1906, he released his research material in a groundbreaking book called, simply, *A Modern Slavery.* Nothing would be the same again in the world of "democratic" chocolate.

~

The British chocolate companies were furious with Nevinson. They argued that the *Harper's* articles were completely over the top and that the journalist had sensationalized conditions in Angola. What's more, the whole series of articles was insulting to the Portuguese, who were key trading partners of Britain. But anti-slavery activists immediately demanded a boycott of cocoa from São Tomé and even Morel thought the articles were compelling, much to the chagrin of his friend and financial patron, William Cadbury.

For the crusading Cadburys with their idyllic settlement on the banks of the Bourn and their campaign for labour reform in British factories, a boycott of Portuguese beans would have been consistent with their corporate values. But the Cadburys faltered. They convinced themselves that Nevinson had exaggerated the situation and that their own investigation through Joseph Burtt would reveal the truth. Whether this was just the public face of a private crisis is a matter of speculation. The Cadburys would keep purchasing São Tomé cocoa and using their influence to persuade the Portuguese to make improvements. In fact, they rationalized that they could have more of an impact on the Portuguese by maintaining trade than by boycotting beans.

Predictably, their powers of persuasion didn't work. So William and his uncle George Cadbury turned to their contacts in the British government for help. This was the land of hope and glory. Surely the government shared their Quaker desire for human rights.

Britain was in a difficult position. The Foreign Office was quite aware of the labour abuse on São Tomé and Príncipe since the anti-slavery activists had been publishing reports, and the government had its own intelligence sources, which corroborated the public record. Politically and morally, Britain disapproved. But civil servants in the Foreign Office were there to serve the interests of the Empire and to protect Britain's status as the economic powerhouse of the world. The moral debates about indentured servitude on Portugal's islands could be threatening to those interests, especially against a backdrop of highly lucrative commerce.

British companies had huge holdings in Africa, including diamond and gold mines in South Africa and Rhodesia. All labour intensive. All cost sensitive. To minimize manpower expenses while avoiding the stigma of slavery, British interests in Africa imported "coolies" from China to work in their diamond pits and mines. The coolies were shipped to the Transvaal with numbers tattooed on their chests and few, if any, ever returned to China. When the newspapers attacked the coolie system as just another way to get around laws against slave labour, British mining industrialists were compelled to find other sources of cheap or free labour. Enter the Portuguese.

In addition to Angola on the west coast of Africa, Portugal was also in control of Mozambique on the east coast, a country that conveniently bordered both South Africa and Rhodesia. Unknown to the general public or the cocoa companies at the time, throughout the first decade of the twentieth century the British government was in protracted negotiations with the Portuguese to have African labourers transferred from Mozambique to the mines of the Transvaal. The British assumed that this transaction could be pulled off without attracting too much attention. But the negotiations were slow and the Portuguese obstinate.

American historian Lowell Satre has recently investigated Cadbury's cocoa sources and found a cover-up in the British foreign office of the early twentieth century. He unearthed documents that reveal a profound interest on the part of British civil servants to keep a lid on the cocoa-slavery debate because of the negotiations they were conducting with the Portuguese for a cheap labour supply from Mozambique. "To a great extent," says Satre, "the gold mines of the Transvaal were equivalent to the *rocas* of São Tomé. Greed and profit dictated both Portuguese labour policy in São Tomé and British labour policy in Johannesburg. Cadbury Bros. was little more than a sideshow to the transactions in South Africa."

But the Cadburys had their own complicating sideshow. In addition to being chocolate-makers, they were also newspaper proprietors. George Cadbury had several papers in the Birmingham area, and in 1901 he purchased the *Daily News* in London to provide an editorial platform for Liberal political views. The paper led the campaign against the Conservative government for allowing Chinese coolies to work in slavery conditions in southern Africa. Cadbury-directed editorials lambasted the government for allowing "slavery by another name" and demanded that the abusive labour practice stop immediately. But the paper was strangely silent on the subject of São Tomé even as other periodicals began to follow Nevinson's lead and write of the atrocities in Angola. Conservative voices in Britain's fiercely competitive and highly partisan media accused the Cadburys of hypocrisy.

In letters to other cocoa-makers, as well as to his Quaker associates and his friend Edmund Morel, William Cadbury urged restraint to the point of deception on the issue of slavery in São Tomé. Play it down, he cautioned, claiming he was assured by high sources in the Foreign Office that the British government was pressuring the Portuguese to mend their ways. Let the Foreign Office do its work without high-minded harassment, Cadbury advised his inner circle.

Did William Cadbury and his Quaker colleagues really believe the Foreign Office was fixing things, or was it just convenient to believe the official line from Whitehall? As individuals, the Cadburys were highly conscientious, genuinely moral, socially engaged. But they also had a business to run and thousands of employees dependent on their actions. They even had a higher goal: pioneering a new philosophy of business. To risk their economic prospects would be to jeopardize the larger mission. They were cultivating other lines of supply, but it would take time before they could divorce themselves from the unsavoury Portuguese slave-drivers. And maybe, given time, the Portuguese would come around under pressure from the Foreign Office. Perhaps they could keep the story from doing any more damage until they could secure another source of cocoa.

But the anti-slavery activists just wouldn't let up, and the Cadburys presented an easy target. The conservative newspapers had a field day watching them struggle on the horns of their moral dilemma. The Cadburys fell back on the justification that they were conducting their own investigation. In fact, Joseph Burtt, the keen and affable researcher who now spoke a smattering of Portuguese, had departed for Africa just as Nevinson was returning, in June 1905. The two investigators actually crossed paths in Africa, Nevinson departing while Burtt was arriving. Nevinson thought Burtt was a decent enough chap but entirely too impressionable and "about the youngest man of 43" he'd ever met. Nevinson concluded that Burtt was out to whitewash the slave system—even before he'd seen it—as the best possible arrangement for poor Africans:

"Thinks the plantations greatly increase human happiness and so on," Nevinson wrote in his diary.

While the Cadburys urged patience and dismissed Nevinson as a blowhard, Burtt spent two years travelling and didn't return to England until 1907. His report took months to write. Once it was completed, the Cadburys kept it from public view until near the end of 1908. Seven years had passed since they'd acknowledged to their board that there was a problem in the cocoa groves of São Tomé and Príncipe, and it was twenty years since the stories of abuse started to fill the pages of the *Reporter*. Even people who supported William Cadbury wondered why it took so long. Clearly, some of the delay can be blamed on the machinations of the Foreign Office since diplomatic contact with Portugal was complicated by political instability, a plague of coups and assassinations in Lisbon. But Britain had problems of its own, and it's safe to assume that the Portuguese missed few opportunities to remind the British of their own moral lapses in southern Africa.

Even though Joseph Burtt had received most of his information in Africa from Portuguese slave traders and cocoa farm owners who had wined and dined the wide-eyed writer during his visit, Burtt still managed to write a damning report. Perhaps the abuse was so widespread and so flagrant that even someone eager to please the Cadburys couldn't avoid being moved to outrage. Burtt's tone was measured, and his voice lacked the passion of the fiery Nevinson, but his bottom line was the same. He told the Cadburys that Nevinson had been right about everything — except perhaps he had not gone far enough. No matter what the Portuguese wanted to call their system, it was simply slavery by another name.

The conservative British press had been hammering at the Cadburys all along. Now, with Burtt's report, the Tory papers could smell the blood of Liberals and reformers, expecially the moralistic Quakers. The Conservatives weren't so much offended by the evidence of slavery as by the hypocrisy of the other side.

The *Standard* led the charge against the chocolate kings with a damning editorial: "It's not called slavery; but 'contract labour' they name it now . . . But in most of its essentials it is that monstrous trade in human flesh and blood against which the Quaker and radical ancestors of Mr. Cadbury thundered in the better days of England."

The Cadbury family was outraged by the bluntness of the accusation, coming as it did on the heels of a dozen less pointed attacks. They had threatened and coerced newspapers to print apologies and retractions in the past, but this time they decided they would sue the *Standard*. But the Cadburys needed to have one crucial bit of business in place before they could subject their reputation to the scrutiny of the courts.

In 1909, just before the libel trial, William Cadbury declared that he was going off to see the operation in São Tomé for himself. His uncle George urged friends and other newspapers not to report on the Portuguese labour issue for the time being lest it endanger William during his travels. William Cadbury had all the access the Portuguese would allow, which wasn't much. But on this same voyage, he made a side trip, which was, quite possibly, the real reason for his journey. He went to the Gold Coast (now Ghana) to investigate cocoa export possibilities there. The first cocoa plants had arrived in the Gold Coast about twenty years earlier and, by the time of Cadbury's visit, the country had the growing capacity to replace São Tomé. The Gold Coast was also a British colony, where the cocoa companies and the British government could conceivably have considerable influence over labour practices. What's more, the Africans themselves were the farmers. All in all, it was a perfect solution to his problem. The Gold Coast would become the source of Cadbury's—and Britain's beans.

When Cadbury returned to England, the Quaker cocoa companies finally agreed to launch a boycott against São Tomé cocoa. The timing was perfect. They had an alternative supply of cocoa. It was the eve of the libel trial they hoped would shut the

Tories up, once and for all. The boycott, they assumed, would strengthen their case against the newspaper.

The trial began on November 29, 1909, and it soon became as much a test of Cadbury's ethics as defamation by the *Standard*. In his book *Chocolate on Trial: Slavery, Politics and the Ethics of Business*, Lowell Satre documents an extraordinary display of legal theatrics. It was a dramatic contest between two of the most accomplished and brilliant lawyers of the time: Edward Carson representing the *Standard*, and Rufus Isaacs representing Cadbury Brothers Limited.

What emerged during six days of testimony and florid oratory from the two barristers was a portrait of a highly principled company brought to moral paralysis for a decade in a genuine confusion of ethics and self-interest. Yes, the company ultimately launched a boycott against São Tomé cocoa—but that couldn't excuse ten years of dithering. William Cadbury could offer few explanations for all the procrastination, except to blame the Foreign Office. He'd been following instructions from important men at Whitehall and he thought he'd been behaving in the national interest. But in the end, the Foreign Office hung him out to dry.

Foreign Secretary Edward Grey, when called to testify, could shed no light on any such arrangement. Much to the astonished chagrin of the Cadburys, Grey claimed he could hardly remember any meetings with the chocolate companies and could offer no explanation as to why Cadbury Brothers had failed to boycott São Tomé years earlier. The Foreign Secretary had been called as *their* star witness.

In the end, the Cadburys had to fall back on their long-standing reputation for fairness and high moral principles over many years of business dealings. In the closing moments of the trial, it seemed that this might be enough. The judge's instructions to the jury urged that, should they find in favour of the plaintiff—that the *Standard* had indeed libelled the chocolate-

makers—they should award "sufficiently substantial damages."
The jury did rule in Cadbury's favour. But the victory was bittersweet. The jurymen awarded damages of "one farthing."

~

Henry Nevinson continued to investigate and to rail against the
chocolate companies in a campaign that was more advocacy
than journalism. In his diary for June 3, 1910, Nevinson recorded
a conversation with two cocoa traders who seemed to confirm
that Cadbury Brothers had cynically avoided any boycott of the
Portuguese until they were satisfied that Gold Coast plantations were ready to meet their needs for raw product. He also
wrote that the Fry company seemed to have finalized a huge
contract for São Tomé cocoa "the very day before the boycott
was announced & continued to draw on it for many months."
During the trial, Cadbury's principal buyer admitted under cross-
examination that it would have been "difficult" and "awkward" to
obtain beans from anywhere else before 1909, but it was still possible, if one wanted to pay a premium. And that was the fundamental problem: The bottom line in business was, as always, the
bottom line.

A number of contemporary scholars, including Satre, have
concluded that it was a lack of alternative bean sources and not
skepticism over Nevinson's report that made the Cadburys delay
action for so long. The appalling corollary is that the Quaker
cocoa companies of Britain dragged their feet and dodged the
issue for nine years before they finally stopped using slave cocoa.

Despite worldwide condemnation of slavery, and laws against
it, as many as eight million Africans died from overwork or were
slaughtered by their masters in the late nineteenth and early
twentieth centuries. Uncalculated numbers perished on the
Portuguese islands while the Cadburys temporized and stalled.
Even after the British companies withdrew, slavery continued on

the islands for many more years, and Angolans were still being forced into labour until the 1950s.

São Tomé was not the most abusive of colonies, nor was Cadbury Brothers the most hypocritical of companies. But Cadbury had elevated chocolate, in the public mind, to a special status—a token of affection, a symbol of simple joy, a sensual yet innocent pleasure. It was Cadbury more than any other chocolate company that had rebranded chocolate and defined its public image. Cadbury's role in slavery and human exploitation was indirect. Their behaviour, compared with that of the pillagers of gold and ivory and diamonds in the Congo and southern Africa, was commendable. But Cadbury's history and its philosophy and its product imposed a higher corporate standard. The company's corporate moral failure left them vulnerable to the jibes of journalists like Nevinson, the mockery of their cynical political opponents and the judgment of posterity: If high-minded Quakers could be tainted by the cocoa business, what realistic hope existed that there could ever be integrity in the world of unrestricted commerce?

Chapter Four

THE GEOPOLITICS OF **A HERSHEY'S KISS**

"All the other chocolate makers, you see, had begun to grow jealous of the wonderful candies that Mr. Wonka was making, and
they started to send in spies to steal his secret recipes. The spies
took jobs in the Wonka factory, pretending they were ordinary
workers, and while they were there, each one of them found out
exactly how a certain special thing was made."

— ROALD DAHL, *Charlie and the Chocolate Factory*

MILTON SNAVELY HERSHEY HARDLY SEEMED DESTINED
for greatness when he was growing up as a poor farm boy on the
eastern seaboard of the United States. But then again, this was
nineteenth-century America where anything was possible.
Milton's great-grandfather had fled persecution in Switzerland in
the seventeenth century, along with other people of the
Mennonite faith, and he had sought refuge for his family in the
New World. The British Quaker William Penn had promised
religious freedom for all in his new colony, and the Mennonites,
feeling quite at home with the pious Society of Friends, settled
among them in Pennsylvania.

Hard-working, dutiful and dour, Milton's mother, Fanny,
taught her son that the only pleasure he should seek was that of
reading from the Bible and that he should struggle to avoid more
frivolous pursuits. But Milton's father had other ideas. Romantic,
whimsical and utterly unreliable, Henry Hershey encouraged
his son to read widely and question everything. Though born a

Mennonite, Henry was preoccupied with the secular world of the nineteenth century, preferring modern skepticism to the certainties of faith. He read the *New York Times* every day, along with any book that he could find among the cornfields and dairy farms of Derby Church, Pennsylvania.

Henry might still have endeared himself to his purposeful and pragmatic wife if he hadn't managed to squander her resources, and those of her family, on various inventions and get-rich schemes. On the somewhat sensible side, he once tried his hand at planting fruit trees. There were trout brooks and canned vegetables—all worthy ventures that went bust for reasons beyond Henry's control. If his wife felt any goodwill towards his endeavours, she lost it when Henry attempted to invent a perpetual motion machine. Fanny Milton was chronically cross but unable to challenge her husband for his vagaries since he was never around. In addition to his other qualities, Henry had a tendency to wander off, usually returning more broke than when he left.

The Hersheys had one other child—a daughter, Serena. When the little girl died of scarlet fever at the age of four, all of Fanny's and Henry's conflicting hopes and dreams for the future came to rest on young Milton. They bickered constantly about his education, and Henry dragged his son from school to school while Fanny insisted that the boy needed to settle down and learn how to run a farm. She loathed her husband's library, and much later—when it seemed he was finally gone for good—she happily burned all his books. For his part, Henry had nothing but scorn for Fanny's faith, calling his fellow Mennonites "the gray-minded people who cannot rejoice."

With so much disruption in his schooling, Milton acquired only the most rudimentary reading and writing skills and had no knowledge of the farm business at all. By the time he reached puberty, his parents concurred (one of the few occasions) that the only hope for the young lad was for him to learn a trade. Henry's love for the printed word persuaded him that his son should apprentice in a newspaper office, but the plan was a disaster. Milton was as unfocused and whimsical as his father and couldn't set his mind to the precise work of typesetting. He managed to jam the machines (deliberately, according to some accounts) and he soon lost his first job. Whatever plan Henry had in mind for Milton after that fiasco, he never got the chance to exercise it. Soon after, Fanny showed him the door, and Henry wandered off to seek his fortune elsewhere.

As far as his mother could figure out, the only thing that seemed to interest young Milton was candy. Every Saturday, when the family took their farm produce to market, Milton would use whatever money he had earned running errands for people to buy himself sweets—nougats, sour balls, licorice and lollipops. But Milton's addiction to sweets also gave Fanny an inspiration: her son would go to work for Joe Royer at his Ice Cream Parlour and Garden and learn how to make candy.

As soon as he arrived at Royer's shop, Milton found his calling. He was no scientist, and he had none of the qualifications of the great candy-makers of the world, but he loved the alchemy of sugar mixed with flavours, the boiling and mixing, the transition, at a specific temperature, from liquid to perfect solid.

His spinster aunt gave Milton $150 to set up his own business, but he proved to have as much aptitude for money management as his father. He sold too many products. Along with basic items such as candied fruit and dried nuts, Milton tried to make and sell a vast range of sweets, including throat lozenges (his father had advised him that these new medicinal candies were the future) and French Secrets—bonbons with sentimental verses written inside the little paper wrappers. Milton couldn't stay ahead of the creditors; in particular, he fell behind in his payments for imported sugar, the mainstay of his enterprise. The business sank into insolvency, and Milton collapsed with nervous fatigue.

Henry Hershey had gone out west, like many restless Americans who sought their fortunes, and Milton soon joined him there. But it was Milton, not his father, who struck gold. The young Hershey got work with a candy-maker in Denver, Colorado, who specialized in particularly fine-tasting caramels. Through stealth and curiosity, Milton learned the man's secret: the Denver confectioner was adding fresh milk to the product. Most caramels were manufactured with paraffin, which rendered them chewy but added little else. Milk made the candy smooth and creamy, even buttery. Milton hurried back east, where he worked by day for a candy-maker and by night for himself, cooking up batches of these caramels. His mother and aunt joined him and, with the last of their funds, they set up yet another business. Since there were no family members left who would lend the young Milton money, this was probably Milton's last kick at the can.

The story from here is the stuff of legends—the mythical American dream realized. An Englishman happened to sample Hershey's wares one day and pronounced them the best caramels he had ever tasted. Would Hershey be interested in exporting his product to England? The order was huge, the profits substantial. Milton Snavely Hershey was an overnight success story.

The Lancaster Caramel Company swiftly grew and became a major enterprise. There were no more cash flow problems. When Hershey went to a major New York bank with a request for $100,000, the bank offered him $250,000. The factory sprawled over 450,000 square feet, and the company soon set up branch plants in three other cities. Hershey's caramels were sold in Japan, China, Australia and Europe as well as the United States. In 1890, at the age of thirty-three, Hershey was a wealthy man. He married a delicate young candy-counter girl named Kitty and set up his family members in big houses. He left his factory supervisors in charge of production while he ventured out to travel the world with his new bride. His aim was to satisfy his fascination with all the things his father cherished: books, theatre, painting and architecture. Milton imagined he could travel and learn for the rest of his life, and he certainly had the wealth to do so. But he became enchanted not with Europe's arts and letters but with its candy business and, in particular, chocolate.

Hershey had already tried adding cocoa powder to some of his caramels, and he had certainly tasted hot cocoa before, but the divine confections sold in Europe were like nothing he had ever experienced. Sweet memories of European chocolate haunted him, and when he saw chocolate-making machinery at the 1893 Columbian Exposition in Chicago he was smitten. Amidst the amusement rides and the cotton candy was a Dresden chocolatier named J.M. Lehmann, cooking up batches of toothsome goodies for the crowds. Hershey bought him out.

He assembled Lehmann's equipment back in Lancaster, and with products from the Walter Baker Company (America's leading cocoa-grinder) in neighbouring Massachusetts, Hershey set up his own modest chocolate-making enterprise in the back of his caramel factory. Though he hired a chemist, Hershey was suspicious of "experts," and he wouldn't follow any of the conventional practices of the time. He was going to reinvent the chocolate business.

A chemist in Switzerland by the name of Henri Nestlé had recently perfected a method for blending dairy milk with cocoa solids to produce a product called milk chocolate. Nestlé had been experimenting with removing some or all of the water from cow's milk in order to make baby formula. But he discovered that condensed or powdered milk would also blend well with cocoa butter. After he teamed up with an entrepreneur and found some capital, Nestlé's milk chocolate became the hottest item on the candy shelf—a smooth, easily digestible sweet treat.

Hershey wasn't above stealing the idea for making creamy caramels, but he wanted to craft an original American version of the milk chocolate. He conducted his own back-room experiments to separate butter from the solids, to condense milk and to blend it with sugar and cocoa butter. In his mind, he was starting from scratch, dismissing the centuries of technique that had preceded him. Hershey wanted to be the Henry Ford of candy—to create a chocolate bar that he would sell for a nickel and that almost anyone in America could afford to buy. And he did it.

Bars of rich milk chocolate, stamped with what would become an iconic name in the candy business—Hershey's—started to roll off the assembly line. Hershey unloaded his caramel business for a million-dollar profit and turned his full attention to chocolate-making. First there were Hershey's milk chocolate bars, then Hershey's milk chocolate with almond bars, then tiny Hershey's Kisses, each individually wrapped and with that distinctive little twirl on top. It didn't matter what the Europeans had done; this was America, and Hershey was a chocolate pioneer.

The Pennsylvania farm boy was soon rich beyond his dreams, but also bored. Like his father, he needed the constant stimulation of new projects and new inventions. His next endeavour would be far more challenging than reinventing candy.

While he was travelling in England and learning about chocolate, it appears Hershey encountered some of the social engineering of the Quaker candy barons. He would certainly have heard of the garden city movement, including Cadbury Brothers' model community in Bournville and though he never did explain the source of his inspiration, Hershey became determined to create a town of his own in the shadow of his candy factory. The idea was presented as his own utopian vision: an all-American community where there would be "no poverty, no nuisances, no evil."

His financial advisors told him he was crazy. But he no longer had to listen to them. He was rich and, experience had demonstrated more than once, he had good instincts. At the dawn of the twentieth century, Milton set about to build what would become Hershey, Pennsylvania. He bought a few hundred acres of corn-fields in his home township of Derry, in the heart of Pennsylvania Dutch territory and started building in 1903. Within two years, the town of Hershey had become one of the most daring social experiments of the age, and true to Milton's expectation, it far surpassed anything the Cadburys or the Rowntrees had achieved back in England. The streets were broad, and every house had expansive green lawns. (Milton would sometimes tour the neighbourhoods to ensure that people were maintaining their properties to his satisfaction). There was indoor plumbing, electricity and steam heat— luxuries for most American factory workers, who were more accustomed to coal lamps and outhouses. All of it was available at an affordable rent or through low-interest loans from the Hershey Trust Bank.

The centrepiece of Hershey was, of course, the factory, where the odour of melted chocolate wafted from the giant copper kettles and infused the town with a surreal cloying sweetness—for candy lovers, even breathing was a pleasure. But there was more: an amusement park with rides; a lake-sized swimming pool; a community centre housing an enormous theatre with a grand marble lobby; a bandstand; a golf course; gardens modelled on those in Versailles; and a network of trolley lines linking up with neighbouring communities. Hershey, Pennsylvania, attracted hundreds of thousands of visitors who came to eat chocolate, listen to music, swim in the artificial lake and envy the people who lived and worked there. For all of his employees, there were insurance benefits, health care and retirement plans. Old-fashioned American capitalists were shocked. *Fortune* magazine called Hershey's enterprise immoral, suggesting that such generosity "saps a community's self-reliance and injures its pride."

What did Milton Hershey want in exchange? Happy, clean-living and above all else loyal employees who would turn tons of cocoa beans into rich milk chocolate and help to make him the king of chocolate in the United States. He got his wish. Within five years of his factory opening, the Hershey Chocolate Company had annual sales of over $5 million, while employing twelve hundred people who worked in shifts, twenty-four hours a day, six days a week, with nary a complaint. It was an industrial miracle, reinforced by Hershey's fervent belief in the idea of progress.

When he and Kitty discovered they couldn't have children, they established an orphanage and took in homeless boys. The children attended the Hershey Industrial School and lived with house parents, where they were better off—at least financially—than most of the children in town. Hershey wanted them to have everything he lacked as a boy.

By the end of the first decade of the twentieth century, Milton Hershey was a living legend—one of the best of the rags-to-riches success stories that made the United States the Promised Land for immigrants. Hershey's generosity was scorned by other capitalists, but he was celebrated by the leading intellectuals and social activists of his time. And in the end, nobody could argue with achievement. His town was a success, business was booming, and he got richer every day.

But as Hershey basked in the success of all his ventures and the praise of his admirers, his fellow chocolate-makers in Britain were getting a different kind of feedback from the public. Muckraking journalists had exposed a sordid secret in the chocolate trade. Chocolate, no matter what the cost in the candy store, had a hidden price in human misery. The candy business was becoming complicated. People in Britain had started asking hard questions about the real cost of cocoa and its sinister sources. Working people were growing impatient with the paternalism of the better bosses—the Rowntrees and the Cadburys—and their cozy arrangements with workers. The king of cocoa in America would find he was not immune from censure and disparagement.

~

The slave trade had ended formally in the mid-1840s, after 250 years of blatant exploitation. Abolitionists and idealists celebrated an important turning point in human history—the triumph of decency and justice. But the victory was deceptive. There were new anti-slavery laws in most European countries and an outright ban in Britain. And yet slavery in other forms continued.

Until at least 1918, "indentured labourers," also known as coolies, were exported to the islands of the Caribbean from Asia. At least a half-million East Indian labourers arrived at British colonies in Jamaica and Trinidad during this time, while Cuba imported a quarter of a million from China. European and American shipping merchants offered work to men and women fleeing famine and depravation in their own countries. They were offered "contracts," as the Portuguese had done for Africans in Angola to circumvent laws against slavery. The indentured labour business was a sham, but the contracts and the acquiescence of frightened, starving people gave the exercise a veneer of legitimacy that managed to fool an all-too-willingly blind world of consumers into complacency.

The labour merchants treated the Asian workers like animals: they were held in pens, branded, chained and herded onto ships that bore a striking resemblance to the African slave vessels of bygone days. The coolies in the Americas, like the Angolans in São Tomé and the Asians in the Transvaal, would have to work for years before they received any pay. If they were lucky, they might earn just enough to make their way back to their countries. Few of them ever tried it. With nothing to return to after years abroad, many of them stayed on beyond their "contracts," clearing land for new plantations to satisfy the insatiable demand for both sugar and cocoa. The indentured coolie system was, as George Cadbury's own newspaper had declared, "slavery under a different name." Yet, here it was, largely unreported, on the cocoa-producing islands of the Caribbean. There was no crusading Henry Nevinson here to take up the cause.

The Cadburys purchased two estates in the British colony of Trinidad in 1897, just as the damning reports about labour abuse in São Tomé were growing too loud to be ignored and as the company was scrambling to find other less controversial sources of raw materials. They also entered a joint venture ownership with the Scottish distillery C. Tennant and Company for the Ortinola Estates in Trinidad, one of the largest on the island.

In the archives of York University in England, Rowntree Company records include files and photos from its own plantations in the British colony of Jamaica. There are also photographs of Cadbury's cocoa farms in Ortinola (oddly enough, published in the Rowntree Company newsletter to show their employees in York what the future Rowntree farms would look like). The pictures reveal rows of miserable-looking workers raking cocoa beans. The ethnicities are mixed, but the photo captions are explicit: "Coolies Sorting Cocoa—Ortinola Estates"; "Coolies 'Dancing' Cocoa—Ortinola Estates." The latter shows about sixty workers standing on a pile of fermenting or drying beans, their stern-faced Creole managers close behind them.

As the British government reduced the tariffs on cocoa beans in order to stimulate the chocolate industry, Britain also allowed contractors in its Caribbean colonies to buy up large tracts of Crown land—most of it virgin rainforests—and to clear-cut the area for more cocoa plantations. To their credit, the British companies invested in the colonies to improve crop quality and attempt to avoid the cocoa tree diseases that had closed down other cocoa-producing regions in Spanish America. But the coolie system was endemic to the region.

Since the days when Spanish monks hid their operations deep in their monasteries and guarded their recipes closely, the chocolate business had evolved a cult of unparalleled secrecy. There were good reasons for it, and they weren't all in the kitchens and the labs, as the São Tomé scandal would reveal. The controversy over slavery drove the companies even further underground, and today it's virtually impossible to pin down exactly where the high-minded Hershey was getting his cocoa beans. It's safe to assume, though, that much of the supply was coming from the Caribbean, taking into account geography and hemispheric politics. The Caribbean was relatively close. And the Monroe doctrine, asserting American hegemony in the region, guaranteed a certain predictable security of trade.

Hershey was one of the few companies in the United States that actually processed cocoa. With the exception of the Baker Company, most of the other—and smaller—manufacturers purchased their cocoa butter and powder from Hershey. But pinning down where Hershey got its cocoa would become even more of a guessing game as the business of commodity trading went global. Traders in Amsterdam, Hamburg and New York were consolidating cocoa beans from the Caribbean and West Africa—a practice known as bulking. Significantly, the Portuguese producers from São Tomé were able to continue a flourishing trade in cocoa beans—concealing slave-made product among supplies from other locations—long after their woeful labour practices had been exposed and the industry agreed to boycott their product.

In 1910, Joseph Burtt, the investigator retained by Cadbury to check on the Portuguese, was asked to testify before a U.S. Ways and Means Committee hearing in Washington to describe what he had seen in São Tomé. He was happy to oblige. He told congressmen that he had found as many as forty thousand Angolans working on São Tomé plantations—in shackles—and that he had seen the bones of the dead lining the slave route from Angola to the island. The committee chairman asked Burtt why the slaves didn't just run away: "What would happen to them? I never had any slaves," said the chairman. "What would happen to them?" Burtt told him he couldn't even begin to imagine, having seen so many corpses and so much death. He never saw a slave attempt to simply run away. "They might be treated like gentleman for aught you know," stated the chairman.

Despite the chairman's facetiousness, the Senate passed a toughly worded resolution: that the U.S. president be given the authority to "forbid by proclamation the entry of cocoa into the United States or her possessions when it is shown to his satisfaction that the same is the product of slave labor."

The Americans were acutely sensitive on the subject of slavery at that time. They had, in living memory, fought a bloody civil war over states' rights, and many Southerners had considered the ownership and employment of slaves to be inviolable. The abolitionists won the cause and the war and, while the realistic among them were undoubtedly aware of the myriad ways to continue enslavement under less provocative terminology, they were determined to make a bold show of opposing it in all its forms.

Labour practices in the Americas were becoming an American responsibility. European influence in the hemisphere was breaking down as a result of independence movements in the colonies and a muscular American policy that prevented the old European powers from doing much about it. Where it suited their interests, Americans were asserting military and economic power in the former European colonies—and nowhere with more enthusiasm than in an old Spanish colony a hundred kilometres off the Florida panhandle.

Cuba was considered central to the "American way of life." American sugar barons had invested tens of millions of dollars on the island, and in the late nineteenth century American capitalists bought Cuban revolutionary bonds issued in New York City to help overthrow Spanish authority.

Cuba declared its independence in 1902, but its sovereignty was a fiction from the start. Washington asserted power over Cuba's foreign relations as well as domestic matters of "life, property and individual liberty." In reality, American sugar barons ruled in Cuba while tens of thousands of Chinese coolies and African slaves, working for subsistence wages, maintained their lush plantations. The real beneficiaries of this arrangement were the lords of the U.S. candy and soft drink industries.

While it's hard to say exactly where Hershey got his cocoa, there's no mystery about where he got his sugar. American businessmen purchased hundreds of thousands of acres of Cuban farmland for sugar crops and flattened the ancient rainforests. Cuba became an importer of basic foods as its farming sector turned into a monoculture committed to a single market. Hershey bought 65,000 acres of sugar fields in Cuba. His holdings stretched so far along the northern coast of the island that he built his own railroad. Near the coastal town of Santa Cruz del Norte in Yumuri Valley, Hershey built Central Hershey Cuba, a town for his workers, just as he had done in Pennsylvania. It had running water and electricity. He provided health services and built a baseball diamond for the town. While it was never quite as grand as the town of Hershey, Pennsylvania, it was far above the standards for the region. But Cuban land was cheap, its labour force captive, and American capitalists such as Hershey ruled as absolute monarchs on their plantations. Through the U.S. control over Cuba, Hershey could secure his sugar supply in such volumes that he actually became one of the largest suppliers of sweetener to the Coca-Cola Company.

In the first decades of the twentieth century, Milton Hershey was at the top of his game, a self-made man with the heart of a philanthropist. His model city in Pennsylvania was part of a sophisticated marketing strategy. A spinoff town in Cuba gave him security in the vital flow of sugar to his factories. He had a virtual monopoly in the American chocolate market. But the world was evolving. A whole new generation of cocoa barons was on the rise—and with them came a new spirit of sophisticated ruthlessness that would overwhelm the visionary Milton Hershey.

~

Forrest Mars, the heir apparent to the American chocolate throne, was born in 1904, the only child in the unhappy and short-lived marriage of Frank Mars and Ethel Kissak. Frank was running a failing candy business in Minneapolis at the time of his son's birth. Soon afterwards, Ethel divorced her bankrupt husband and sent Forrest to live with her parents in the then remote Saskatchewan mining town of North Battleford.

Forrest proved himself to be the ace student in his one-room prairie schoolhouse where his teachers were convinced he would go places. After graduation from high school, the only place to go was back to the United States. There were few educational opportunities for a poor prairie scholar in early twentieth-century Canada, but the University of California at Berkeley saw Forrest's potential and gave him a partial scholarship.

Forrest was too restless and too ambitious to sit for any length of time in a classroom. His real calling was in sales, and he was soon making a small fortune as a campus wheeler-dealer, buying and reselling any merchandise he could get his hands on, from neckties to cigarettes. The Berkeley campus proved too limited, and he started peddling his wares on the street. Forrest was the archetypal American salesman. He had his father's passion for business, and eventually the two linked up in Chicago. The circumstances weren't auspicious—Frank had been arrested for illegal advertising. His hapless daddy bailed him out.

Frank had been running a relatively successful chocolate business in the 1920s when his son resurfaced in his life. Forrest's mother had more or less poisoned her son's memory, but still, father and son had a lot in common and decided to go into business together. Forrest would later insist that he gave his father the concept for the chocolate bar that turned the small company into an empire. The young Mars claims he invented the idea for solidifying a malted milk drink and then coating the nougat filling with chocolate. It was the birth of the Milky Way, an instant winner that turned a profit for the Mars men of $800,000 in its first year on the market. The bar was quickly followed by another nougat-filled chocolate-coated treat—Snickers. It was another home run, which would be repeated with Three Musketeers.

The magic couldn't last. Blood and genealogy aside, Forrest Mars hated his father and, more significantly, couldn't stand to share the glory of their chocolate creations with anyone. "I told my dad to stick the business up his ass," Forrest later claimed. Frank gave Forrest $50,000 and the rights to sell the Milky Way in Britain. They went their separate ways and never met again.

Unlike the pious Milton Hershey, who had to figure everything out for himself, Forrest Mars had a knack for appropriating the ideas of other people. He went to Switzerland and got a job on the Toblerone factory floor, where he absorbed everything he possibly could about the high-end chocolate manufacturer before going on to get a job at Nestlé. He learned a lot—most usefully never to allow outsiders near his own factories. In later years, he outlawed visitors to his plant and kept outside work crews under strict control when they were on the premises. They were compelled to enter and leave the plant wearing blindfolds. Mars knew from his own sleuthing how common and how rewarding it was to spy.

After Nestlé, Forrest Mars went on to Britain with a plan to compete in the big leagues there. But by the 1930s, Cadbury Brothers, recovered from its public relations disasters of the early decades of the century, was a vast multinational operation, with plants throughout the former British Empire. Rowntree was also booming, thanks to the popularity of its Kit Kat and Aero bars and the ubiquitous Black Magic chocolate boxes. With the $50,000 his father had handed him, Forrest set up a little operation north of London, in the town of Slough, where he began to make a modified version of the Milky Way. He called it the Mars Bar.

Forrest was, at heart, an empire builder. He was soon expanding into other lines, including dog food. By the eve of the Second

World War, he was the third largest candy manufacturer in Britain. Then, faced with war, the British government imposed a special tax on foreigners that made it unprofitable to stay. It was time to head for home anyway. Frank Mars was dead (Forrest didn't attend his father's funeral), and Forrest figured the time was right to take over the family business. He had the experience. He had the expertise. It would take all that—and all his bravado and guts—to survive a looming crisis in candy land.

~

They had names that would strike terror into the hearts of cocoa producers: "witches' broom," "capsid," "swollen shoot," "black pod rot," "cocoa wilt." These were the vivid names of diseases that rampaged through the cocoa plantations of the Caribbean in the first half of the twentieth century. Just as Mexico had lost its advantage in cocoa production when its crop was virtually wiped out, now the new plantations in the Caribbean were facing the same fate. Disease devastated the economies of the islands and forced chocolate-makers to look elsewhere for their products. Africa became the logical choice, even for Milton Hershey.

By the 1930s, cocoa was well established in West Africa, still ruled by the European powers. France controlled Côte d'Ivoire; Nigeria was under British authority. Both produced some cocoa, but no colony was as productive as the land called the Gold Coast—also under the administrative sway of the British. The Cadburys, after the scandals of São Tomé and the Portuguese, had developed productive plantations there in partnership with independent African farmers, and the Gold Coast now led the world in cocoa production.

In 1936, there was a hiccup on the international commodities market. The global crop yield was less than anticipated. Prices for cocoa beans jumped to a record thirteen cents a pound. Milton Hershey panicked. Worried that the value of beans was going to rise even further, he started hoarding. He was buying and stockpiling all he could get his hands on when prices tumbled in 1937. He panicked again and calculated that if he bought up even higher quantities, he could take control of the pricing mechanism by manipulating supplies. It was a brave but deeply flawed idea.

Word got around that Hershey was the only purchaser in the market, buying everything available at his own inflated price. Soon he was buried in offers to sell. It went on for months before Hershey realized that he was buying nothing. He'd played into the hands of market speculators who were gambling that Hershey would one day soon have to unload the cocoa at a significantly lower price than he had paid for it. Then they'd buy it back. It's called futures trading, a phenomenon that would now take over commodities markets like cocoa and make fortunes for those who knew how to play the game. But Milton Hershey didn't understand it, and he lost $10 million.

According to the archives of the company, Hershey was profoundly resentful that gamblers had had him. "He was not the type to show anger," said one anonymous employee quoted in archival documents. "But he never forgot what he thought was the whole world against him. He was bitter."

In the end it didn't matter. With war looming, the British government seized direct control of Gold Coast cocoa—and most other commodities throughout the empire—and began to regulate prices and shipments of beans for the "war effort." The price controls were good for the manufacturers; they had a predictable supply of cheap raw materials. As always, the economic burden landed on the people at the bottom, the primary producers in distant, undeveloped lands.

Hershey and the other chocolate-makers were able to manipulate farmers in Africa, but their control at home wasn't quite so secure. The times were changing. Democracy in the marketplace, and on the factory floor, was cutting into the historic influence of the old-style capitalist proprietors. The effect of good intentions and proprietary munificence was just about exhausted.

~

Workers in Europe and North America took decades to find their common voice and the means to exercise collective power. But unions were gaining strength and workers were demanding concessions as a matter of fundamental rights, not the goodwill of benevolent capitalists. Milton Hershey was at a loss to understand the strife that was becoming part of the labour-management dialogue in the United States. Workers were going out on strike, turning violent when they didn't get what they were asking for. Managers were employing goons and Pinkerton security agents to intimidate ordinary working people and to physically harm them when necessary.

Hershey had built a town for his workers; he had tried to anticipate their every material and spiritual need; he extended credit when they ran low on money, and gave them stores to spend it in; he entertained them and made sure their children grew up in a stable, moral environment. During the Depression, he used his profits to start make-work projects and keep his people busy. The residents of Hershey, Pennsylvania, hardly knew there was an economic crisis destroying people in less fortunate American communities. And so it came as a shock when Milton Hershey faced his first strike. What more could they want from him?

The answer was simple. Hershey had never allowed his town to incorporate; he had run the place virtually as his fiefdom. There was no mayor, no municipal council and no government.

It was 1937 and communists were agitating. Labour organizers from the Committee for Industrial Organization (CIO) began holding secret meetings in a neighbouring town, and before too long Hershey's workers were on the march along with everybody

else. They demanded working hours consistent with other chocolate factories (the Hershey work week was sixty hours) and contracts that specified wages and benefits. Hershey had no idea how
to handle the uprising and left it up to his lawyers while he
retreated to his home on the hill overlooking the town he had
built from scratch. It was a lonely, silent place since his beloved
Kitty had passed away. From the empty mansion, he watched
what happened in horror.

Six hundred workers seized the factory building and chained
its doors. Within days, the labour action turned violent, with
Hershey loyalists and supporters physically beating the striking
workers. The first effort to unionize failed when the Hershey
labour force decided the CIO was too left-wing and "un-American"
for their taste, but shortly after, they joined the kinder, gentler
Bakery and Confectionery Workers International Union. They
continued to profess deep loyalty to their boss, but union leaders
persuaded them that the days of authoritarian management and
company towns were past. They had nothing against Milton.
He'd proven his decency and commitment many times over. But
he was mortal. They'd be foolish to expect that his altruistic values would live on after him.

Disgruntled workers noted that Milton Hershey spent more
money on each of his orphans than they could spare for their
own children with the wages they were earning. Hershey was a
benevolent dictator. His subjects wanted both the benevolence
and a union.

The company eventually signed a labour agreement with
the American Federation of Labor, while the Bakery and Confectionery Workers International Union won the right to represent the Hershey workers. These were the dying moments of
paternalism in the labour force and the end of an unsustainable
experiment in benevolent capitalism. The world was changing,
and Hershey felt less and less a part of it. After the strike, he spent
much of his time in Cuba, where he had a palatial home and

where, at least for the time being, men with money could still thrive and call the shots, a simple world with simple, undemanding people.

~

Milton Hershey was tired and dispirited in the war years. Cutthroat commodities traders dominated the market, and his own labour force—his children—had turned against him. Hershey's president, William Murrie, gradually took charge of the business.

For fifty years, Murrie had been the loyal man-in-the-shadows of the Hershey empire. Hershey was dreamy and preoccupied with his social engineering projects, while Murrie was a solid manager of day-to-day affairs. Murrie, like Hernán Cortés centuries before, saw the caloric value of chocolate and persuaded the authorities in Washington that it had strategic value for the war effort. Chocolate became part of the soldiers' survival kit, as it had once been for both Aztecs and conquistadors. During the 1940s, most of Hershey's production went to war department contracts, and a billion chocolate bars were packaged for the soldiers. The chocolate was for nutrition, but also for morale. What could better lift the warrior spirit on a distant battlefield than a familiar Hershey's Kiss? The sweet deal with the U.S. government allowed Hershey to thrive throughout the war years and to maintain a monopoly over American cocoa. The Hershey company had all the quotas while other chocolate-makers had to make deals with Hershey.

It was Murrie, not Milton, who was at the president's desk the day the Hershey head offices had a strange, uninvited visitor. For years, Hershey had provided the chocolate coating for Frank Mars's Milky Way bar, Three Musketeers and Snickers. But there was a new Mars in town—Frank's boy, Forrest Mars. He was back from Britain with an idea: a chocolate that would "melt in your mouth and not in your hand." Forrest Mars showed up in Murrie's office with small round candies in all the happy hues of the rainbow. They were filled with chocolate. He'd discussed the candy with the British Rowntree people, who called them Smarties. He, of course, would come up with a better name.

Forrest Mars wanted Hershey to produce the chocolate for this new line of candy in the United States but he needed Hershey's access to cocoa. And he wanted something else. Forrest Mars asked that William Murrie's son, Bruce, become his associate in the business. It was a great opportunity for the young business school student though Bruce Murrie would figure out only much later that Forrest Mars was using him as a conduit to his dad. By then Hershey had become Mars's principal supplier and Bruce was deeply involved with what most of the chocolate world came to know as the industry tyrant.

An abusive and self-centred man, Forrest Mars also happened to be a brilliant businessman. Claiming to have the U.S. licence to produce Smarties, he created M&Ms—the two M's representing Mars and Murrie. And Mars, Inc. would go on to make billions of dollars, eventually eclipsing the Hershey legacy.

~

Milton Snavely Hershey died in 1945. Typically, most of his shares in the company were left in trust for the operation of the Hershey orphanage. Thousands came to pay their last respects to an industry giant and a capitalist anomaly. Milton Hershey had become a sad, reclusive man in his eighties, a relic from another age, unprepared by nature for the cutthroat industry that Forrest Mars would thrive in.

Following the war years, chocolate companies became deeply secretive and highly competitive. An age of innovation and invention was overtaken by one of acquisition and merger. J.S. Fry & Sons was folded into Cadbury Brothers, which eventually merged with the soft drink empire Schweppes. The last member of the Cadbury family to sit on its board of directors retired from the position in 2000.

The Rowntree family at first resisted merger. The patriarch of the empire, Joseph, once wrote a memorandum stating that his company was not a mechanism to generate money but a trust, given by God, to be in the service of others. Such ideas went out with garden cities, and by the 1930s there were no Rowntrees running the affair. Professional executives replaced the family. Rowntree merged with the toffee manufacturer McIntosh, then the whole lot was acquired in a "dawn raid" by Nestlé.

Mars has remained a private company to this day, even as it moved to the head of the pack in the United States, with multi-billion-dollar profits. Mars family members are among the richest people in the United States, each worth as much as Ross Perot. Mars, Inc. expanded into manufacturing all types of food, including Uncle Ben's Rice (with the friendly liberated slave on the box), and, in keeping with Forrest's earlier ventures in Britain, pet food such as Whiskas, Sheba, Kal Kan and Pedigree (high-quality pet food is a curious sideline of many chocolate companies).

Swiss chemist Henri Nestlé sold his enterprise long before it became an international conglomerate. The Nestlé instant coffee product Nescafé emerged as a staple for soldiers in the U.S. military, and the company actually made money during the war, when many other food-makers were suffering. The company became the subject of an international boycott when it was accused of aggressively marketing instant powder formula for infants and contributing to a drastic decline of breast-feeding in the developing world. The boycott was huge, lasting from 1977 to 1984, but Nestlé recovered and aggressively gobbled up Maggi seasonings and soups, Libby's foods, Stouffer's and San Pellegrino, along with pet food companies including Ralston Purina and Friskies.

The chocolate business, predictably, has shifted from family-run enterprises to corporations and multinational conglomerates, and a fiercely competitive industry has consolidated into large monopolies and cartels. Most of the cocoa companies have entered collective umbrella organizations that provide professional spokespeople to deal with thorny issues such as "Where do the beans come from?" and "Under what conditions do those workers live?" No company wants to answer directly, as George Cadbury was willing to do in his own newspaper.

In recent years, the dirty work of buying and selling cocoa beans has become the domain of giant food conglomerates such as Cargill and Archer Daniel Midlands—anonymous corporations that are able to deal with the imperatives of the industry, particularly the constant, pulsing pressure to find cheap sources of beans so they can keep prices reduced. Low prices are what consumers consider fair, even if their affordable goods create injustice elsewhere. And into the coming decades, cocoa would continue to claim its victims.

Chapter Five

NO SWEETNESS **HERE**

"The playing field was essentially bequeathed to the African
seekers of power whose ethical and humane political antennae
were nonexistent . . . There would be no sweetness here."
— PETER SCHWAB, *Africa: A Continent Self-Destructs*

FOR MUCH OF THE TWENTIETH CENTURY, BRITISH
authorities claimed that their agents had introduced cocoa to the
Gold Coast, and an early version of the *Encyclopedia Britannica*
even describes Ghanaian cocoa farms as an English colonizer's
initiative. The British not only had little to do with bringing
cocoa to West Africa, but also almost destroyed what the Africans
had achieved with great effort.

The lion's share of the credit for introducing *Theobroma* cacao
trees to the region goes to an African named Tetteh Quarshie.
Born to a land-owning farm family in Gold Coast, Quarshie was
trained by Basel missionaries to be a master blacksmith, a trade
that allowed him to make a reasonable living. He travelled to
other colonies for work and eventually found himself on the
Spanish slave island of Fernando Po (now Bioko).

Quarshie was fascinated with the strange crop that European
merchants obsessed over and Angolan slaves laboured and died
for. The short, broad-leafed *Theobroma* tree, with its large
gourd-like pods growing right from the trunk, was unlike anything Quarshie had ever seen in Africa. But more interesting,
he realized that it produced possibly the most perfect cash crop

imaginable. The tree thrives in a mixed farm operation and it flourishes best when surrounded by other crops, especially food-producing ones. Since *Theobroma* needs shade, the tall banana plant with its broad canopy of leaves is a perfect neighbour; yam and cassava crops around its feet contribute to a nourishing sponge-like mulch, perfect for retaining moisture and a habitat for the tiny mites that pollinate the fragile cocoa flower. A sterile plantation-style monocultural environment — such as what are often the conditions for coffee and rubber — is disastrous for cocoa. And there is no machine that can cultivate or harvest cocoa as effectively as the human hand. Compact, family-run mixed farm operations are ideal for *Theobroma*, and for Africans.

The peripatetic Quarshie returned to his village in the Gold Coast after six years abroad, carrying with him precious cocoa seeds. He propagated them and then distributed stock as well as seeds to other farmers. The climate and soil in the Gold Coast were perfect for the variety he brought home with him — the Forastero, a hardy and prolific variety of "food of the gods."

Quarshie couldn't have foreseen when he planted his cocoa seeds in the late 1870s that thirty years later, when the trees were mature and bearing fruit, dramatic circumstances would place him in the middle of a confluence of developments in Europe and America. As international consumers clamoured for chocolate bars and cocoa, Caribbean and Latin American plantations had become disease-ridden and incapable of meeting the new demand. And anti-slavery crusaders were blowing the whistle on the Portuguese islands in the coastal areas where Quarshie had worked for the Spanish. His timing turned out to be perfect. Enter Cadbury, looking for scandal-free beans, and soon the cocoa farmers of Gold Coast were enjoying a brisk trade.

The British government, for its part, hardly seemed to know cocoa was growing in its colony until the trees were mature and Cadbury came along. At the time, British interest in its African colonies was centred on the lucrative mines in Rhodesia and South Africa. But with a new market for *Theobroma* from the mineral-depleted Gold Coast, the British government quickly clambered on board.

A review in the *Journal of Economic History* entitled "Cocoa in the Gold Coast," published in 1966, documents the extent to which the colonial administrators of the early twentieth century misunderstood both the importance of cocoa and the science of cocoa cultivation. Once they became involved, British bureaucrats railed at the farmers for what they considered to be sloppy and inefficient agricultural practices. They insisted that the farmers raze the existing forests to create large plantations, then plant their trees in long, neat rows, and scrupulously weed and ditch to create dry and tidy fields, clear of all unattractive debris. The farmers argued that the trees required disorder—the shade of other trees and plants, the tangle of weeds and mulch. But the protests of Africans were met with derision from the bwanas. "The producers of cocoa in this colony and the Ashanti are natives in a most elementary state of civilization whose sole aim, as yet, appears to be the attainment of the maximum amount of money for a minimum expenditure of energy, however uneconomical the system," said one report from 1916.

The same "sessional paper" laments that cocoa production was much better managed on the Portuguese islands of Príncipe and São Tomé because the colonizers used coercive means, something the report's author suggested the British colony might consider: "Peaceful persuasion by the few available officers of this Department is not often successful . . . legislation appears essential to impress necessary cultural reforms upon a people incapable of taking the necessary measures to ensure the future prosperity of the industry."

Despite British bureaucratic meddling, the Gold Coast became the world's leading cocoa bean exporter by 1920. The seeds and the know-how spread to other farming enterprises—large and small—

throughout equatorial Africa. African farmers not only had another cash crop, along with coffee and palm oil, on which to depend, but also one that was compatible with their various farming operations.

The Gold Coast gained its independence from Great Britain in 1956, the first West African country to do so, and its founding president, Kwame Nkrumah, renamed the country Ghana, after an ancient African kingdom. Independent Ghana would grow rich—at least for a few decades—on cocoa.

Nkrumah was a charismatic African nationalist who was no admirer of his former colonial masters. He'd done hard jail time for his left-wing views and for political agitation. But he was part of a new generation of African leaders determined and obviously able to throw off the suffocating mantle of colonial power. It was, at first, an optimistic breath of spring in Africa, fragrant with the anticipation of freedom and self-rule. Nkrumah declared: "We are going to demonstrate to the world, to the other nations, young as we are, that we are prepared to lay our own foundations."

As president, Nkrumah took over the cocoa marketing board from the British and soon after attempted to create a cartel through which cocoa producers could collectively fix the price of the beans. The big chocolate companies had been through it all before. Milton Hershey had put an end to such shenanigans in the 1930s and his company would help to do it again. The Hershey archive reveals some of what the company did to crush this nascent African movement when it reared its head in the early 1960s. "Everybody in the company worked on that one," said Richard Uhrich, the man in charge of buying for Hershey. "We all had to agree because this required borrowing a lot of money."

Uhrich was interviewed as part of an oral history project at Hershey, and a transcript of his remarks in the Hershey archive is revealing: "We bought—oh such tremendous quantities of cocoa beans that you couldn't believe it," Uhrich says of one buying spree in 1965. "We bought them with no place to store them when they started arriving [laughs] so we had to do all kinds of things." Uhrich describes how they rented warehouse space in an old hosiery mill, a former train car factory and even an abandoned mushroom plant in order to stock the thousands of tons of beans from Africa. "When this stuff started arriving, oh my gad [*sic*], we were working around the clock to unload these things. They were coming in so fast you couldn't believe it. Trainloads of them were coming!"

The company sat on the beans until the price started to climb and then they flooded the market. The result was predictable. That was end of Africa's cocoa cartel.

The bottom fell out of the price of cacao beans in the 1970s while Ghana was heavily in debt. Nkrumah had been ousted, his promises of a new Africa supplanted by cynicism and disappointment. His own corruption and incompetence had doomed his messianic project for a new African democracy. Many farmers abandoned cocoa in favour of food crops that fetched less money but were not subject to the power of the chocolate companies.

Some Ghanaian farmers tried to stick it out. The problem was, as accommodating as *Theobroma* is of other crops, it is also a finicky plant that requires perfect growing conditions and a great deal of tender care. Expensive pesticides and herbicides increase its longevity and productivity, but as the big cocoa companies controlled the price of beans, the cost of maintaining the tree was often more than the cocoa was worth. Instead of tree husbandry, many Ghanaian farmers simply cleared more rainforests and planted more trees, abandoning the fallow farms behind them. As the rainforests disappeared, severe drought became common; finally, in the early 1980s, devastating fires destroyed most of Ghana's cocoa crops.

With a shrug, the chocolate companies did exactly what they had been doing for centuries: they moved on in search of a new frontier, new resources to satisfy the now globally entrenched chocolate addiction. They found what they were looking for just next door, in Côte d'Ivoire.

~

Rising out of the dense, steamy tropical forest like an apparition, Our Lady of Peace Basilica, on the city limits of Yamoussoukro, Côte d'Ivoire, rivals the Vatican both in dimension and pretension. By papal request, the dome is not as high as that of St. Peter's. But the gold crucifix atop the cupola thrusts into the African sky just far enough to make the entire structure even taller than the church in Rome. No pale imitation of the original, in many ways the African version is more magnificent. The architect had the advantage of the modern materials and technology of the 1980s and was able to construct a lofty, egg-shaped shell almost entirely out of stained glass. A total of 7,400 square metres of windows contains three dozen biblical scenes, each one crafted by the most talented glassworks artisans in all of Europe.

Inside, seating places among the rows of polished wooden pews have individual air conditioners, giving worshippers the luxury of forgetting they are in the midst of hot, humid equatorial banana and cocoa plantations and allowing them to focus on communing with God. There is also standing room for eleven thousand people inside the church, and a plaza (again reminiscent of the Vatican) in front of the grand doors can accommodate another 300,000 faithful. Sprawled out beyond the plaza is a generous parking lot. Given that the population of Catholics in the whole of Côte d'Ivoire totals not more than a million (and precious few of them have cars), spread over a country of 320,000 square kilometres, a casual observer might well wonder what the basilica is really all about.

The church's construction was commissioned and lovingly supervised by Côte d'Ivoire's founding father and long-term president Félix Houphouët-Boigny, who is referred to as "Le Vieux"—literally meaning "The Old Man," but signifying something more beatific. He wanted this tribute to the Virgin Mary built at any cost, and it's still difficult to learn the final price tag. Estimates are that it ran to US$300 million before completion. Labourers had worked on the project twenty-four hours a day for several years. Most of the construction was done in strict secrecy. The architect was an Ivorian citizen of Lebanese descent, but all the artisans and craftsmen were foreigners, and portraits of the chief designers—all French—are incorporated into one of the stained glass tableaux, along with God's humble servant, Houphouët-Boigny, featured at the feet of Christ.

Aside from the fifteen hundred Ivorians who worked on the building and grounds, the basilica's creation had almost nothing to do with the people of Côte d'Ivoire, except that they paid for it—not just at the time of construction but for years afterwards. The church was financed, according to the president, through a "deal with God" but more accurately through massive amounts of foreign funds that Houphouët-Boigny was able to borrow based on the country's substantial cocoa stock. At the time of completion in 1989, the bottom had fallen out of the price of cocoa and Côte d'Ivoire was spiralling down into economic chaos. But that had no effect on the extravagance of the project. Our Lady of Peace Basilica represents everything that Le Vieux was all about: it's a monument to his ego and political success— both enormous—and to his close relationship with both the mother church and France, his political patron.

Yamoussoukro, Côte d'Ivoire's capital city, where the basilica stands, is also mostly make-believe—a modern metropolis commissioned by Houphouët-Boigny and built upon the site of Ngokro, a tiny village that was Le Vieux's birthplace. It's also where his body is now interred in his massive former palace, a complex surrounded by five kilometres of protective walls, plus an artificial lake with real crocodiles. To drive through Yamoussoukro (and one must drive because, unlike in almost all other African cities, nothing is within a comfortable walking distance) is to enter a surreal world. Six- and even eight-lane roads are completely free of vehicles. On one afternoon, the only car I saw in a stretch of over ten kilometres was a single taxi containing two men from China on their way to a Chinese–Côte d'Ivorian joint venture project.

In the tradition of Bournville in England, Hershey in Pennsylvania, and even Montezuma's ancient Aztec capital, the city of Yamoussoukro is a monument to paternalism, megalomania and chocolate. But unlike those other places, Yamoussoukro has little to do with the people who live there. All important government buildings are on the outskirts of town; the president's monument to himself is off limits to the public; the alligator lake is smothered with tangled water vines; the highways lead nowhere useful. Sunday mass at the basilica is presided over by middle-aged white priests from France who give communion to the few hundred faithful scattered among the pews who bother to make the trip out into the woods. But then, chocolate has nothing to do with Ivorian lives, either. Nor does the history of how their country came to be called Côte d'Ivoire or how it came to be the largest single producer of cocoa beans in the world.

~

Félix Houphouët was born to a prominent family of landowners in 1905—a year after France had declared Côte d'Ivoire a part of its West African colonies. Houphouët trained as a doctor, but though he was able to work as an assistant, or auxiliary as the position was called, he could never be a full-fledged licenced practitioner in the French colony as an African. In the 1930s, he gave up medicine to work on his father's cocoa farm. Enjoying the privileges of his established family, part of the influential Baoulé clan, he became chief of his home district and quickly came up against the colonial authorities.

In 1885, the continent of Africa had been divvied up among the European empires at a conference held in Berlin. King Leopold's enterprises in Congo had unleashed a frenzied rush for ownership of the resource-rich "dark" continent. German chancellor Otto von Bismarck called the European powers together to discuss how they could share ownership of Africa in an orderly, gentlemanly fashion, avoiding the messy conflicts usually associated with competing interests. Bismarck wanted clear-cut rules and good manners to prevail. Britain laid claim to the Gold Coast and Nigeria in West Africa, plus large swathes of territory from Cairo to Cape Town. France grabbed the rest of West Africa, from Algeria to Côte d'Ivoire, or Ivory Coast (named after the commodity of most interest to colonial merchants). Belgium's King Leopold already had Congo; Germany, Portugal and Italy gobbled up whatever remained.

The artificial borders established at the Berlin Conference defined territories according to imperial interests, but they also divided kingdoms and millennia-old connections between regions and the diverse populations of Africa. Tribes could find half their members under one colonial administration, half under another. Even relatives could be ruled by different European governments. No regard was given to the effect these arbitrary divisions would have on native people. The rationale of empire was subordination of lesser places and peoples to the needs of the colonial masters.

West Africans didn't make things easy for the French colonials. Côte d'Ivoire resisted occupation for years, delaying France's plans for resource extraction. As a result, for much of the first half of the twentieth century, France was playing catch-up with her competitors, chief among which were British interests in the Gold Coast and Nigeria. Great Britain also had the advantage of better port facilities on the Gulf of Guinea.

Though both the French and the British seemed to understand little about the growing conditions of their territories, the skill of African farmers, coupled with the enterprise of colonial merchant houses, as well as the exploding demand for tropical products, were making the West African countries along the Gulf of Guinea among the most valuable of the African colonies. In the decades after 1920, crop exports from the Gold Coast and Nigeria increased nine hundred per cent; those of French West Africa grew by well over a thousand per cent.

France was mainly interested in cocoa and coffee from Côte d'Ivoire, but the French came smack up against the old problem of labour. For reasons the colonial barons could never quite grasp, Africans did not want to work for them, especially without compensation. The solution was an old one as well. The French introduced laws that forced Africans to toil on their cocoa plantations. France imposed a poll tax on all its colonial subjects, one that could be paid only in French currency, and the only way to earn the currency was to work for the French.

Ivorian farmers, such as Houphouët's family, grew their own cocoa, but they had to compete with French colonial landowners for access to hired farm labourers. Migrant workers, the backbone of cocoa farm productivity, were available first, and often exclusively, to the French. If that wasn't enough of a competitive advantage over the homegrown venture, the French instituted a two-tier price structure that gave more money per pound to French-produced beans than to African ones.

Félix Houphouët might have lived out his life in obscurity as a modestly successful farmer in colonial Africa if he hadn't been spurred into politics by these discriminatory French policies. In 1944, he launched the Syndicat Agricole Africain (African Farmers Union), a rather elitist organization of indigenous landowners who wanted access to the same recruited manpower. He was supported by the African governor of the region, who was seeking a better deal for African cocoa and coffee producers and who also wanted limits to the political influence of a number of racist colonists (many of whom were pro-Vichy fascists).

When France resisted the union and continued to favour French farmers, the Syndicat Agricole Africain (SAA) attacked the farm-conscription policies implemented by the French to coerce Africans into working their plantations. In later years, the union would be celebrated for liberating West Africans from forced labour, though that had hardly been Houphouët's original intention.

Europeans had many theories about how best to "manage" their colonial populations, all reflecting their credo that imperialism was a kind of moral crusade. The British pontificated on the "White Man's Burden," the French on *la mission civilisatrice* and the Germans on *Kultur*—all of which were about bringing civilization and enlightenment to people who were considered semi-formed and living in darkness. No matter how noble-sounding the mission, the colonists were profoundly bigoted both in theory and practice, even as they were under pressure, by human rights activists of their time, to reform.

To demonstrate its post-war enlightenment, France allowed its first colonial election in 1945: fourteen African candidates vied for one seat in the French Constituent Assembly. With support from the SAA and his Baoulé tribesmen, Félix Houphouët-Boigny (he added Boigny to his name when he entered politics; in the native language it means "irresistible force") was successful, and he became a sitting member of the French Parliament.

In Paris, Houphouët-Boigny aligned with the French left, and in particular the French Communist Party, which supported his call for the emancipation of Africans. Houphouët-Boigny's Parti Démocratique de la Côte d'Ivoire (PDCI) was progressive in a number of areas wildly popular with Africans: it called for rights to full citizenship, plus access to health care, education, roads and farm modernization. Running in elections in the late 1940s, the PDCI received unprecedented public support—Houphouët-Boigny won his first election for the French assembly in 1945 with fifty per cent of the popular vote; he won re-election with ninety-eight per cent—and began to use its power and influence to harass the colonial government.

Economic conditions in Africa spiralled down in the post–Second World War period as the empires channelled all resources into rebuilding their own countries. Wartime wage and price controls were lifted, and the price of commodities from Africa plummeted. By then the system was stacked against primary producers anyway. Brokers in London and New York had perfected their techniques for manipulating supply and demand. Prices bottomed out, to their own advantage and to that of their buyers—the chocolate companies. At the base of the cocoa chain, African farmers were earning less and less for their beans while paying ever-increasing prices for the pesticides and herbicides required for the European-imposed farming techniques.

In 1949, the PDCI finally provoked Ivorians to take to the streets to protest deteriorating economic conditions. Colonial empires, including France, had been forced to fight intransigent tribes in the early decades of settlement, but popular civilian demonstrations of this size were unheard of and a threat to colonial authority. French troops put down the insurgencies with brutal force, killing an unknown number of protesters (the official count was fifty-two) and arresting as many as three thousand—though Houphouët-Boigny used his diplomatic immunity as a member of the French assembly to escape incarceration. Houphouët-Boigny's party and his personal strength only became stronger.

As word travelled in Africa, Houphouët-Boigny's support base broadened from his own tribe and region to include a wide cross-section of Ivorians of all ethnicities and then to include other French colonies. The farmer's union—the SAA—was developing into a pan-West-African rally and was threatening French hegemony throughout West Africa. France fought Houphouët-Boigny both in the street and at the ballot box, giving wide financial and political support to selected opposition parties and making it legally impossible for those without colonial support to organize.

Houphouët-Boigny was not by nature a revolutionary but rather a businessman. He enjoyed power, and he wasn't about to move his PDCI party underground. He also feared that France would do less, not more, to help develop Côte d'Ivoire if the militancy continued. In 1950 he made a pragmatic tactical manoeuvre—a complete political U-turn from radicalism to moderation. He renounced all connections to the French Communist Party (he claimed the link had never existed in the first place) and made it clear that his intentions were to work closely with the colonial administration. He put forward his policy plainly: "A new page has been turned. On it, let us write a resolution to make Africa the most splendid and the most loyal territory in the French union."

Houphouët-Boigny's deference to Paris paid large dividends. Côte d'Ivoire received preferential treatment in the French colonies, with protected markets for its cocoa and coffee and access to large amounts of French aid. By 1956, Houphouët-Boigny had managed to become the first African to hold a ministerial portfolio in the French government. While many of his supporters considered him a sellout, Houphouët-Boigny—the "irresistible force"—saw himself as the champion of his people. His close ties to the French administration meant that European businessmen went to Côte d'Ivoire to court his patronage, and he soon became the darling of the colonial merchant class.

On August 7, 1960, Côte d'Ivoire became an independent nation, with Félix Houphouët-Boigny as its first president. Since the PDCI was willing to work closely with its former colonial master, France helped to ensure that there was no political opposition to the party during elections. The new constitution gave complete executive power to the president.

In order to appear representative, and to placate those who might cause him grief, Houphouët-Boigny included opposition members and youth-wing agitators in his government. But window dressing notwithstanding, Côte d'Ivoire would be run more or less as a dictatorship under Houphouët-Boigny, with no free press, no opposition parties and no democracy. What the people got in exchange was the strongest economy in sub-Saharan Africa—what came to be called the African miracle. In Houphouët-Boigny's own words, "We must get down to work on the basis of discipline, which I hope will be freely accepted: but I will impose it if necessary because our country must succeed."

Le Vieux was an autocrat with a vision. He literally put Côte d'Ivoire to work, encouraging rural people to convert all available land to grow crops, both for cash and for food. Virgin rainforests metamorphosed into cocoa farms overnight. He invited people from other West African countries to come and open up new territory—to make Côte d'Ivoire rich. In 1965, five years after independence, half of the labour force was classified by a government survey as made up of "foreigners."

Few Ivorians objected to these outsiders being included in their miracle. The foreigners came from Mali, Upper Volta (later Burkina Faso) and Guinea, where crop failure and the encroaching Sahara Desert made them desperate for work. They were more than willing to do the hard toil while Ivorians moved to the cities to take advantage of more education and to seek employment as the clerks and petty bureaucrats serving the much more influential group of "foreigners" in the country—the French.

Unlike the situation in most of colonial Africa, French citizens came to live in Côte d'Ivoire by the tens of thousands, building luxurious neighbourhoods for themselves, complete with shopping areas where all the goods of Paris were available. They enjoyed the sprawling coastline of the Gulf of Guinea, with its glorious beaches, where they built themselves resorts staffed by young blacks eager to find wage-earning jobs.

The government's 1965 survey shows that eighty-five per cent of all managers in the country and eighty-one per cent of senior staff

were Europeans, while Ivorians filled almost the same per centage of junior clerical jobs. If Ivorians demonstrated any unhappi-
ness with the imbalance of opportunities, the Houphouët-Boigny
government quickly suppressed it. Preventative detention and
deportation were common tools of the state. Freedom of speech
was tolerated only when it was in support of the party.

France loved the economic liberalism of its former colony,
coupled with its iron-fisted leadership. Houphouët-Boigny was
rewarded with guaranteed markets and low-interest loans from
European banks. This was the kind of post-colonial African
Europeans and Americans longed for: an administrator who was
firm with his own people but open to outside investment.
Houphouët-Boigny became senior statesman more for the
Europeans than for Africans (he maintained strong relations with
the apartheid government of South Africa). He wore three-piece
suits and a perpetual look of Zen-like serenity on his fleshy face,
though a little furrow on his brow suggested a man always concerned with large matters of state. But he didn't neglect his people. The consummate benevolent dictator, he was rewarded by
the obedience of his citizens and the generous support of his
former adversary, the government of France. It was truly a miracle, entirely built on the world's endless appetite for chocolate.

Cocoa wasn't just an export crop. For its founding father,
cocoa *was* Côte d'Ivoire. The backbone of Houphouët-Boigny's
party was formed by rural cocoa growers and traders. Baoulé
tribesmen still dominated the old cocoa-producing areas where
Houphouët-Boigny was raised, but outsiders were opening up
new frontiers throughout Côte d'Ivoire. In the countryside, a network of mostly Dioula people—Muslims from northern Côte
d'Ivoire or the bordering states of Mali and Upper Volta—were
the party bosses in each region, appointed by Houphouët-Boigny.
While it was resented by some, especially Houphouët-Boigny's
own Baoulé tribesmen, Le Vieux's patronage of the Dioula was
shrewd. They were the most able cocoa farmers in Côte d'Ivoire,

and they had access to the itinerant labour from their home countries that was so necessary to the success of cocoa production. In addition, the Dioula shared a common religion with Muslim cocoa merchants and middlemen, increasingly French-speaking Arabic business tycoons from Algeria and Lebanon.

Houphouët-Boigny created a fixed price for cocoa beans, giving farmers a guaranteed income even when the market price was low. The state borrowed from European banks to make up the difference. Rural communities had purchasing power for the first time, and Le Vieux's most loyal and devoted followers were in the countryside. Even if France was still, essentially, running the show and Frenchmen had all the best jobs, this was the best country in Africa for its citizens. There was ample food and virtually no malnutrition.

Côte d'Ivoire was already well on its way to becoming the world's leading cocoa producer even before fires devastated much of the farming district of Ghana in the 1980s. It now took the lead, following in the steps of Mexico, Venezuela, the Portuguese islands and the Gold Coast. Le Vieux was determined to surrender that number one status to no country.

The great eighteenth-century thinker and writer Alexis de Tocqueville identified a volatile social phenomenon that came to be called the theory of rising expectations. Among its tenets is the idea that improved living conditions sharpen the appetite for more improvements delivered faster. People are rarely satisfied with the pace or the extent of progress. Such was the case with Houphouët-Boigny's economic miracle. Côte d'Ivoire's gross national product doubled within a decade of independence, but people wanted more, faster. Even dictatorships require a certain level of satisfaction among the oppressed, and Houphouët-Boigny's economic success depended on a motivated and contented society. Ivorians had full bellies, but they wanted better lifestyles. They resented the Dioula, who controlled the land in the regions, and they hated the French, who ran the commercial affairs of all their cities.

Houphouët-Boigny's miracle was already something of a mirage. He was subsidizing the price of cocoa beans and attempting to win the hearts and minds of his citizens with massive public works projects, many of them laudable, some laughable, but all of them built with borrowed money. New roads, bridges and telecommunications systems made a modern state out of a colonial backwater. A small coastal fishing village—a swamp, really—called San Pedro was transformed when Houphouët-Boigny decided to turn it into one of the largest, deepest ports on the West African coast, almost exclusively for the purpose of shipping cocoa to the world. Before-and-after photos are astonishing: construction workers completely remade the coastal landscape, building a bustling commercial centre from a cluster of mud huts. Transport ships from Holland, France and America soon lined the harbour, ready to carry away millions of tons of beans to chocolate lovers everywhere. But the cost of the port created massive public debt.

Among Houphouët-Boigny's wackier projects was the Hôtel Ivoire. Built in the principal Ivorian city of Abidjan, the hotel became one of the ritziest operations in post-colonial Africa, a miniature city on the side of a lagoon. The hotel's casino and multiple restaurants, swimming pools and shopping plazas were for the exclusive use of Europeans (lest Ivorians became corrupted). There was even a *patinoire*, which Houphouët-Boigny boasted was Africa's only ice-skating rink. But the cost of keeping the ice frozen in a place where the temperature rarely dips below thirty degrees centigrade, and where the humidity is often eighty per cent, seemed the height of folly.

Abidjan itself became one of the most remarkable cities in the developing world, with bold modern buildings poking the African sky with their asymmetrical shapes and guzzling electricity to keep the hermetically sealed offices cool. The price of cocoa on the international market was on a constant roller coaster ride—all too often on the downslide—but it was the government, not the farmers, who absorbed the losses. Côte d'Ivoire was deeply in debt long before Houphouët-Boigny began to build his final monument to himself, the basilica.

As cocoa and coffee prices nosedived in the late 1980s, Houphouët-Boigny was desperate to increase the value of his beans. Because Côte d'Ivoire was the biggest single cocoa exporter in the world, Le Vieux was deluded, as others had been before him, into thinking he actually had power in the marketplace. The world of commodities had changed drastically in a few decades, and a small country could exert very little influence on markets. World market prices were determined by commodities brokers who never saw a bean in their entire lives, along with a few powerful multinational corporations who had their own tactically managed stockpiles.

Houphouët-Boigny tried his best to manipulate the international cocoa trade but commodities investors and big cocoa companies seemed to have all the influence over the market. Finally, in 1987, the African miracle maker made his most desperate bid yet to save what was left of his country's wealth. He declared Côte d'Ivoire insolvent, unable to pay its massive debts—now totalling US$4.5 billion—and reneged on his debt repayment schedule. At the same time, Houphouët-Boigny blocked all shipments of his cocoa to international markets, a boycott he managed to sustain for two years. He literally shut down the economy of his country, and its government offices ceased to function. As documented in a bestselling book published in France in the 1980s, *La guerre du cacao: Histoire secrète d'un embargo,* the president launched a virtual cocoa war: Le Vieux against the giant multinational chocolate companies and the banks. In his final salvo, the president secretly secured a large grant from his former colonial masters in Paris in exchange for contracts awarding all of Côte d'Ivoire's beans to two giant French companies. It was high-stakes poker played with some of the most skilled gamblers on the planet.

It was the French media that exposed the secret arrangement, and the deal subsequently collapsed. With only one commodity propping up his entire economic miracle, Houphouët-Boigny's wager bankrupted the country even further. Farmers weren't paid, prices soared, local businesses withered. It was a total failure for Houphouët-Boigny and a complete victory for multinational cocoa companies, who had proven that even the biggest cocoa-producing country in the world couldn't push them around. What's more, the banks moved in on Le Vieux to make sure there would be no more reneging on payments. They had a new weapon to use on difficult countries such as Côte d'Ivoire.

~

It is generally accepted that the Bretton Woods delegates in July 1944 honestly intended the World Bank and the International Monetary Fund (IMF) to become benevolent forces in the postwar universe. It was a time of high optimism, an opportunity for men of vision and determination to create structures that would prevent a recurrence of the political and economic chaos of the preceding decades. Today, after more than a half-century of experience, benevolence is not a word that springs easily to the lips of clients of these two international financial institutions. Bullying and manipulative policies in the developing world have left a wake of disillusionment and bitterness, along with real economic hardship. The currents of anger run particularly deep in Côte d'Ivoire.

By the late 1980s, the World Bank and the IMF had evolved into the most powerful international institutions in history as they increasingly came under the sway of neo-liberal American monetary and foreign policy, devised in Washington D.C. and, often derisively, labelled "the Washington consensus." Driven largely by the ideological vision of U.S. President Ronald Reagan and his economic advisors, and that of his political soulmate,

British prime minister Margaret Thatcher, the two institutions became instruments of a hard-line movement to impose rigid capitalist and monetarist policies on floundering Third-World economies—of which there were many, thanks to the mismanagement and corruption of autocratic indigenous leadership.

That the fiscal policies and economic programs imposed on client states were generally more beneficial to banks, treasuries and corporate officers of the developed world only deepened an already widespread cynicism in the struggling nations of Asia, Latin America and Africa. The IMF, and in particular the World Bank, whose leaders are chosen by Washington, were soon regarded as the henchmen of Reaganomics ideology. Liberalization was the buzzword of the day, driving the demand for an end to marketing boards, domestic regulatory agencies, protective tariffs, subsidies and any program that might compromise the "natural" dynamic of the global marketplace.

Developing countries whose leaders had attempted to stave off ruin by accumulating massive debts—which often served to cover up their own greed—now turned to the World Bank for salvation. Côte d'Ivoire had become one of the most indebted countries in the world, and Félix Houphouët-Boigny lined up with the others for financial assistance.

The World Bank and the IMF had only one prescription for all the debtor nations that showed up in their waiting rooms: the shock therapy of liberalization. The bankrupted countries would have to dismantle their agricultural boards, cease to provide any subsidies to industry and desist from anything but the most nominal role in their own economic affairs. The directives insisted that all government programs be slashed or eliminated; that civil service be cut to the bone; and that health care, education and public infrastructure be reduced to a minimum. People were told to expect to pay user fees even to see a doctor. Currencies had to be devalued. Debtor nations found themselves growing crops for export while importing most of their food (mainly from the U.S.).

State enterprises were privatized and sold (usually to foreign multinational corporations), and commodities floated on the open market, where they would usually sell for the lowest price possible. These were called Structural Adjustment Programs — SAPs — an acronym that perfectly described what SAPs do to the lifeblood of suffering societies.

Houphouët-Boigny took his medicine — or, rather, his citizens did. Côte d'Ivoire turned itself over to the two institutions in 1989, just as the basilica reached completion, taking six World Bank Structural Adjustment Loans over the next five years and attempting to absorb the excruciating pain of the SAPs. The World Bank zeroed in on agriculture, and in particular the cocoa industry. Houphouët-Boigny had established an agency called CAISTAB — Le Caisse de Stabilization — to guarantee a base price for cacao farmers no matter what the unpredictable commodities markets were doing. Under the shock therapy of liberalization, CAISTAB had to go.

Farmers, many of whom were uneducated, with no access to stock market figures, found themselves stranded, tossed rudderless onto the sea of Reaganomics liberalism. The cocoa market became a free-for-all, and the farmers, without CAISTAB's subsidies, started to lose large amounts of money. Small-business loans had been available in the past, but under the SAPs these no longer existed. The purchasing power of the producers and the small businesses they depended on began to collapse as the Côte d'Ivoire currency lost value on the foreign exchange markets. And to top it all off, the international market price for cocoa beans dipped to its lowest in decades.

None of this had any effect on the chocolate companies and multinational food exporters — quite the contrary. The prices were low, and farmers were increasing their yields in a desperate attempt to generate more income. Cocoa exports from Côte d'Ivoire increased as the price sank. At the same time, more countries, mostly in Asia, were now producing cocoa with the encouragement of the World Bank and the IMF, flooding the market with beans and driving down prices even further.

Liberalization triumphed all through the 1980s and '90s, while cocoa values rode the market roller coaster with little regard for economic reality. The United Nations Conference on Trade and Development (UNCTAD) listed cocoa among the most volatile and unpredictable commodities in the world. It declared, in one of its otherwise cautious reviews, that the ideology of liberalization was the direct cause of the freefall in the price of cocoa.

Commodities exchanges in London and New York became the custodians of the lives of Ivorian cocoa producers thousands of miles away. Speculators played the hedge market, guessing what price cocoa beans might fetch in the future and basing their predictions on myriad factors such as weather, disease and pestilence, world stock supplies and war. A rumour of a possible *coup d'état* could send prices soaring, while wild speculation about a bumper crop could push prices in the other direction. By purchasing futures, a company with accurate information can lock down prices that turn into bonanzas when predictable circumstances come to pass. But only people with money to spare can play these odds. And when the commodity is as vulnerable to caprice as cocoa, competent speculators can—and do—make a lot of money quickly.

Throughout the latter part of the twentieth century, Côte d'Ivoire lost its miracle. Multinational corporations took control of the industry through the leverage of SAPs, and by the end of the 1990s a small handful of foreign firms controlled almost all of Côte d'Ivoire's cocoa production. The Belgian and Swiss giants Barry Callebaut and Nestlé and the American food conglomerates Cargill and Archer Daniels Midland cornered world markets, becoming suppliers to the European and U.S. manufacturers that had run the business since the previous century.

Félix Houphouët-Boigny continued to lose strength over the two and a half decades of his presidency. Near the end, he belatedly offered his people some elements of democracy, including open elections to assuage their other woes. But with the jobless rate soaring, along with inflation, a free vote was little comfort. As an octogenarian, he retreated to his artificial capital and his Vatican in the jungle. He passed away in 1993, just a few years after Pope John Paul II consecrated Our Lady of Peace Basilica. Houphouët-Boigny wouldn't see Côte d'Ivoire descend into war and chaos, nor would he know that his precious cocoa sector would fall victim to some of the most corrupt and criminal exploitation in Africa.

By the end of the millennium, Côte d'Ivoire was one of the most indebted nations on earth, even as it supplied almost half of the world's cocoa to the multi-billion-dollar industry and helped to satisfy the world's addiction to chocolate. Cocoa farmers slid deeper and deeper into poverty, and they began to look for cheaper ways to produce their beans. They turned to the same old scourge that has plagued cocoa growing since its inception — slavery.

Chapter Six

THE **DISPOSABLES**

"In the old days slaves were expensive; you kept them for their
whole lives, you took care of them. Today they are cheap; there
is a glut of slaves and when you've used them you throw them
away if you don't want them any more—they're disposable."
                                        —KEVIN BALES, *Free the Slaves*

ABDOULAYE MACKO SETTLES HIS LARGE FRAME INTO
an armchair at the Grand Hotel in Mali's capital city of Bamako
and looks about to see if he knows anyone in the lobby. His
caftan robes are fraying, and his once elegant white shoes are
worn through in several places. He has the appearance and
demeanour one would expect from an out-of-work diplomat in
the Republic of Mali who is trying to keep his place in society. It
has been five years since he had to suspend what came to be his
driving mission in life: liberating conscripted child workers from
the cocoa farms of Côte d'Ivoire.

Macko orders a plate of buttery croissants and a big bowl of
café au lait, consumes everything with zeal and orders more.
I was warned by a local aid worker who knows Macko that he is
a freeloader and would probably ask me for money. But aside
from the obvious fact that he's famished—he had left at dawn
and travelled two hours on public transportation to keep our
appointment—the unemployed civil servant seems to want little
more than a patient listener for a long and disturbing story. And
I am more than willing to oblige.

Macko had been the Malian consul general in Bouaké, in central Côte d'Ivoire, until his government recalled him in 2000. He never really learned why he was withdrawn and then "retired," but he can guess that it was because, in the eyes of his political masters, he had caused too much trouble. I had confirmed this much prior to our conversation.

Macko is a classic whistle-blower. In the late 1990s, he began to hear stories that disturbed him greatly. Bouaké is in the heart of the cocoa-producing sector of Côte d'Ivoire, where thousands of Malians—tens of thousands at peak season—live and work on the farms. In addition to the large numbers of people who came to Côte d'Ivoire from Mali and other poor West African countries under the benevolent eye of Félix Houphouët-Boigny and who have farmed their own plots of land for as many as four decades, a small army of Malian men and older boys descend into the fertile cocoa belt each season to earn extra money as hired labourers. It has been a mutually beneficial arrangement for decades.

But Macko learned of another category of labour that he couldn't quite fathom. What his informers described sounded a lot like slavery, and what made the stories even more horrifying was that it seemed the slaves were children. Surely it wasn't possible! Slavery and all the euphemisms for it—bonded labour, conscript, coolie—had, supposedly, ended long ago. There had been laws against that type of thing for years.

The tribes of what is now called Mali have a long, even ancient, history of itinerant labour, and stories of migration are embedded in their history and their mythology. At the end of each domestic harvest period, after new seed is planted on their own farms, it's traditionally time to leave home and look for work elsewhere for a period of a few months. Malians often call the workers "sequoias," referring to a migrant bird that heads south at the same time. It's so common for people to move around looking for work that most families are not surprised when even the youngest declare they are leaving in order to make some money. People presume that other Malians will keep an eye on them. It's the Malian way to look after one other, whether they are travelling to the next village or a neighbouring country or, in modern times, seeking new lives in Europe or North America. Children and teenagers have, for ages, commuted safely within this custom-sanctioned system, often watched by uncles, aunts and cousins of their extended families

But Macko heard about child labour that didn't fit this traditional pattern. It certainly had similarities, but these were stories of boys, some as young as nine, who were working on farms where they had no relatives. This information alone was enough to trigger alarm bells for a Malian. Macko also heard they weren't being paid. The witnesses, Malian men employed as transporters for the cocoa beans, came to tell the diplomat they were witnessing situations in which very young boys worked at gunpoint. It was difficult to obtain details—they weren't encouraged to pry into what seemed to be a clandestine system. But the *pisteurs* managed to talk to some of the young people and learned details of their plight.

The farmers, or their supervisors, were working the young people almost to death. The boys had little to eat, slept in bunkhouses that were locked during the night, and were frequently beaten. They had horrible sores on their backs and shoulders, some as a result of carrying the heavy bags of cocoa, but some likely the effects of physical abuse.

There was also evidence of more sinister activity. The *pisteurs* were convinced that the farmers were paying organized groups of smugglers to deliver the children to their cocoa groves, and they told Macko that the Côte d'Ivoire police were being bribed to look the other way. The child traffickers worked in teams: a Malian man along with one from Côte d'Ivoire, and often a third from Burkina Faso, a country that was also a source of child workers.

Macko could have ignored what he heard, or passed on the information to the authorities and washed his hands of the whole affair. After all, it was probably only a small number of boys. Malians are survivors. Eventually, they'd solve this on their own. And most of the complaints were likely just exaggerations. Who would dare use slave children in the 1990s? Instead, Macko became deeply preoccupied with what he heard and, in time, obsessed with rescuing the boys.

As a diplomat, his own activities were circumscribed, so he commissioned Malians in the region to investigate the allegations and eventually he had a network of spies that included *pisteurs*, shepherds, sharecroppers and farmers, some Malian, others Burkinabè. From his network, Macko learned that many people were aware of what was going on; some of his informants had even seen the abuse first-hand. As the investigation deepened, more and more people came forward with distressing stories. Macko was convinced there was a substantial contingent of child labourers, all working under horrendous conditions.

He invented reasons to visit cocoa farmers and, while among them, made casual inquiries about the itinerant Malian workers. How were they performing? Were they well? All normal concerns of their government's representative. Some of the farmers told the consul general that the child workers on their farms were members of their own families, or that they were relatives. It was plausible, since children of extended families in agricultural communities frequently work alongside the adults. Then there were farmers who admitted openly that they had paid money for the children—and what of it? The farmer would compensate whoever delivered the labour force. He'd get his money back through their labour. He'd pay them wages once those original costs were recovered—if there was enough money to go around after the harvest and the systemic manipulations of cocoa traders. But Macko knew that, without family members looking after their interests, the children were at the mercy of the farmers. Given what he knew of human nature and the cocoa business, it was highly probable that few of the young workers, if any, were being paid at all.

Macko asked if he could visit with the children. When permission was denied, he invoked diplomatic privilege and asked the Côte d'Ivoire police for an escort. At first, the authorities were reluctant. Macko suspected that many of the cops were on the take, but after a few unannounced visits to the farms, even the police were seeing the sordid picture. Sometimes the children ran away when they saw the police arriving. They'd been warned in advance that the police might show up to arrest them and that they should flee to avoid the terrors of detention. Eventually word spread among the children that there was a brave Malian official who was trying to help them. Gradually, the children started talking.

Many of the details of this story have been related to me by Macko, but they are more than confirmed by other accounts, including those of the police. At our meeting at the Grand Hotel, Macko pulled out a heavy sack from beside his chair. He had brought photo albums, all meticulously organized and labelled. It might have been a family memoir, but his folders contained documentary evidence of what he discovered on the farms.

The photographs are startling. Page after page reveals groups of dusty, frightened children, without footwear, dressed in scanty clothing, unsmiling faces revealing poignant details that illustrate the story the former diplomat is telling. There are scores of boys in the pictures, ranging in age from about ten to eighteen; dozens of the photos show the shoulders and backsides of the youths with their open sores and cuts. It's difficult to know which wounds were from beatings and which were from carrying the heavy sacks, but the sores were all untreated. Most of the boys had been on these farms for months or even years before Macko found them. His most depressing discovery was of a boy who was nearly dead. "I saw something hidden under a pile of leaves. At first I couldn't believe it, but it was a child. He was sick, his pants were covered in his excrement, and they had left him out in the field to die."

Macko says he liberated only a portion of the young workers, and he believes there were many more he was unable to reach, probably there to this day. But the ones he did reach are home now. Their harrowing stories are seared into their memories, and his.

~

Malick Doumbia tells me he was fourteen years old when he decided he would take control of his own destiny. The cotton and corn were planted, and the rains were yet to begin. But the village food supply was already depleted and there would be little to eat until the next harvest. The sub-Saharan climate had been changing for about a decade, and now, in the first months of the twenty-first century, environmental conditions were deteriorating rapidly. Even the more humid and verdant parts of southern Mali, where Malick was growing up, recorded some of the lowest rainfalls in memory.

Malick was hungry. He wanted more in his life. He had seen other children from his region go away to work and come back later with money in their pockets and Malick was determined that he would do the same. One afternoon, without telling his parents, he simply walked away, heading to the main road that led to the market and hitching rides all the way to the teeming city of Sikasso.

Sikasso is a major crossroads of the sub-Sahara. One way leads towards Guinea, Sierra Leone and the huge port cities of Monrovia, Freetown and Dakar on the Atlantic Ocean. In the other direction, towards the east, Burkina Faso is only ten kilometres away; southeast leads to the prosperous farms and industries of

Ghana. Directly south of Sikasso is the road to Côte d'Ivoire, the African miracle—for decades regarded as El Dorado, the most prosperous and promising nation in West Africa.

Malick loved Sikasso, bustling with noise, people, odours both familiar and foreign, multi-storey buildings, cars and minivans going in every direction. The bus station kiosks were crammed with riches such as he had never seen: beautiful cloth sarongs; colourful shirts and pants; mangoes, bananas and oranges piled high on the heads of women hawking their wares; pens, pencils and books; newspapers covered in words he could not read; and delicious food he could not afford—delicate little fried donuts, cashew nuts, candies and bags of brightly coloured sugar water. Malick had no money, only the few clothes he was wearing, and he had no idea what to do next. Then a man from a car rental shop at the bus station approached him with an offer too tempting to refuse. Malick followed him.

Travelling by night, they meandered by car through the back roads and pathways of southern Mali. Malick and other boys travelling in the same vehicle were told to stay very quiet until they arrived in Korhogo, a city in another country. This was the promised place Malick had heard about. This was Côte d'Ivoire.

The tropical air became thick and humid; the vegetation around him dense and impenetrable. They had nothing to eat—in fact, Malick realized he had consumed almost nothing since he left home. Finally, a stranger came for him. Money changed hands between the man who had taken him from the bus station and the stranger. The transaction completed, Malick and another boy were told to leave with this individual. They had jobs now and would be paid. The bus station man told the boys they should work hard.

For the next several years (he's unclear how many), Malick slaved on a cocoa plantation. He had never seen a cocoa tree before, nor its strange green, yellow and red pods that sprout directly off the tree trunk. With a machete-like tool, hooked on the end, he lopped off the fruity gourds. He then hacked through the thick rind to expose the pulpy, pale seeds inside. He scooped them out and piled them on a rack to ferment and dry. This was the essence of chocolate destined for the pleasure of young boys and girls in another distant world.

Malick had no idea what the beans were or why anybody wanted them. He only knew that, if his keeper wasn't looking, he could scoop a handful of the slippery, raw bitter-tasting seeds with their mild-flavoured pulp from the pods right into his mouth and chew quickly. The beans and the juice refreshed him and gave him energy to complete the day's work. He was never paid and rarely fed, living on a diet of green bananas and yams, which the boys would grill for themselves on a fire. At night, he was locked up with the others. The children and teenagers became ill; some of them died. After many months, Malick asked to be paid, and he was beaten. He never asked again.

One day while clearing land in the forest, Malick saw his chance to flee. Côte d'Ivoire's rainy season often produces violent storms—heavy clouds cover the sky, blocking out the sun almost completely. Malick and some other boys waited for their chance. They had heard about a man from Mali who might help them. He worked in something called a consulate, and it wasn't far away—if they could only get there. As the storm turned the day almost as dark as night, the children ran for their lives, eventually making contact with Macko's network. In time, they joined others liberated by the consul general, who transported them all back to Sikasso, in southern Mali. It took weeks for Macko to sort through all the names of the boys; some children could no longer remember where they were from. Some had been away from home for years, while others had joined the labour pool in more recent years. None of them had ever been paid for their work.

Broken, sickly, confused and poor, Malick returned to his village years after he had left. He tells me his parents were glad to see him, but unhappy that he had come back with nothing, except diseases they would have to pay to treat. Malick learned that Macko had returned to Mali hundreds of children who had suffered his fate, but that an unknown number—possibly thousands—were still working on the plantations in Côte d'Ivoire.

~

In the village of Sirkasso—about thirty kilometres of rough back roads from Sikasso—Aly Diabate and Madou Traoré were making plans for their futures when I went to find them in 2005. They are young men now, lean and muscular, but their families remember when they disappeared in the late 1990s and then returned years later, sad and broken.

They explained to me their decision to go. Everyone had known about a boy from the village who had gone to Côte d'Ivoire to work on a cocoa farm and had returned with a bicycle. Diabate remembers that he and Traoré were extremely covetous. (The two learned only later, when they were home again after their ordeal, that the boy with the bike had gone to work for a relative who had guaranteed his safety.) Diabate and Traoré concluded that if they could get to Côte d'Ivoire, wherever it was, they would come back with money.

Diabate and Traoré were fourteen and fifteen years old respectively when they left during the night. They commandeered Traoré's father's bicycle, believing he would forgive them when they returned with an even better machine, and peddled the stolen bike all the way to Sikasso. They had a few West African francs between them, but they quickly realized their stash wouldn't last long. "In the city, you need money for everything," says Diabate with a world-weary air. "In the city, you have to pay money to pee, and you pay a fine if you do it in the wrong place. In the countryside, you pee wherever you want."

A man the boys came to know only as Solo approached them in the bus station and asked where they were going. "'I can't hire you, but my older brother can get you jobs,'" Diabate recalls the man told the two boys. "He said we could make as much as 150,000 [West African francs—about US$140] in Côte d'Ivoire if we went with him." It was a staggering sum of money for the boys, and they were more than interested. They opted to go with Solo, travelling by night to Korhogo, where they were installed in a stranger's house that already had many children. The boys don't remember who was in charge at the place, but the next day, Solo came back with another stranger.

"He gave us to the man," says Traoré sadly.

"No!" Diabate corrects him sternly: "He sold us to the man."

The fact that the two young teenagers were sold is something Diabate and Traoré understand only in retrospect. At the time, they had no concept of what was normal or fair in the world outside their village of Sirkasso. Their only objective was to get jobs and make money. They were accustomed to grown-ups making decisions and had no real reason—yet—to suspect that these men were any different than others they had encountered in the course of their short lives. They followed their "owner" because they simply thought that this was how people got work.

For two days they travelled on a bus with other boys and some girls before arriving at the farm. People called their new boss Le Gros (the Big Man), referring to his paunch, but the boys remember only his cruelty. Le Gros had paid 50,000 West African francs for the two of them, and he wanted his money back—in labour. The boys from Sirkasso met about twenty others in the same predicament and learned that no one was ever paid. They slept in a rectangle-shaped mud hut that initially had windows but when some boys found they could escape during the night, the windows were sealed shut. Diabate and Traoré remember eating mostly bananas, though they would gobble up the cocoa beans, as the others did, whenever they got the chance.

Many months passed, and the boys forgot what the purpose had once been for this adventure. Le Gros's own children went to school, while the slave boys rummaged in the garbage for clothes and footwear and ate what they could scrounge. Life became a struggle to exist, then hardened to despair. They gave up thinking of escape. Though they were under constant threat of beatings if they were caught trying to flee—and they had seen boys treated savagely—they were actually spooked by a belief that they were under a spell. The farm managers told the boys they were held in place by magic and they could not break the enchantment. When a boy was caught trying to leave, his tormentors would demand to know how he had learned the secret of the incantation. The psychological torture was almost as effective as the physical abuse.

The boys suspect they would still be there—or more likely they would have died by now—if it hadn't been for Abdoulaye Macko. Rumours of the consul general's investigation had spread over a large area of western Côte d'Ivoire, where the cocoa farms are concentrated. One of the boys managed to get word of their plight to Macko's office in Bouaké, probably through one of the diplomat's many spies. "Macko came with the police," recalls Diabate. "The boss told us to run away, and we went and hid in the forest." The boys had been convinced that if the police found them they would be punished. "But a week later, Macko came back alone," says Diabate. "Kids were sick. We were really tired. He told us he was there to help us escape and not to hurt us."

The boys were so completely unaware of their own condition that they had no idea how they must have appeared to an outsider. "Macko cried when he saw us," Traoré remembers.

~

Macko tells me he eventually learned that the farmers had deals with an elaborate network of traffickers, and he began to understand that the real villains in the story were not the farmers but the crime rings who brought the children to the farms. The boys may have left their family farms voluntarily and even joined up with the smuggler of their own volition. "They were just kids who needed money for their families," says Macko. They didn't bargain for the kind of exploitation they experienced. He believes many of the cocoa farmers were also caught in an unbearable squeeze. Though some of the farmers were surely taking advantage of the desperation of the poor, most of those who were buying the children had been driven to do so by their dire economic straits. Preying on the hopelessness and needs of both groups, the middlemen were the ones making the profits.

These "job brokers," as they called themselves to the authorities, took advantage of a system of trust that had existed among Malians for generations. Many of the farmers may have genuinely believed (or wanted to believe) that they had a fair deal and that the boys were to be paid by the brokers. And certainly not all the farmers abused their workers to the degree that the vicious Le Gros did. But the sale of these children and their inability to leave the farm until they had recovered the fee paid to the brokers amounted to conscripted labour, no different than the notorious coolie system of another century.

By the time Macko was repatriating children, the system of child trafficking in the region was well established and actually known to international agencies. In a 1998 report, UNICEF describes in exact detail how the transactions are worked out. "Recruiters," as the United Nations calls them, seek out children at the bus station and on the busy roads leading out of Sikasso, gathering as many as possible, often using minibuses to transport them to Côte d'Ivoire. The recruiters prefer to perform their dirty work on market days, when traffic is dense and no one asks too many questions at the border.

In what the report calls the "arrive and pay system," the recruiter and the transporter split a fee of about 50,000 West African francs for each child while the farmer openly commits to pay the child 80,000 for his labour, hence making the system quasi-legal. But the child must first of all reimburse the recruiters' commission and then he's charged a daily fee for room and board. Most often, there's nothing left at the end of the year to pay the child, after all the hidden costs are cut from his wages.

UNICEF and others knew of the system for years, but had not been able to stop it. Local authorities were rarely interested in getting involved, with the bold exception of Macko. He pursued these middlemen tirelessly, harassing authorities on both sides of the border to investigate the networks. He learned even more about the elaborate trafficking operations: a Malian member of the team would recruit the children while Ivorians with the right papers would take the boys over the border at night and install them in safe houses, first in Korhogo and then further south in Bouaké — right under the consul general's nose.

What was most interesting for Macko about the smuggling rings was the women who were involved. In fact, they were probably the ones who initiated the organizations in the first place. Malian women often went to Côte d'Ivoire to buy goods that were not available in their own markets. They would transport their wares, mostly food but also some textiles, back to their shops and stalls over the border. But the vehicles they used, rented cars or minivans, travelled empty on the trip to Côte d'Ivoire. Mali has nothing of interest to sell to Côte d'Ivoire — except cheap labour. The women saw a chance to make some extra cash: They would gather up children along the route. There never seemed to be a shortage. Border guards weren't suspicious; it appeared to be normal traffic, young boys travelling with mothers and aunties, and if questions were asked, everyone understood that a little baksheesh — a small bribe — would see them through. In Korhogo, the Malian women found houses where they could warehouse the boys (and some girls, who would be sold in the larger cities as domestics and prostitutes, as well as cocoa workers) until the traffickers came to get them. The business started informally, but blossomed into a full-scale enterprise supplying workers not just for coffee but also cotton. New "specializations" developed in the world of crime. Middlemen began to transport the children in larger numbers, while the women specialized in temporary lodgings.

As he learned more, Macko became more and more aggressive in his pursuit of the people smugglers. And they became more devious. They operated at night, and moved the children in smaller groups, sometimes using motorbikes and transporting children a few at a time through the backwoods. Macko initiated many arrests of smugglers, and a few high-profile cases were actually prosecuted by Ivorian courts.

Aly Diabate and Madou Traoré finally made their way back to Sirkasso, with Macko's help. They had earned no money and had even lost the bicycle Traoré had taken from his father for their adventure; they were ecstatic when Macko gave them money to buy another one. Even more rewarding, they saw Le Gros, whose real name they learned is Lenikpo Yeo, taken away in chains by the police. The farmer was charged with assault and was convicted, but he spent less than a month in jail. The witnesses who could have testified against Le Gros—all children— were not around. They had gone back to Mali.

~

For three years, from 1997 to early 2000, Abdoulaye Macko continued his mission to locate and liberate children who had straggled into bondage. NGOs set up safe havens for those who returned. But the circle of concern was limited in scope. Authorities with more clout than Macko were reluctant to acknowledge the extent of the problem he was helping to expose and Malian authorities in Bamako were almost as uncomfortable about the situation as the Ivorians were. Almost all of Mali's trade and commerce came from its association with Côte d'Ivoire. The money sent home to Mali by immigrants who had gone to work in Ivorian cocoa was substantial. Mali didn't want to disturb a mutually beneficial arrangement, but it was becoming difficult to ignore the dark side of the deal.

In a 2000 report on human rights in Côte d'Ivoire, the U.S. State Department estimated, with startling candour, "that 15,000 Malian children work on Ivorian cocoa and coffee plantations . . . Many are under 12 years of age, sold into indentured servitude for US$140 and work 12-hour days for $135 to $189 a year." This was the strongest and most authoritative public statement yet. According to the State Department, during 2000 alone (and probably thanks to Macko), approximately 270 children were repatriated to Mali from Côte d'Ivoire. How many others were still working on the cocoa farms, not being paid for their efforts?

Under pressure from the United States and the United Nations, the governments of Mali and Côte d'Ivoire signed an accord called the Bouaké Agreement, in which Côte d'Ivoire grudgingly agreed to be more vigilant in watching the border and to help repatriate the remaining children on its cocoa farms. But Ivorian officials were reluctant to concede that the problem was as widespread as the reports suggested and argued that child trafficking, if it existed at all, was the work of foreigners, specifically, Malians and Burkinabès. Ivorians, the government claimed, were not involved. Declaring the problem under control, the governments of Mali and Côte d'Ivoire moved on to silence their critics and prevent any further aggravation. Abdoulaye Macko was removed from his post and ordered to return to Mali but he wouldn't stop campaigning on behalf of the children. Soon afterwards, he lost his job. "The economy of Mali depends on Côte d'Ivoire for its survival," Macko explained to me. "Côte d'Ivoire has us by the throat. And I was making too much trouble."

~

Brian Woods and Kate Blewett are self-described "advocacy" journalists, and they unapologetically claim that their ambition is to change the world through their TV documentary reporting. In the late 1990s, Blewett and Woods teamed up with the American activist Kevin Bales, head of Free the Slaves in the United States, a sister organization to Anti-Slavery International in Great Britain. Their objective was to make a film that would expose abusive child labour in three sectors: the rug-making industry in India; the domestic workers employed by the diplomatic missions of the United Nations in New York City; and the cotton industry in West Africa. The third part of the assignment changed after the film crew arrived in Côte d'Ivoire in 2000 and found themselves in the midst of cocoa season and a swirl of NGO reports on the existence of child trafficking for cocoa farms.

The film they produced, *Slavery: A Global Investigation*, was sensational in all respects. "We literally walked onto plantations and found slave after slave after slave," Blewett explained in an interview. They encountered teenagers and boys who told them they had not been paid even after a year's work. The young people described beatings, starvation diets and foul living conditions, and they revealed their lacerated backsides. In the most controversial and effective moment of the documentary, a young cocoa worker tells the interviewer, "When people eat chocolate, they are eating my flesh." To make sure the viewer hasn't missed the point, there is the background sound effect of a whip cracking.

One of the people they interviewed for the film, Diabe Demeble, president of the Malian Association of Daloa, a major city in western Côte d'Ivoire in the heart of cocoa land, made the controversial (though not provable) statement that ninety per cent of the cocoa farms probably used bonded child labour or slaves.

The filmmakers also talked to farmers who readily admitted that they had paid money for the boys but saw nothing wrong with what they regarded as a business arrangement. They presumed that a deal had been struck between the "job broker" and children. The wounds on the boys' bodies, said the farmers, were the results of fighting among themselves. As for the locked bunkhouses—well, that was necessary only to protect the boys from outside dangers.

While the original plan had been to uncover the indentured servitude of children in the cotton industry, the documentary's cocoa farm revelations likely had far more impact when the film was presented to the British public on Channel 4 in September 2000. In the apathetic, often cynical court of public opinion, it's difficult to move people with stories of tragedy from Africa any-more. Famine; AIDS; child soldiers trained to maim, mutilate and kill—all combine to numb the sensibilities of comfortable television viewers. But children being exploited and abused for *chocolate*, enslaved to produce the primary ingredient of a luxury for children of the developed world—the story packed a punch even the filmmakers could not have predicted.

The public was stirred. The British media covered the story of the film and its findings extensively. Outraged viewers and readers inundated the British chocolate industry with complaints and a threat of a boycott. The United Kingdom Biscuit, Cake, Chocolate and Confectionery Alliance (BCCCA), for its part, released a care-ful statement: "We do not believe that the farms visited by the pro-gramme are in the least representative of cocoa farming in Côte d'Ivoire although the claims cannot be ignored." Ivorian govern-ment officials dismissed the documentary as rubbish.

The fact remained that reports of indentured child labour and the trafficking of children into cocoa farms had been emerging from West Africa for years, though the industry had chosen to ignore them, just as chocolate manufacturers a century earlier had disregarded the reports from São Tomé until they were forced to confront the brutal reality.

While the chocolate companies and the Ivorian government went into damage control, NGOs and human rights activists moved to take advantage of the publicity and public outrage. Aid agencies from several countries, including Germany, France and Canada, convened a meeting to devise an action plan to rescue children from Ivorian farms. The director of Save the Children Canada, Michel Larouche, declared, "There are two scenarios. One is that all the children will be expelled . . . or we will have to change our strategy and pull them out of the plantations. Either way, we will do it."

Among the NGOs working in the region, Save the Children Canada took the lead to establish a kind of recovery house called Horon So (translated as Freedom House) in Sikasso. Over the four and half years of its existence, Horon So became a temporary refuge for more than two hundred repatriated and intercepted children. Horon So and Mali Enjeu, another local agency, also endeavoured to stop children at the border and prevent them from crossing. The aid agencies started local programs to educate young people about the dangers of venturing to Côte d'Ivoire. But many of the children ignored the warnings. Life in Mali was desperate, and they were willing to play "the lottery" (this is what aid workers call their willingness to believe they will be one of the lucky ones to get gainful employment). Mali Enjeu workers were not surprised when they intercepted the same child more than once.

More revelations of child exploitation in Côte d'Ivoire farming and stories of how young labourers continued to be spirited out of Mali and Burkina Faso emerged following the Blewett-Woods documentary. Kevin Bales of Free the Slaves says he hired local people to go into an Ivorian market, where the "job brokers" were known to ply their trade, and pretend to be looking to buy conscripts. Within a half hour, Bales's agents say they had managed to purchase two children for the equivalent of $40 each.

The BBC's Humphrey Hawksley delivered a mind-boggling story in April 2001 about a ship, the MV Etireno out of Benin, that was allegedly carrying a cargo of as many as two hundred children, some as young as six, destined for work in Côte d'Ivoire. When the vessel was finally captured, the captain and his crew were arrested, but only forty-three children and adolescents were still on board, and authorities said all but a few of the young people were accompanied by adults. Aid agencies scrambled to find out whether the original report had been a false alarm or if the children had been unloaded at sea after the captain learned he was about to be arrested. A more plausible story, reported by the BBC, was that the *Etireno* was confused with another ship, name unknown, that possibly did manage to dock, undetected, with a cargo of children.

Despite the growing controversy, Ivorian authorities dismissed child trafficking as a limited activity, practised by a small group of criminals, and they insisted that very few Ivorian cocoa farmers were using children illegally. But only months after the controversial BBC report, the Knight Ridder news agency produced the most explosive series yet on child exploitation in cocoa. The two reporters, Sudarsan Raghavan and Sumana Chaterjee, found that it was relatively easy to locate victims of child trafficking in Côte d'Ivoire's cocoa-producing areas. They interviewed many of them. Even as Malian authorities claimed to be maintaining a constant vigil on the border, Raghavan and Chaterjee discovered that child-trafficking rings continued to work, undeterred by legal action and foreign publicity. The Knight Ridder crew met Madou Traoré and Aly Diabate soon after Macko had liberated them, and they interviewed the notorious Le Gros. Though they borrowed heavily on what other journalists had already uncovered, Raghavan and Chaterjee had the advantage of access to a U.S. audience. For the first time, the sordid story cracked American indifference and generated a public outcry in the world's most lucrative market for cocoa products.

Just as Henry Nevinson had managed to stir an indifferent British public with his articles in *Harper's Monthly* a hundred years earlier, the Knight Ridder series presented similar damning information: chocolate—the innocent, inexpensive little treat—

came to North America from the hands of underfed, ill-treated African children who toiled in bonded servitude. A $13 billion industry in the United States, controlled by a small group of corporations who obtain their principal product from hundreds of thousands of unmonitored African farms, was suddenly jangled to consciousness by a major international wake-up call.

~

To this day, Abdoulaye Macko is still looking for work, but he has never regretted what he did. As for the boys he rescued, they remember him with the greatest fondness. "He was very good to us," Traoré told me. "We hope he is happy and doing well."

I didn't have the heart to tell them what has become of their saviour, or that today he lives in economic circumstances only slightly better than their own.

Chapter Seven

DIRTY CHOCOLATE

"Mars, which enforces a vow of secrecy on every person
who works for it, has often been compared to the CIA. This
analogy is overstated. Mars, Inc. is far better at keeping
its operations secret than the CIA."

> —JAN POTTKER, *Crisis in Candyland: Melting the
> Chocolate Shell of the Mars Family Empire*

IN 2001, AS THE LATE JUNE HEAT BEGAN TO MAKE LIFE
unbearable for people working on Capitol Hill in Washington,
the representative for congressional district seventeen, compris-
ing the New York counties of Bronx, Westchester and Rockland,
was just getting ready to pack up his work for the July fourth hia-
tus. Congressman Eliot Engel wasn't looking for more to do, but
when the Knight Ridder articles crossed his desk, he was genuinely shocked. Child slavery was the secret ingredient of
American chocolate—that was the upshot of the newspaper
reports. "The more I looked into it, the more it raised my concern," the congressman told me in an interview about how he got
involved in the politics of cocoa.

A run-of-the-mill agricultural appropriations bill was just about
to go to a vote in the House of Representatives, and Engel decided
he might be able to do something quickly. He attached a rider to
the bill, proposing a labelling system for chocolate that would
proclaim the candy to be "slave free" if it could be documented
that the product hadn't involved the work of exploited children.

"It would be just like the certification on cans of tuna that say 'dolphin safe,'" Engel explained. To his profound amazement, the rider passed the House of Representatives in a vote of 291 to 115, with even a sizable number of Republicans voting in favour of it. Congress authorized a budget of $250,000 for labels.

The U.S. chocolate manufacturers were blind-sided. At first, the companies expressed shock about reports of slavery while insisting that they had nothing to do with the practice. Although the two U.S. chocolate giants, Mars and Hershey, conceded that Côte d'Ivoire did supply them with a lot of their cocoa (industry observers say most of America's cocoa is Ivorian), the companies insisted that the cocoa chain was outside their control. There are about 600,000 cocoa farms in Côte d'Ivoire. No one would be able to prove which chocolate was "clean"—to use the buzzword that the controversy developed—and which was tainted by the use of slave labour.

"Their attitude surprised me," Engel said of the conversations he initially had with company representatives. "Industry people came to my office. They were hostile and belligerent. I was going to put people out of business. I thought they would say, 'We don't think this is a problem but we'll investigate.' Instead it was all about the bottom line."

The public relations problem for big chocolate was acute. Hershey Park, a sprawling tourist attraction of midway rides and food concessions that was now at the centre of Milton's Pennsylvania town, had become a wholesome holiday destination for American families. Controlling interest of Hershey Foods was in the hands of the charity that Milton Hershey had established. M&Ms were sold in schools, and Mars had partnerships with publishers to market its wares through books for children, using cartoon characters. Skittles, Reese's Pieces, Hershey's Kisses, Aero, Kit Kat—these iconic treats would now have to pass a test of their moral qualities. All were subject to the labelling requirement, from chocolate Easter bunnies to the boxes of candies sold door to door to raise money for school equipment. U.S.-based chocolate companies and foreign subsidiaries Hershey, Mars, Cadbury and Nestlé, as well as the large U.S. food conglomerates, Cargill and Archer Daniels Midland, faced the possibility of enormous losses from investors and from an American public that, when confronted with injustice, has been known to flex its considerable purchasing muscle. Basketballs and Barbie dolls had become issues in previous fights with child labour activists. Sports and toy manufacturers had come out of the ring with more than a few bruises. How could the candy companies hope to win?

Eliot Engel's House amendment caused a stir in the hot Washington air but after he teamed up with Tom Harkin, a Democrat in the Senate, the labelling idea became a full-blown windstorm. "Harkin was in a position to do profound things," says Pete Leon, the Legislative Director for Congressman Engel. Senator Harkin introduced a revised version of the Engel amendment into the Senate that had much bigger teeth and four times the money available to enforce the legislation. "Industry was worried when the amendment passed the house," says Leon, "but it really flipped when the Senator got involved."

Harkin presents himself as a small-town boy from Iowa who is willing to take on big international human rights issues—though in some cases he's done so with disastrous consequences. In 1992, Senator Harkin had first introduced the Child Labor Deterrence Act, which proposed a U.S. ban on importing products made with child labour. The legislation ultimately failed to pass Congress but even the threat of such a boycott sent a chill through industry worldwide and had devastating consequences, particularly in Bangladesh, where the country's garment manufacturers abruptly dismissed about fifty thousand child workers. Most of the children had been supporting their familes and were subsequently forced to turn to other more dangerous and less lucrative employment—some in rock crushing and many others in prostitution. It was perhaps a well-motivated gesture on the part of the senator, but it demonstrated some of the unintended consequences of benevolence.

The potential for a similar outcome was very real in Côte d'Ivoire. A ban on cocoa could devastate that country's economy and affect the entire region. Itinerant workers from all over West Africa depended on jobs in the Ivorian cocoa sector. Human rights workers, who had been trying to get the U.S. Congress interested in the worst forms of child labour for years, now worried that grandstanding by publicity-seeking congressmen might actually make matters worse. The reality is, in much of the world, children work. The trick is to identify the fine line between human rights and economic necessity—and the tolerance of morally sensitive consumers who like to have their issues served to them in clear black and white terms.

All of the-back and-forth with human rights activists and the congressmen convinced the chocolate companies that they were going to have a hard time proving they had "clean" chocolate if the "slave free" label system went into effect. At first, the umbrella organizations for big chocolate glossed over the issue. Susan Smith, the vice president of public affairs for the Chocolate Manufacturers Association (CMA), said, "A lot of us grew up on farms and we know it's normal for children to work." She speculated publicly whether children were really being exploited in Côte d'Ivoire, or whether the news accounts were sensationalized. "The boy was probably paid to say that 'you are eating my flesh,'" one cocoa company executive remarked, off the record, when I mentioned the Blewett-Woods documentary to him. "There's no way that he would know to say that unless he had been coached." Regardless, the boy did say it, and the media that covered the story now quoted him widely.

Big Chocolate tossed the political hot potato in the direction of the Côte d'Ivoire government: it was the government's responsibility to guarantee clean cocoa, the industry insisted. But the government in Yamoussoukro only deepened the public relations crisis when it blamed the problem on "foreigners." A letter from Côte d'Ivoire to the United Nations asserted that "the noble, courageous, proud and assuredly hospitable people of Côte d'Ivoire" produce most of the cocoa in the country. "Of the ten per cent of foreigners [meaning people from Mali and Burkina Faso] involved in agricultural activities, two or three per cent engage in child trafficking, many of whom [child labourers] also join the ranks of street children in the cities." The communiqué fixed all of the blame on the immigrant population, the Dioula, many of whom had come to Côte d'Ivoire at the invitation of Félix Houphouët-Boigny. Malian and Burkinabè farmers were the likely culprits, according to the Ivorian government, since it was they who had access to the children from their own countries.

There is a modicum of truth to these assertions, since the poorest farmers in Côte d'Ivoire are those from Mali and Burkina Faso. Many are sharecroppers—farmers who don't own land but only use it and they would be the most desperate for cheap labour. Ultimately however, the argument had limited credibility: only a few months after Côte d'Ivoire signed the Bouaké Accords, authorities arrested thirteen child traffickers, several of whom were Ivorians. And Ivorians were prominent among the farmers who were not paying their child workers—Abdoulaye Macko had pursued many of them. Racist arguments were hardly going to help the Ivorian government protect its industry or help the chocolate companies defend their reputations.

Faced with a public relations debacle, Big Chocolate called in the lobbyists. The CMA retained the services of one-time presidential candidate Bob Dole and paired him up with retired Democratic senator George Mitchell. The two savvy politicians, both former majority Senate leaders, argued on their clients' behalf that chocolate companies could not possibly know what was happening on 600,000 cocoa farms. But according to a source on Capitol Hill, Dole and Mitchell also advised the chocolate companies to try to broker a deal—to get the pesky

NGOs and the high-minded congressmen onside before things got out of hand. The lobbyists voiced concerns, according to the source, that "too many reporters are willing to go to Africa and get kids to say on record that they're slaves."

With their powerful connections, Dole and Mitchell seemed to make an impact. Their political timing was also providential. There were elections coming in 2002 and people running for office — candidates who needed money and knew it wouldn't be wise to step on the toes of potential corporate donors. According to official records, Harkin's election war chest had $12,000 from Archer Daniels Midland, as well as $35,000 from sugar companies and another $20,000 from the dairy industry, one of the key players in the chocolate business. Championing children's rights was a good idea from an image point of view, but this was perhaps not the year for a senator who was chairman of the Senate's Agricultural Committee and whose political base was in the farm fields of Iowa to take on the giants in the food business. Before the anti-slavery rider on the agricultural bill could clear the Senate, the politicians found a way to compromise with Big Chocolate.

The Harkin-Engel Protocol, as it came to be called, would be one of the first fully voluntary arrangements for regulating industry in U.S. history and certainly the most ambitious. The cocoa companies agreed to accept a six-point program designed to eliminate child slave labour in the cocoa chain. The chocolate manufacturers, plus the cocoa exporters and importers and the government of Côte d'Ivoire, would work alongside the NGOs and the International Labour Organization (ILO) to set up a monitoring and verification system. It was a moral undertaking; those who signed on were not legally committed. The transnational corporations also agreed to a vague avowal to help improve the lives of cocoa farmers and to get more African children into schools, the oversight for which would come from the ILO.

Each step of the six-point program had a deadline supposedly leading to the final abolition of abusive child labour in the cocoa supply chain by July 1, 2005, when they would have "credible, mutually acceptable, voluntary, industry-wide standards of public certification consistent with applicable federal law, that cocoa beans and their derivative products have been produced without the worst forms of child labour." If the industry failed to eradicate "the worst forms of child labour" on cocoa farms within that time, the politicians would revert back to plan A: the much-feared "slave free" labelling system.

Anita Sheth of Save the Children Canada, a veteran activist and champion of child rights on West African cocoa farms, complained that wording in the agreement appeared to be deliberately vague, and there were holes in it large enough to drive a truck through. Sheth now believes the early efforts on the part of the NGOs to reform the industry were hampered by inexperience and ignorance. No one really knew what they were talking about, she says: "We needed a proper definition of what we were trying to solve." Words like "slavery" seemed overblown and raised the hackles of both industry players and Ivorian authorities. The language slowly evolved until it included the palatable euphemism "the worst forms of child labour," a legal description of compulsory labour that comes from the directives of the ILO. It was certainly a less sensational term than "slavery," and many children's rights activists wanted to crank down the rhetoric of the debate. They were worried that their own campaign might do more harm than good. Says Sheth, "What we wanted was to take the hazards out of the work and not the child out of work. There are circumstances in which children should be able to have jobs—and they want to have jobs."

In addition to more enforcement of laws against child trafficking, Sheth wanted the industry to enforce a comprehensive ban on work that was too hard for children to do, such as carrying heavy sacks or using tools, such as machetes, that they aren't old enough to handle. The protocol, as she understood it, was also supposed to cover work that kept children out of school or that exposed them to health hazards such as agricultural chemicals.

Nowhere in the agreement does it suggest that the cocoa companies might simply undertake to make sure the farmers received a decent price for their beans. And yet almost every critic of the industry has identified the key problem: poverty among the primary producers. Farmers seek, and exploit, the cheapest forms of labour possible because of economic necessity. Time and sophistication equipped all the other players in the chocolate production chain to extract a satisfactory return for their investment of work and capital—everyone except the farmers on the bottom of the pile. Sheth throws up her hands at this failure: "How effective will the Harkin-Engel Protocol be in the long run when it doesn't address the direct correlation between low prices paid to farmers for their cocoa beans and the type and quality of labour employed?" The prime minister of Côte d'Ivoire had warned cocoa companies when the child trafficking scandal first emerged that the manufacturers would have to pay about ten times more for their cocoa if they really wanted to end forced labour.

One labour leader who was involved in the inside talks to establish the protocol says off the record that every time he would ask, "Why not just pay a better price for beans?" of the industry people in the room, "the lawyers for the chocolate companies would snap to attention and announce that it was against U.S. law to price-fix. There was just no way around these guys."

From a public relations point of view, the protocol was a brilliant coup for Big Chocolate. It bought them some time and possibly did away with the threat of labelling—all they had to do was make a show of compliance, and then drag their feet for a while. The politicians would go away, seduced by some other issue of the moment. Eliot Engel denied that the protocol was a climbdown from his originally aggressive and principled reaction to what he'd learned about life in the cocoa groves. The industry got a clear message from the legislators: "They know we mean business, and we do," he said in an interview after the protocol was signed. The deadline structure is rigid, he declared, and failure to meet each milestone will mean that that U.S. legislation will once again become likelihood. Big Chocolate had committed itself to having "clean" cocoa by July 1, 2005, and Engel confirmed that they would find a way to independently verify that exploited child labour was not one of their ingredients.

To help sell the initiative, the chocolate companies retained the services of a who's who of public relations firms. According to *La Lettre du Continent*, an African-based newsletter for the European market, the lobbying industry experienced a mini-boom, thanks to the Harkin-Engel Protocol: Powell, Goldstein, Frazer & Murphy represented Cargill; while Barbour Griffith & Rogers and Hogan & Hartson worked for Nestlé. Other firms opened files for the Chocolate Manufacturers Association—fronting for Hershey and Mars—and still others worked for the Ivorian government.

The NGOs had never managed to take effective control of the issue and were no match for this kind of mobilization. Their uncoordinated efforts had been all over the map, complain some aid workers. "We were playing 'coalition politics,'" says one activist, who criticized the protocol as an escape hatch for the industry but who also blames the aid agencies and human rights activists for capitulating along with the politicians. The Harkin-Engel Protocol appointed (critics would say co-opted) the NGOs who were involved in the child labour issue to be the watchdogs of the process. A number of American NGOs endorsed the protocol through their own umbrella organizations, declaring it the best possible solution to the problem.

Anita Sheth took a hold-your-fire position, concluding that, if the deadlines were not met, she and others would resume the pressure later. But Kevin Bales of Free the Slaves, who was an advisor and a signatory to the protocol from the NGO side, was immediately effusive in his praise for the deal, calling it a model for other manufacturing sectors: "If other industries acted with such social and moral responsibility, we would be much nearer to freedom for the 27 million bonded worldwide," reads a statement from Bales.

Only one major U.S. organization publicly broke ranks with the NGOs and rejected the protocol. The International Labor Rights Fund (ILRF) is of the old, take-no-prisoners school of political agitation that eschews any compromise with industry. The fund was founded in the mid-1980s by a Methodist minister, at a time when the aggressive and often ruthless expansion of American corporations into the developing world had coincided with a complete lack of concern on the part of the international labour movement in the plight of workers in those countries. Trade union bosses in Central America were being murdered yet no one seemed interested in their cause. The newly-minted International Labor Rights Fund stepped into situations that were just too hot for any other group to handle.

Twenty years later, the ILRF is still marching to its own drum, resisting any compromise with industry. While many activists in the human rights business argue in favour of cooperation with big business, even insisting that "partnerships" with their adversaries are essential in the modern world, the ILRF refuses. The fund has filed eight specific lawsuits in as many years and has initiated a number of charges against big corporations, including an attack on the world's largest oil company, Exxon Mobil.

Natacha Thys, a young human rights attorney working for ILRF, was the first in the organization to flag the serious flaws in the cocoa protocol. "I thought the congressmen were on the right track with the labelling plan," she says of the proposed law that would force Big Chocolate to get a "slave free" stamp before selling their wares in the United States. "That idea was punitive. It had teeth. My feeling was why go through this whole process and sign on to it if, in the end, no one is going to enforce it?" Thys was alarmed, but not surprised, when so many other American aid agencies and activists endorsed the protocol. She says, "Other NGOs who don't deal with the corporate world were naive about how adversarial business can be. 'We can dialogue,' they all said. But those of us who fight corporations—we know their m.o. And we know how to deal with them."

In the spring of 2002, the ILRF dispatched Haitian-born economist Marx-Vilaire Aristide to West Africa to find out what was really happening on cocoa farms. It was the first of many trips to the region that allowed Aristide to infiltrate the cocoa chain in ways no other researcher had done, making connections with farmers, workers, *pisteurs* and children, and he was able to discover how the job brokers buy and sell children for farm work. Aristide concluded that the children, even those who were being paid, were forced to stay until the end of the season. Farmers told Aristide quite frankly that the business of child labour bondage was a reality, and necessary for their survival. For the child brokers, the trade was so brisk, and the chances of being caught so slim, that it was worth the theoretical risk of punishment.

In May 2002, based on Aristide's research, the ILRF filed a petition to the United States Customs Department demanding an investigation into cocoa entering the country from Côte d'Ivoire. All cocoa imports to the United States should be stopped, the claim stated, pending completion of the investigation because of the strong possibility that the importers were in contravention of U.S. law. Since 1930, the United States has prohibited the importation of goods produced with slaves. "The burden is on the industry to prove that it's not using child labour," declared Bama Athreya, deputy director of the ILRF. The organization argued that the onus had to be on the transnational corporations, not the cocoa farmers, to stop the odious practice, because they were the only ones with the power to do so. Chocolate is a big international business, Athreya argued, and farmers have no control over the supply chain. For the ILRF, the Harkin-Engel Protocol was a dead letter: "Whatever the chocolate manufacturers claim to be doing about this, we cannot leave a problem as serious as child slavery to voluntary private efforts, particularly when there is a federal law on the books to combat it," said Athreya.

The ILRF threatened to upset the apple cart so carefully loaded by the collaboration of congressmen, Big Chocolate executives, the government of Côte d'Ivoire and a network of well-intentioned NGOs. The agencies that endorsed the protocol approach regarded the ILRF petition skeptically and grumbled that the labour rights organization was employing guerrilla tactics that would only create more trouble. The effect the ILRF petition was likely to have, said the dissenters, was to get Ivorian cocoa banned from the U.S. market, an act that would bankrupt Côte d'Ivoire and throw everyone out of work.

It was a risk the ILRF seemed willing to take. Athreya said she believed an actual boycott would never happen, since Big Chocolate would capitulate before it lost access to its prime ingredient. The companies would be forced to prove to U.S. Customs that their cocoa was clean, rather than being able to hide behind a deal made in the backrooms of the industry and Congress. It was effectively the beginning of a game between the ILRF and the U.S.-based transnational cocoa companies to see who would blink first. The stakes were high: the fate of tens of thousands of Ivorian cocoa farmers and their desperately poor employees hung in the balance.

While the ILRF followed its own course, the circle of protocol supporters only got larger. International organized labour, led by the ILO, along with a broadening number of non-profit groups, plus cocoa companies outside the United States—and the governments of cocoa-producing countries—all met in July 2002 in Geneva, where they agreed to make the Harkin-Engel Protocol global, under Swiss law calling it the International Cocoa Initiative. What had been a gleam in Congressman Engel's eye a year earlier had developed into a bureaucracy with a thick alphabet soup of initialisms representing dozens of organizations, some newly invented.

Big Chocolate rejected what its officials considered the hearsay reports of overexcited journalists. And just as the Cadburys had hired an investigator in the face of Nevinson's disclosures a century before, the companies initiated their own inquiry, assigning the International Institute of Tropical Agriculture (IITA), a Nigeria-based institution, to find out just how many children worked on cocoa farms in Côte d'Ivoire, Ghana, Cameroon, Nigeria and Guinea, and to report on their working conditions. While the industry calls the study "independent," the World Cocoa Foundation—Big Chocolate's philanthropic front—actually played a key role in its development, while the U.S. government provided much of the funding. The ILO, already on side to the protocol, helped to design the questions. When the Cadburys wanted their own version of events in West Africa, they openly handed over a wad of cash to the man of their choice. In the contemporary world, such transactions fall under the auspices of a dozen public sector "partners."

After some months of research in West Africa, the IITA concluded that assertions of child exploitation on cocoa farms were exaggerated and the problem was not as pervasive as media reports claimed it was. There was poverty, certainly, but most—if not all—of the children on farms worked in conditions that were normal in their culture. "Everyone was pretty surprised by all the wild figures being thrown around," said Jim Gockowski, who led the study, referring to the earlier suggestion by the U.S. State Department that fifteen thousand children had been victims of trafficking. He told the *New York Times*, "By and large, the cocoa industry didn't deserve the rap it got." He pointed out that everyone knows "that African kids help out on farms." The IITA published only a summary of its findings, not a full report, and it never explained how it obtained any of its numbers.

The NGOs and labour rights activists who had endorsed—or in some cases signed—the protocol were livid. Anita Sheth learned, through Save the Children's field offices in West Africa, that IITA researchers had been "uneasy" when interviewing children about what they did on the farms, and often didn't ask them hard questions. And she was told that the researchers relied without skepticism on testimony from the farmers, who were allowed to supervise all interviews. In some cases, the farmers spoke on behalf of the kids. Sheth dismissed the IITA study in a report: "Save the Children Canada believes that the IITA study results do not accurately reflect the . . . practices of child labour and child trafficking on Ivorian cocoa farms."

Anti-Slavery International complained that the methodology of the survey was skewed. The researchers didn't actually investigate child trafficking but simply questioned child workers about their "level of satisfaction in the job."

All of the surveying for the IITA report was done in the cocoa-producing countries of Ghana and Côte d'Ivoire, not in the labour-producing countries throughout West Africa. One aid worker in Mali says he was surprised that the IITA people never came to investigate reports that an estimated one hundred Malian children were crossing the border every week. It may or may not have been the intention of the IITA to take the legs out from under the child labour activists, but that's the effect the report had, much to the satisfaction of industry players.

Despite all the limitations, the questionable research and the conservative point of view, the IITA study did acknowledge a very large problem. The survey reported that 284,000 children worked in hazardous conditions on cocoa farms in West Africa, over two-thirds of them in Côte d'Ivoire, where they were required to spray chemicals without proper protective equipment and to clear areas using machetes that they couldn't always manage. The report said most of the children toiled under the supervision of their families and relatives, making them ineligible for the bonded labour or slavery category since this work fell into the category of family "chores." But it also concluded that 12,000 of the children were working on farms where they seemed to have no family ties and that about 2,500 may have been smuggled into the country for the purposes of working on these farms.

There was enough alarming news in the study to point to a larger systemic problem, but the chocolate companies preferred to focus on the study's conclusions that showed previous investigations had exaggerated reports of child slavery. A plethora of media reports, mostly in the sympathetic business press, heralded that the "child slave" issue in the cocoa chain was a crock. "Sigh of Relief for Chocolate" declared the influential Dow Jones Newswire. The industry has "done its homework," affirmed its business reporter Enza Tedesco, who reported, "Some market participants say they are completely exonerated."

Speaking anonymously to selected reporters, chocolate industry officials sprinkled quotes through the media: "They'll know now," said one nameless cocoa dealer, referring to the public, "that it's not big plantation owners with thousands of laborers slaving under poor conditions, but rather small crop holders with heads of households trying to feed their families." The dealer goes on to suggest that people should eat more chocolate instead of boycotting it so that the farmers in Africa can make more money and poverty in West Africa can be eradicated. A quote from another "relieved" cocoa industry expert said that the hazardous working conditions for children are just part of the culture of those countries and are not abusive by African standards. "The fact that the kids don't go to school is not because they're being kept at home working," claimed the expert, with not a hint of irony. "It's because there are no schools."

What's remarkable is that the news from the IITA report came as such a comfort to the chocolate companies. A conservative, and by many accounts inadequately researched, report still concluded that hundreds of thousands of children were working in hazardous conditions; that they were poor and unable to go to school; and that many of them had probably been installed in their jobs by child traffickers. But somehow, as long as they were not called "slaves," and as long as the numbers were in the modest hundreds of thousands, there was no issue. That children in undetermined numbers were suffering from poverty so extreme that they would "volunteer" to accept the tender intervention of child traffickers; that their parents were willing to sell them to anonymous middlemen rather than struggle to feed them for another day; that cocoa producers were so desperate to make a living that they'd resort to the bondage and imprisonment of children to maintain an affordable labour force—none of these unchallenged findings seemed to bother the leaders of the industry that solicited the information.

On August 28, 2002, with information from Save the Children Canada workers at Horon So, Malian authorities arrested three men caught transporting dozens of children over the border. They'd paid local people between 25,000 and 30,000 West African francs for each child. The detention of these suspects revealed to all that, in spite of international concerns and publicity, the criminal industry was still quite active. Border police in Mali complained that smugglers were difficult to locate since communities often covered for them. Families received desperately needed money from the "brokers," and they had convinced themselves and their neighbours that it was all for the best, all part of the faint hope that their kids were really going off to work and would prosper and one day return to share the fruits of their good fortune. How could parents admit that, in reality, they were selling their children into a modern form of slavery?

The arrests came almost concurrently with the IITA study, but that didn't mitigate the triumph in the press releases from the industry. Ivorian authorities argued that the detentions only proved that the Bouaké Accords were working and that there was no longer a significant problem with trafficking.

With the authorities in Africa making arrests and the Harkin-Engel Protocol in force, the child labour issue was well on its way to having being "dealt with," as one industry player described it. It was back to business and a well-established tradition of privacy among the titans of chocolate. There was no longer any purpose to be served by talking to the public. The corporations refused requests for attributable interviews after the protocol was signed, deferring all comment to the World Cocoa Foundation (WCF). Bill Guyton of the WCF became the face and voice of Big Chocolate, an unflappable, even-tempered young man who exudes profound concern for children. He insists that the industry is doing all that it can. "We will put a system in place to monitor child labour in the cocoa chain and we will take corrective action," Guyton says in every interview. "But you can't chase down every bean," he adds, with prudent caution and a smile that tells you it's almost absurd to think otherwise.

Long-deceased Cadburys would envy the effectiveness of modern lobbying and message management. Had it been available in their time, they certainly could have avoided much of their bad press. And contemporary leaders in the cocoa business might have felt a private satisfaction that, in the ranks of their critics, there was no one with the dogged, uncompromising commitment of Henry Nevinson. On the contrary, they had the advantage of a modern phenomenon called pack journalism.

Like tropical fish, reporters often swim collectively in one direction and then abruptly turn to go the other way. Just over a year after the explosive Blewett-Woods documentary and the florid reporting that followed it, journalists went back to the children and the aid workers who had been interviewed by earlier journalists and filmmakers, but this time to challenge their veracity. The most prominent report to rise from this revision showed up in the pages of the Sunday *New York Times Magazine*.

A young maverick reporter named Michael Finkel was making a name for himself at the magazine for daredevil trips and unorthodox reporting methods. He landed his first cover story after he joined the desperate passengers of a rickety Haitian refugee boat as they attempted a death-defying escape through shark-infested waters to the United States. After this exclusive, Finkel was off to cover violence in Gaza and, soon after that, he investigated the illegal market for human organs—all sensational stories that won him high praise in some circles but criticism in others for being a bit of a stuntman.

In the spring of 2001, the *New York Times Magazine* handed Finkel a copy of the Blewett-Woods documentary on slavery in Côte d'Ivoire and a file from the British-based Anti-Slavery International along with an assignment to investigate child labour in the cocoa fields. He showed up in Côte d'Ivoire in June 2001 and then hooked up with the Malian Association of Daloa, the same group that had informed Blewett and Woods that ninety per cent of cocoa farms used child conscripts as part of their labour force.

The association set up interviews for Finkel with teenaged boys who had escaped the drudgery of bonded farm work. Finkel says he quickly grew skeptical of the stories he heard from the boys because they all seemed to be saying the same thing—as though they had been coached. One boy talked of his beatings on the farm, but Finkel doubted the boy's sincerity. He asked to see the scars from the thrashings, but the boy said his wounds had healed. Finkel asked others to show him scars, but apparently no boy could present a single unsightly blemish.

Finkel also disclosed that, while it's routine to "present timely gifts or to grease a few palms" in the course of one's work in such countries, the fixers and facilitators he met in Côte d'Ivoire were more aggressive and more greedy in their pursuit of fees and bribes than he normally experienced and that made him more suspicious. "If you listened to certain members of the Malian Association and took notes and tilted your head just so—well, yes, there was slavery," Finkel wrote. "If journalists are willing to pay good money to see slaves, it seemed as though some official with the Malian Association was more than willing to provide them."

All of this was enough to convince Finkel that he was in pursuit of the wrong story. "I changed my tack," Finkel explained in

his eventual exposé. "Rather than looking for slaves, I was looking for liars." A less dogmatic approach might have been to seek
out both slaves and liars, since both probably existed in the cocoa
fields. But Finkel clearly felt he'd been duped, and that the issue
to be investigated wasn't child labour but deception.

When he returned to the United States, Finkel told his editors
that, instead of writing about slavery, he wanted to write a piece
about how journalists see what they want to see and how NGOs
perpetuate errors to suit their own interests. His editor thought
that a better idea would be to write a feature describing one boy's
story; people could then decide for themselves whether the children are really slaves. Finkel complied. The headline that eventually appeared with his story, which ran over a large photo of a
sad-faced teenager, asked: "Is Youssouf Male a Slave?"

In the article, Finkel describes Male's life, writing as though
he was speaking from the boy's own point of view. Using this
emotive technique, Finkel raises doubt as to whether Male was a
slave or just another victim of conventional and systemic poverty.
The story strongly suggests that Male had been manipulated by
NGOs such as Save the Children Canada, that, according to
Finkel, used the Blewett-Woods documentary to indoctrinate the
children while they were at the Horon So refuge. The boys were
persuaded that they were enslaved against their will, suggests
Finkel's story, even though they were probably just poor kids
looking for jobs and a chance to buy American goods such as
Nike running shoes, as Youssouf Male apparently did.

Finkel's piece, published in November 2001, at the height of
the Big Chocolate public relations campaign, was a bonus for
revisionists and a blow to the NGOs' fragile work to stop child
trafficking and bonded labour. Save the Children Canada was
outraged, as Finkel's story made it appear as though the organization had been coaching the children. But Anita Sheth saw something even more troubling about the article. As she read "Is
Youssouf Male a Slave?" it seemed to Sheth that the details about

the boy's story didn't quite add up and she instructed her field office in Mali to find Male to ask him some questions. Sheth discovered more than she'd bargained for. Finkel's story about fabricated facts had its own fishy smell and contained numerous glaring errors—he was even wrong on the dates he said he'd been at Horon So. What was even more intriguing was that the photograph of "Youssouf Male" was really someone else, Madou Traoré, the boy from Sirkasso who had stolen his father's bike and run away to the cocoa groves with Aly Diabate.

Finkel was just returning from covering the war in Afghanistan when Anita Sheth finally tracked him down. She told him she'd found his article confusing. Could he explain some facts? Finkel complied. When his attempt to clarify his story provoked further questions from Sheth, Finkel finally admitted that he had created a composite character based on a number of the children he had interviewed. He eventually confessed, in a series of emails, that he hadn't actually seen Youssouf Male at Horon So, nor had he ever witnessed children watching the Blewett-Woods film. Male, he said, was just one of the boys he interviewed. (Sheth has Male on tape saying he never met the American journalist.) Finkel pleaded with Sheth in emails and phone calls not to expose his liberties with the truth. The *New York Times* was being rocked with scandal over other journalistic lapses. He'd surely lose his job. His small children would suffer. (Sheth would later learn he had no children.)

Sheth told him that Save the Children was interested only in the truth—his article, loaded with lies, was damaging to the organization. If the *New York Times Magazine* would simply publish a correction, including the correct name on the photo, that would be enough. Privately, she thought this would probably be sufficient to get Mr. Finkel fired.

In order to get the photo corrected, Finkel had to come clean with his editors, who quickly became suspicious: If he'd falsified the identity of his main character, what else might be fabricated?

Finkel admitted to the composite character and said he was only trying to present a realistic picture. Everything else was true, even if it never happened. But his editors didn't accept his defence of creative licence. They banished Finkel from the magazine and published a lengthy correction of the facts in the next edition. Months later, the magazine reported that it had closely double-checked all previous articles by Finkel and had found no other serious discrepancies, certainly none on the scale of the Youssouf Male story.

In a bizarre tell-all memoir that includes details of the incident, Finkel admits it was the single biggest mistake of his life. "I thought I'd get away with it," he writes in *True Story*, a book about his troubles, for which he is purported to have received a $300,000 advance. In his account, Finkel weaves the details of his journalistic disgrace with another narrative—about a felon who stole Finkel's own identity to escape prosecution for murder. Of his article for the *New York Times Magazine*, he says, "I was writing about impoverished teenagers in the jungles of West Africa. Who would be able to determine the main character didn't exist?"

Finkel confesses that he wrote the article under a strict deadline that compelled him to stay awake for three days, high on amphetamines, and that he'd found himself short on research material for the story. He had come back from Côte d'Ivoire only with the intention of exposing the shoddy practices of other journalists and the NGOs, not the story of one boy's dilemma, as his editors subsequently requested. Finkel admits that he considered flying to Toronto to try to bribe Anita Sheth and Save the Children Canada. He thought US$10,000 in cash might be enough to buy their silence. But he still maintains that, while the narrative may have been fictive, the story itself was true.

A number of newspaper and magazine articles about the Finkel debacle, published after his book was published, supported the idea that sometimes the truth is larger than the sum of the facts—and sometimes facts get in the way of truth. Whatever such apologies do for the state of American journalism, the labour issues of West Africa took on another layer of confusion.

The Finkel saga may seem tangential, but it reveals a number of disturbing elements that are germane to the narrative of exploitation in the world of global commerce: the tendency to manipulate facts from remote and undeveloped places to advance unrelated interests; the ripple effect of misinformation on political and corporate interests; the vulnerability of gullible victims to the polished and frequently self-interested inquiries of outsiders; the ease with which important issues can be dismissed by bad reporting and never recovered, no matter how much the dissembling is exposed.

Ultimately, in the months and years to come, the news story of "slave" children in the cocoa chain would take a back seat to the more pressing story of the "global war on terror." A few journalists, such as Humphrey Hawksley of the BBC, continued to uncover stories about trafficking, but his was a more personal mission: "There's something about this particular story that got under my skin and stayed with me. I can't leave it," he admits. But the journalistic pack had moved on.

Whenever there were questions about child labour in chocolate, the industry referred inquirers to the Harkin-Engel Protocol, which promised the world it would have "clean" chocolate by July 1, 2005. As part of the protocol, the corporations had started investing money in small ventures to make the lives of farmers better and to encourage them to send their kids to school.

One project that I visited in Côte d'Ivoire provides a little tree nursery so that children can cultivate their own cocoa crop. It also funds a small vegetable garden near the school where children are encouraged to grow their own food. From what I saw, the garden, at best, might feed fewer than half of the students in the school for a few days per week. Directors of the little enterprise maintain that the tree nursery will eventually generate money to pay for more food, a necessary development since the chocolate companies have made no commitment to long-term funding of either the nursery or garden.

As for the school building itself, it was crumbling. The playground reeked with the sharp odour of urine—there was no latrine. Yet this project was offered as an example of cocoa company largesse. The school, and several others like it, is conveniently located near Abidjan's international airport. The teachers who run the little school canteen say they have a lot of visitors from abroad—people interested in seeing signs of progress. In truth, this small showcase project is an improvement over the situation in other schools only because the norm in Côte d'Ivoire farm communities is so pathetic. Compared with the massive amount of aid the oil companies pour into African countries to mollify local people and their governments, the investment from Big Chocolate in projects like this is minuscule. "I've seen some dreadful companies in dreadful places but few as stingy as these," says the BBC's Hawksley, speaking of his own investigations.

The Harkin-Engel Protocol, endorsed by the chocolate industry in 2001, at least acknowledged the existence of a child labour issue on West African cocoa farms. But any initiatives to deal with the abuse amounted to window dressing. Ultimately, the exploitation of children on the cocoa farms of Côte d'Ivoire would be impeded not by any good intentions on the part of politicians or corporate executives but by a factor neither group could control.

War.

Chapter Eight

CHOCOLATE SOLDIERS

"Whenever there is cocoa there is trouble."
—A COCOA FARMER IN SOUTHWESTERN CÔTE D'IVOIRE

JUNE IS A DISTRESSING TIME OF THE YEAR FOR THOSE who live in the fallow farmlands of Mali. The air buzzes with heat and singed dust. Scrawny cattle nose around in the few clumps of greenery, seeking whatever is left to eat. As they await the rains that may or may not come in sufficient quantities—or at all—people take on an air of quiet desperation. Especially now, as the Sahara continues its relentless spread southward, transforming large expanses of overused and depleted soil into sandy, sterile desert.

Forlorn families sit listlessly in their yards, listening to the distant rumble of a thunderstorm that always seems to promise rain for someone else. Their fields can feed them only for about nine months of the year. By June they are reduced to eating just one meal per day. And still, in the cooler part of the morning and before the fatigue of hunger sets in, they bend once more over the exhausted earth to coax the tiny plots of land to life, just one more time, planting their meagre seed and asking Allah, please, to send the rain.

It's at this time of year that Malians of all ages abandon the parched fields, pack a few belongings and wander off to look for work. But in June 2005, more Malians were coming back than going. They returned with terror in their eyes and with stories to tell that were beyond the imaginations of the listeners.

~

Kader Ouattara was twenty years old, a sturdy young man with a lot of plans, when he left his village in southern Mali and headed for the Promised Land. The year was 1987, and Ouattara was responding to an appeal from the iconic African statesman Félix Houphouët-Boigny for ambitious farmers to come and put the Ivorian land to work, to turn jungles into farms. This was the West African dream, and Ouattara would be part of it.

"My father had engaged a wife for me," he explains to me bashfully. With his willing young bride at his side, Ouattara emigrated to Côte d'Ivoire.

He learned the rules of his new country quickly. "You had to find a host who would welcome you and then would invite you to share a part of his land," says Ouattara.

Robert Sho is the Ivorian who gave Ouattara his first break. "We were working with him at first, cutting bush and growing trees," he explains. "And then he showed us another field to cut—one part for him and another part for me." Ouattara insists the arrangement was always very friendly, as it was throughout the cocoa region. The indigenous farmers needed outside labour, especially the durable northerners from Mali and Burkina Faso, and there was plenty of land to share.

Ouattara worked his seven hectares while also toiling in the field of his patron. Through enormous personal effort he eventually saved enough to strike out on his own—to stop working for Sho and dedicate himself entirely to his own enterprise. That was part of the arrangement. But Ouattara was soon ready to expand even further, to grow more cocoa. By then it was the 1990s, and there were few areas in the overcultivated south-central part of the country left to develop. Cocoa was losing its value on international markets, and Ivorians were becoming less willing to share with outsiders. They cleared land for themselves and tried to stave off their creditors by producing more beans and employing the cheapest labour possible to harvest them. Amicable arrangements between Malian immigrants and Ivorians such as Robert Sho became rare.

When Félix Houphouët-Boigny died in December 1993, Ouattara began to sense a new hostility towards the immigrants. The xenophobia became more overt as post-Houphouët governments began to preach a doctrine called Ivoirité. The term was vague, and took on many interpretations, but it came to mean that no one but those of pure Ivorian blood should enjoy full civil rights in the country. In practice, it meant that the immigrants who had been invited to take part in the economic miracle would no longer have any legal claim to the land they worked and lived on. At least, that is how Ivoirité was interpreted by people in the countryside. Ouattara says there were never any clear laws or directives, but Ivorian property owners took the racist policy as a licence to exploit their immigrant neighbours. "They would give you land," Ouattara explains. "You would clear it and prepare the soil [for cocoa]. And then you would find someone else has claimed it and they are planting on it."

The worst cases were perpetuated by the Guere people, says Outtara, natives of central Côte d'Ivoire. "Even if the Guere gives you land, his family will come along and take it back. The Guere people told us they wanted to make a census so that they would know whose fields to take." Such a census would presumably allow the Ivorians to know who was a foreigner, even if a family had been in the country for generations.

Ouattara heard there land was still available in the southwest, near the Liberian border, that no one had yet cleared and that would be suitable for *Theobroma*. A lot of Malians and Burkinabès had already relocated to this virgin territory, far from the more densely populated parts of the cocoa belt, and were attempting to start their farms again. But this was a perilously precarious place to be.

Just over the border, Charles Taylor, the mercurial warlord-president of Liberia, was conducting a reign of terror. Refugees from Taylor's killing sprees escaped into Côte d'Ivoire, and it often seemed a real possibility that the Liberian conflict would, itself, spill over soon. Ouattara didn't know which way to turn. He was alarmed by the rancour and resentment of the Ivorians around him, and he feared the racist policies of Ivoirité, but he was also troubled by the threat of war. In the end, Ouattara gathered up his young wife and their one child and headed west, where he took up residence in a community made up almost entirely of Malians.

Blolekin is a village about thirty kilometres from Liberia, on the edge of the thick, dark rainforests and stunning national parks of a region called Man. Ouattara felt secure there. Not only did his countrymen surround him, but many of them were members of his own family. "My uncle was head of the village," he says.

But peace in the region was an illusion. In September 2002, rebel soldiers from northern Côte d'Ivoire launched a *coup d'état*, sweeping down from the Malian border almost to the port city of Abidjan. They were later beaten back to Bouaké in the centre of the country, but the fighting continued. The rebels were of Malian descent, and they were reacting to the discriminatory policies of Ivoirité that had, among other evils, pitted the mostly Muslim north against the mostly Christian and Ivorian south. The front line between the two sides was now drawn through the heart of the cocoa belt.

Kader Ouattara listened to news reports of the war on the BBC and worried that his village would eventually become a battle zone. Blolekin was inside Ivorian-held territory, and he knew that its people, as Malians, would be regarded as enemies.

Almost simultaneously, fighting broke out to the west of their village, near Liberia. But Ouattara quickly realized it was not the same war. "It was about religion in the north," says Ouattara— meaning Muslims fighting against Christians. "In our region, it was about land." Ouattara says the Ivorians used the excuse of the conflict with the north to launch a land grab, forcing immigrants off their valuable property.

To make matters worse, Liberian mercenaries crossed the border to capitalize on the chaos and to further destabilize Côte d'Ivoire. Ouattara was terrified of these well-armed and savage warriors, many little more than boys. The soldiers were willing to help land-grabbing Ivorians drive the Muslim farmers off their land for a per centage of whatever value they could confiscate. The Liberians systematically moved through village after village in a campaign of ethnic cleansing.

As they closed in on Blolekin, Ouattara didn't know what he would do. His wife was heavily pregnant, and he wasn't sure she would be able to run when the time came to flee. During a night of thunderstorms, while nature's violence whirled and crashed around them, she went into labour. The midwife, trapped by floodwaters from the storm, never arrived. After hours of agonizing labour, Ouattara's wife gave birth, but then, soon after, she died. The newborn boy was sickly and feverish, but Ouattara couldn't find a doctor. He watched helplessly as the child slowly perished. There was hardly time to bury his wife and infant before Kader realized he and his surviving son would have to flee before they too were victims — not of nature, but of a military campaign to rid the land of people like him.

The assault on Blolekin came before dawn. Liberian mercenaries and Ivorian troops first attacked the little village with artillery. "Then the soldiers entered the village. They ordered people out of their houses and told them to bring all their money. And then they blew up our houses." Ouattara was stunned as the big guns reduced the mud huts to nothing while the soldiers stood around and laughed.

As their houses crumbled, civilians fled into the surrounding bush, but the soldiers chased them down. Now the sounds of both artillery and small-arms fire were overwhelming. "We would hide at night and move by day," says Ouattara. The people of Blolekin met with others from surrounding villages, all heading

north, into territory held by Muslim rebels. From there, the survivors were able to make their way back to Mali.

In late fall of 2002, fifteen years after he had left Mali,
Ouattara was back in his home country, penniless and broken-
hearted, his dreams incinerated. He told me his story one June
afternoon in 2005, delivering the narrative in a single, steady
stream of memory. He is a strikingly handsome man who would
appear younger than his thirty-eight years but for the furrows on
his brow. He is nearly deaf because of the bombardment that
destroyed his peace in Côte d'Ivoire. At his side, Ouattara's
young son stands erect, watching with concern as his father
speaks to a small delegation of strangers about their terrible
flight. Ouattara attempts to reassure the boy, gently stroking his
hand while his relatives gather around to listen to the story
they've surely heard many times before. They are sad for
Ouattara but also for themselves. They once depended on his
earnings from the land in Côte d'Ivoire for survival. They have
but one sustaining hope: that Ouattara will one day go back to
reclaim his land in Côte d'Ivoire. When the war ends. If it ends.

When Ouattara finishes his story, the relatives silently stare
out into their barren fields and listen for the thunder.

~

The death of Houphouët-Boigny in 1993 left a power vacuum in
Côte d'Ivoire. The old man had been too self-absorbed to have
properly arranged succession before his death—if rational succession in an autocratic state is ever possible. In fairness, it would
have been difficult for anyone to administer a country where
unemployment was growing exponentially; where drought and
overcrowding were ravaging farmland; where foreign debt was
exploding; where government institutions were being disman-
tled; and where the high expectations of a population had been
thwarted. The entire economy rested on one industry—cocoa—

and the president had learned he had absolutely no control over the price of beans. Houphouët-Boigny, like most megalomaniacs (even benevolent ones), had failed to groom a successor. His death left the country in chaos.

Henri Konan Bédié was Houphouët-Boigny's immediate, but temporary, political heir. This new president had none of his predecessor's charm or charisma, and Bédié attempted to control the country through fear and intimidation. It was he who first introduced the toxic policies of Ivoirité, more as a political manoeuvre than as an actual law. He allowed authorities throughout the country free rein to harass immigrants and generally discriminate against them. When UNICEF first approached the Ivorian government to deal with the abuse of Malian boys on cocoa farms, the lukewarm response from the politicians was, in part, due to the prevailing attitude that "outsiders" had no political rights. Bédié gambled that his own incompetence might escape detection if he turned the immigrants into scapegoats.

Bédié's pathetic efforts to govern by racism might have been temporarily popular, but his insatiable appetite for personal wealth estranged him from the population and drove the country further into debt. Bédié blamed the foreigners for all the country's woes, but international financiers weren't persuaded by his protests. In 1998, the IMF, the World Bank and the European Union suspended all aid to the country. A year later, the Ivorian military mutinied and Bédié was tossed out in a *coup d'état*. General Robert Gueï became the new president of Côte d'Ivoire. He was no improvement.

General Gueï may have disagreed with Bédié on many issues, but he took a fancy to the concept of Ivoirité, enshrining Bédié's policy in laws restricting full citizenship to people born of "pure" Ivorian blood (meaning that both parents must have been born in Côte d'Ivoire). The problem was that Houphouët-Boigny had been so successful in recruiting outsiders into his Ivorian Miracle that nearly a third of the population of Côte d'Ivoire was now made up of foreigners or their descendants. This substantial minority were now, officially, non-citizens, even those who had never been outside the country.

The general didn't last long either. Gueï was soon run out of town by the equally grasping and power-hungry Laurent Gbagbo. Under pressure from the international community to hold elections, Gbagbo went to the polls. But he was elected president principally because he had his only important adversary, the northerner Alassane Ouattara, eliminated from the electoral race. Ouattara is a Muslim whose heritage goes back to Burkina Faso. According to the policy of Ivoirité, Ouattara wasn't a citizen even though he was born in Côte d'Ivoire, so Gbagbo declared him ineligible to run. It was a move of breathtaking opportunism, but the international community, wanting peace in West Africa seemingly at any cost, turned a blind eye. Gbagbo's two predecessors had both been overthrown, and France, principally, wanted another strongman in power. The cunning Gbagbo, backed by his devious and ambitious wife, Simone, would fit the bill.

A few months after Gbagbo was installed, international human rights groups including Amnesty International reported on a mass grave found in Yopougon, north of Abidjan, in the heart of cocoa country, where Cargill runs its major cocoa-processing plant. When the grave was opened, investigators found the bodies of fifty-seven Muslim men who had all been known supporters of Alassane Ouattara. The men had been killed, according to witnesses, by the Ivorian gendarmerie. Gbagbo promised an inquiry, but no one was ever found responsible for the crime. It was only the first of many mass executions in Côte d'Ivoire.

In the cities, principally Abidjan, a new generation of educated and ambitious young Ivorians was waking up to the reality that Houphouët-Boigny's economic miracle had come to an end. They'd missed out on the country's brief moment of glorious prosperity, and they weren't happy about it. Their deep resentment became a political resource to be exploited by young radicals who rose to prominence on promises that they would restore the golden age of Le Vieux. A charismatic and fierce young university student named Charles Blé Goudé, who came to be known as "The General," mobilized thousands of angry young men into a militia group called the Panafrican Congress of Young Patriots. Simone Gbagbo was an open supporter of the militia and a covert financial backer of its leader. The students emulated the brash style affected by the American gangsta rap movement, wearing baggy tracksuits and gold chains, and they declared the martyred African-American icon Malcolm X to be their hero.

Blé Goudé was only one of several youth militia leaders based in Abidjan. The militias tyrannized immigrants and vandalized French business establishments. The General proclaimed that foreigners, both the immigrants from neighbouring countries and those from France, had too much economic influence in Côte d'Ivoire, and that the time had come for true Ivorians to take control of their nation's destiny.

The United States, the United Nations and South Africa advised the Ivorian government to cool the young radicals and their racist rhetoric and to restore the rights of Côte d'Ivoire's immigrant population before the volatile situation got out of hand. But Gbagbo refused. That's when the Muslims from the north took matters into their own hands.

On September 19, 2002, all the trouble that had been building since the death of Félix Houphouët-Boigny finally erupted in a full-scale insurrection. Government soldiers who supported northern opposition leaders mutinied in three key cities: Abidjan in the south, Bouaké in the centre and Korhogo in the north. Three hundred people died in the early fighting, and General Gueï was assasinated, along with his wife, his son and his grandchildren, presumably by government troops loyal to Gbagbo who blamed Gueï for helping to stage the uprising.

Gbagbo's forces managed to beat back the mutineers from Abidjan, but the territory from Bouaké to the northern borders of Mali and Burkina Faso fell under the control of a rebel group called Mouvement Patriotique de Côte d'Ivoire (MPCI). Côte d'Ivoire was severed, with Muslims in the north and Christians (as well as animists) in the south. The country teetered on the brink of anarchy. This is when Kader Ouattara and his fellow villagers fled Blolekin as it fell into the hands of marauding thugs, many of them from Liberia, and government soldiers. Four hundred thousand people, all considered non-citizens under Ivoirité, joined Kader Ouattara in his flight. Forty-eight thousand returned directly to Mali, while more than half of the refugees fled to Burkina Faso. The rest vanished into Ghana, Togo and Benin.

Fearing the possibility of another Rwanda, where Hutus exterminated 800,000 Tutsi in a racist frenzy in 1994, France offered Gbagbo military assistance. The concern was genuine, but it was clear that France was also taking care of its own national interests. More than sixteen thousand French nationals lived in Côte d'Ivoire at the time, while an estimated eighty per cent of Côte d'Ivoire's economy was owned or controlled by French transnationals, who earned 2.5 billion euros a year there.

France negotiated a ceasefire line between the south and the north and sent a military force to back it up (as well as to guard French citizens and their enterprises). About seven hundred French troops landed a week after the outbreak of civil war, and they quickly brought the insurrection under control. Within months, France had three thousand troops in its former colony, making it the largest French military operation in Africa since Opération Turquoise, when French troops entered Rwanda first to rescue Europeans and then to prevent reprisals against the Hutu *génocidaires* (France's traditional allies).

As international mediators and neighbouring African countries pressured Gbagbo to develop a peace plan and power-sharing arrangement with the northern rebels, France put hundreds more soldiers on the ground. They were heavily armed and had impressive air power and artillery to back them up. Another six thousand lightly armed United Nations peacekeepers, mostly from other African nations, controlled a "zone of confidence" around the ceasefire line.

The MPCI rebel movement in the north was, at least in the beginning, a fairly disciplined and professional operation whose members were well-trained former soldiers of the Ivorian army. Apart from occupying half the country, they'd made little trouble for the French or the Ivorian government. Civilians who lived in their occupied territories went about their business with minimal disruption. The northern territories they occupied had few resources of value to the Ivorian economy. But the "other war," the southwestern uprising that Kader Ouattara and the other farmers had been caught in, was an entirely different matter. The fighting there was over cocoa. There was great wealth at stake in that region. The cruelty of the conflict intensified accordingly.

During a decade of waging war in Liberia, Charles Taylor had created a military force of unstable and often psychotic soldiers. Some young men and boys recruited by Taylor's men were allegedly required to kill their parents as a form of initiation. Taylor was attempting to destabilize the entire region. His political and military ambition was to expand his authority into neighbouring countries and to create a Greater Liberia. Côte d'Ivoire was one of his targets, and Laurent Gbagbo's political problems were, for Taylor, an opportunity.

While the Muslim rebels fought for control of the north, two unrelated rebel groups emerged in the southwest: the violent and ironically named Movement for Justice and Peace (MJP) and the Mouvement Populaire Ivoirien du Grand Ouest (MPIGO). These two forces had been loyal to General Gueï and now wanted to help overthrow Gbagbo. Charles Taylor was only too happy to help them. He provided the rebels with weapons and murderous manpower. The anti-Gbagbo rebels and the Liberian mercenaries had a common objective: to grab as much of the fertile cocoa-producing country as possible. Taylor would, in the process, establish a beachhead inside the country.

But a number of independent observers in the country believe that, for Taylor, the prospect of controlling cocoa profits was paramount. It would be a replay of his lucrative foray into the diamond fields of Sierra Leone. In the past, gems had financed his military projects; cocoa would be Taylor's newest currency. The little brown beans were potentially as valuable as the "blood diamonds" that subsidized his delusional dreams of glory.

Taylor's equation of cocoa, guns and power wasn't entirely original. President Gbagbo also relied on cocoa profits to finance the Ivorian army, and the rebels in the west saw cocoa as the key to their own financial and military prospects. He who controls cocoa—and the port of San-Pédro in the southwest—will rule the country.

Immigrant farmers were trapped at the confluence of a vicious and unpredictable power struggle among forces of the central government, anti-government rebels and Liberian mercenaries. Loyalties changed, but there was one consistent factor: the immigrants. All the parties to the conflict in the southwest targeted them. Government troops and local gendarmeries had instructions, which they gleefully fulfilled, to harass the foreigners. The police demanded of them proof of citizenship, which they did not have, and deeds to their properties, which they had never acquired.

Faced with ethnic cleansing and the corrosive policies of Ivoirité, Kader Ouattara and the others who had settled in the Promised Land had few options but to run away.

~

Roger Gnohite is a large beefy man who wears a wide-brimmed felt hat in defiance of the equatorial heat. A towel stuffed inside the crown hat absorbs most of the inevitable sweat. The headgear is a contemporary fashion statement in this part of Africa, a display of assumed American bravado, though such a fedora is rarely seen in the United States except in old Hollywood gangster films. It's hard to tell how much of the gangster image is a reflection of reality and how much is vanity. Gnohite's office walls are lined with photos of himself as active sportsman and also as influential politician, hobnobbing with Ivorian dignitaries, the most prominent in the gallery being Le Vieux himself.

Gnohite is the mayor of Gagnoa, a prosperous, bustling town whose trade in cocoa and coffee has continued without interruption throughout the civil war and ethnic pogroms. The giant Cargill enterprise and other transnationals have busy operations here, and the mayor is determined to keep his region peaceful. Gnohite's authority extends beyond Gagnoa to include the sprawling cocoa-growing region all around.

I went to see Mayor Gnohite in the spring of 2005. A ceasefire agreement between the north and the south was holding, while UN and French soldiers kept things quiet in the zone of confidence. But in the southwest the savage killing, with its undercurrents of racism, continued. The immigrants who remained in the region had armed themselves and were attempting to hold their ground as both government soldiers and hired mercenaries fought for control of the valuable cocoa groves.

I was told that Gnohite was the man to see if you wanted to look into the face of Ivoirité. The mayor is notorious among the immigrant population. They believe he has incited youth gangs to roam the countryside and terrorize the "foreign" farmers. The mayor has made it quite clear that the *allogènes*, as the immigrants are called in French, have no deeds and no rights to the land, no matter how many generations they have worked the fields.

Isn't this a betrayal of the values of Houphouët-Boigny — values that he professes to share? I ask him.

"No," says the mayor. "Le Vieux would have wanted Côte d'Ivoire protected." Gnohite states openly that the *allogènes* are known sympathizers of the Muslim rebels; hence, they are enemies.

"Doesn't that send a message that outsiders have no right to protection here?"

"I am a man of the people," he answers. "I protect everyone. No one is forcing people to leave. But if they are causing trouble, they have to go back to where they came from."

"But innocent people are being killed because of their ethnicity—what is Gnohite going to do about it?" I ask.

"This is not ethnic cleansing," he answers, actually laughing at the question. "We are all mixed together—not like Hutus and Tutsis. That kind of thing could never happen here." If there are such reports, then "this is the fault of the media making things up. Western journalists fabricate these stories," he says.

Ange Aboa, the journalist from Reuters who is travelling with me as my guide, shakes his head in amazement when we leave the interview. "If that is the official voice of Côte d'Ivoire," said Aboa, "you can only imagine the unofficial one."

Ten kilometres to the north of Gagnoa, in the town of Ouragahio, we get a clear illustration of how both official and unofficial voices of racist doctrine affect the lives of vulnerable people. In a house on the edge of town, Kassoum Cissé sits among the few possessions left to him. According to his identification papers, he's seventy years old, but he looks much older. His eyes are sunk deeply in his thin, weathered face, and he shifts his scrawny haunches uncomfortably on a rough wooden bench. His ethnic roots are Burkinabè. Cissé issues an order to the young man who brought us here, and he disappears to fetch some plastic chairs and orange pop for the visitors. We site under the shade of a giant mango tree while Cissé explains the troubles.

How did a community that had lived in harmony for generations suddenly turn into a murderous melee? A year ago, Burkinabès in this area suffered a series of deadly raids that have never been properly investigated. According to one story, an *allogène* woman who lived in the community of Broudoume took some sand from a sacred forest in order to practise witch-craft. The local Bete people, the tribe from which Gbagbo descends, found out about it and drove out all of the eight hun-dred or so immigrants in the region. According to the Bete, those same immigrants returned at night and murdered Bete villagers.

Another, likelier, version of the story, and one that is consis-tent with other reports from this region, attributes the violence to a record harvest, coupled with higher than usual cocoa bean prices. In this account, government authorities encouraged indigenous Bete tribesmen to expel all of the immigrants on the eve of the cocoa harvest. According to newspaper accounts, another seven hundred people were evicted from neighbouring villages. No matter which version explains the outcome—and whether or not there were reprisal attacks by the victims—the operation seemed to have official sanction. Police failed to inter-vene to help the immigrants. In fact, there were reports of immi-grants being removed from buses and summarily executed by policemen.

Kassoum Cissé is a respected tribal elder and the only resi-dent of Ouragahio who would agree to speak to us about the vio-lence that Mayor Gnohite describes as an invention of foreign reporters. As he ponders questions, Cissé wipes his face with a long sunburnt hand in a gesture of resigned despair, staring into space before he answers. He tells of the bands of young men who recently came door to door with guns, threatening every-one in the village and robbing them. The youths, probably members of the Young Patriots, were neither soldiers nor police, and they carried only small arms, in some cases hunting rifles. But no authorities came to protect the *allogènes* as the hooligans burned their houses and forced them to flee into the bush.

Cissé says he knows of ten people killed in just one attack. He escaped, along with others. They've returned to the village, but no one goes to work in the fields for fear of ambush. The area west of Ouragahio is under siege as we speak, with most of the former residents huddled in displaced persons camps. The violence is spreading through the cocoa area, and Cissé doesn't know how much longer his village can survive it. I presume some of the villagers are now armed in anticipation of an inevitable showdown.

Even though he has identity papers to say was born in Côte d'Ivoire, Cissé's birth village is in the Ivorian north — in rebel territory. That alone makes him a likely rebel sympathizer and collaborator in the eyes of the gendarmerie. Cissé assumed he had legal title to the land his father came to clear just after the Second World War. But the family never had a valid deed, according to the law as it is now understood. It was *un achat traditionel*, Cissé explains. A kind of old-fashioned gentleman's agreement, worked out between local people, which everyone once honoured. Not anymore. Mayor Gnohite had spoken of these deals with contempt, referring to them as "gin-soaked informalities" that have no standing in law.

The sudden move to invalidate the *achats traditionels* came as a shock to the people who grow cocoa here. Under new regulations, which the government claims were in existence all along, only farmers possessing citizenship cards can own land, and no outsider can obtain such papers. Those who do manage to hold precious residency cards often have to watch in horror as the police destroy them.

The International Crisis Group (ICG) reports that, within days of the northern uprising, security forces moved into the rural communities and began to systematically arrest "sympathizers" among the immigrant population. According to an ICG report, these forces began a "campaign of mass destruction of shanty towns." Police raided mosques and assassinated imams, and people who spoke out against Gbagbo's regime or about the dirty work of his soldiers, would simply "disappear."

As the economy tumbled and French businessmen shipped their families back to France to escape the violence, jobs in the cities disappeared. Young men, university educated but without employment prospects, returned to the countryside, bringing their disappointment and their bitterness with them. They had been indoctrinated in the language of hate that was percolating in the universities, finding strident voice through militia leaders such as Charles Blé Goudé. Now these angry young men returned to the countryside where their fathers or grandfathers had once farmed. Encouraged by local leaders such as Mayor Gnohite, they demanded that the land be taken back from the immigrants who farmed it, though in many cases their families had abandoned claim to the property long ago. It didn't matter. The young men were determined to be masters in their own house, as The General had instructed them.

Not all Ivorians wanted the immigrants gone. Many of the indigenous farmers needed the *allogènes* and hopefully waited for their return from the displaced persons camps—they couldn't produce a cocoa crop without them. On at least one occasion, Ivorians had gun battles with each other over immigrant labour.

Some of the *allogènes* didn't flee but fought back. There were many reprisal killings. In a deadly game of tit for tat, opposing groups ambushed each other's villages at night. As village-level violence became commonplace, the militias from the Liberian border area pursued more ruthless means to drive the immigrants from the land. International aid workers, who continued to work in the area, reported hideous scenes of carnage: headless corpses, houses full of women and children set alight, women raped, livestock slaughtered, fields burned, widespread looting. The UN peacekeeping forces rarely ventured into this chaotic environment, leaving only aid workers and missionaries to try to protect people. The NGOs and religious orders offered refuge in their own compounds, but even these were raided.

Jacques Seurt, a passionate human rights worker with the International Organization for Migration was among the last Europeans to leave the area near Blolekin. Seurt has lived in Côte d'Ivoire for years, and he has come to regard it as home. I met him in Abidjan, shortly after he had fled southwest Côte d'Ivoire for his own safety. As a Frenchman in the region and a protector of the immigrants, he knew he was a potential target of the paramilitaries. But he stood his ground until it became suicidal to stay. He has a look of fear stamped on his face as he tells of the relentless attacks he witnessed.

Seurt remembers a time, not so long ago, when Côte d'Ivoire was the most peaceful and prosperous country in Africa. It was more than that, Seurt insists, on further reflection. There was a generosity of spirit in the country, a sophistication and gentility. Seurt speaks of a distressing shift in Côte d'Ivoire since the war that he describes as "a rupture"—a break with the codes of civil society, where Ivorians had coexisted with *allogènes* and the French lived almost as natives. That was the old Côte d'Ivoire he loved. But everything has changed, and Seurt talks ominously of what he sees around him now: "ferocious faces where the anger is palpable."

Was Côte d'Ivoire to become another Rwanda? The next Liberia? Sierra Leone? Congo? Most observers play the macabre game of trying to guess which type of hell Ivorians might be heading for. Jacques Seurt wonders if Côte d'Ivoire isn't an African version of Yugoslavia, a country that was once the model for the region, prosperous and educated and multi-ethnic, but shattered in a few short years by poverty, racism and greed.

The Frenchman's fear is surpassed only by his fascination at one intriguing development: No matter how fierce the fighting, the trucks that transport the cocoa beans always seem to get their cargo to the port of San-Pédro and then onward to the candy counters of the Western world. "I don't know if it was bribes, or pre-arrangements with the rebels. But the path was always clear for the cocoa transporters." Nothing, not even war, seems to inter-fere with the availability of the developed world's favourite treat.

Rumours circulated that the big cocoa trading companies were making a financial killing, thanks to the war. The London-based company Armajaro purchased 204,308 tons of cocoa beans in July 2002, gambling that the price of beans was on a rising trend that could only accelerate in the event of conflict. Even before the war broke out, a scant two months later, industry watchers specu-lated that the firm was trying to "squeeze" the market in anticipa-tion that prices would go even higher. Armajaro dismissed the timing as coincidence, but it still managed to make an estimated US$90 million profit on the transaction.

Gbagbo's government increased taxes on cocoa in the areas over which he still had control, the southeast and central areas of the cocoa belt. His enemies did the same in the west, through the unofficial tax system of bribes and extortion. Much of the income from cocoa went to weapons dealers and corrupt govern-ment leaders. Gbagbo's government negotiated ceasefires while diverting cocoa profits to weapons merchants in Israel, Ukraine and Germany. Even though the United States was officially urg-ing Gbagbo to stop the fighting, the involvement of Charles Taylor was enough to persuade the Bush administration to per-mit deliveries of firepower to the Ivorian government.

Meanwhile, the big cocoa companies got their product to mar-ket while they encouraged other equatorial countries to consider boosting their own cocoa production lest Côte d'Ivoire continue the freefall into chaos. As history has illustrated, countries and cocoa groves come and go, but the appetite for chocolate is forever.

~

In January 2003, France brokered a peace plan called the Linas-Marcoussis Agreement (named after the rugby training centre out-side Paris where it was signed), an agreement many believe was forced on Gbagbo and his Front Populaire Ivoirien (FPI) party. It was a power-sharing arrangement between the north and the south, but it actually gave extraordinary influence over the entire country to France. Everything that affected French interests—industry, business and investments—would be protected, while northern rebels would get control of key ministries in the government.

France was accused of engineering a "constitutional *coup d'état*," an argument hard to refute since France was hardly a disinterested negotiator in the process. Youth organizations in Abidjan launched anti-French rallies, calling on the United States to protect Côte d'Ivoire from "French terrorism." While the president was compelled to sign the agreement, his wife, Simone Gbagbo, the Lady Macbeth figure in the presidential court, made ominous suggestions that the French would be better off if they simply left the country, sooner rather than later. Foreign companies started pulling out as the political temperature rose. Presidential reassurances were not enough when the first lady and the increasingly aggressive youth gangs were sending out ominous signals that contradicted them.

International news agencies moved their West African bureaus to Senegal. Human rights organizations and relief agencies closed up shop as aid money was diverted to countries with more stable regimes. Philanthropy loves security, and Côte d'Ivoire was becoming dangerous. People with the courage to stay on, such as Jacques Seurt, found it increasingly difficult to get to the rural communities affected by the violence.

Reports of child slavery in cocoa persisted but were now explained as part of a campaign by France to blackmail Côte d'Ivoire with threats of possible boycotts. It was a twisted argument, but all problems in Côte d'Ivoire were now blamed on the French. Gbagbo accused Western journalists and the NGOs of trying to destabilize the price of cocoa by "feeding" stories to the media about child labour. The best evidence Gbagbo had of this was alleged indifference by the media to child slavery in cotton, which many human rights workers inside the country thought to be more pernicious and widespread than child slavery in cocoa. It was further proof of Western efforts to manipulate cocoa prices so speculators could make even bigger profits on the futures markets, for which therre was some evidence. All of the rumour and innuendo fed into a climate of paranoia towards outsiders—an outsider being anyone the Gbagbo regime didn't like.

Child trafficking did become less of an issue in West Africa during the war, not because it was a fiction of journalists or because police had stemmed the tide, but because it became more dangerous to smuggle children into the cocoa belt of Côte d'Ivoire. The traffickers would have to cross the front line of a civil war, heavily guarded by two armies and two international military forces. One of the attractions of child smuggling in West Africa, according to UNICEF, had been that it carried so little risk. Crime loves easy targets, and Côte d'Ivoire had become a minefield of perils.

Despite the peace agreement, Gbagbo was emboldened by all his new cocoa-financed weaponry—bold enough finally to bomb the northern rebel stronghold of Bouaké in an aerial attack on November 5, 2004. It was a blatant violation of the ceasefire, and Gbagbo delivered it right in the heart of what the Linas-Marcoussis Agreement called the "conciliation zone." The French were not looking for a fight, and Gbagbo might have got away with it had he not managed to kill nine French soldiers and an American aid worker. Within twenty minutes, France retaliated with its own aerial attack and wiped out Côte d'Ivoire's entire air force—a tiny but impressive fighting fleet, purchased from the proceeds of cocoa sales.

Within days, a spontaneous but clearly orchestrated wave of violence swept the country. The epicentre was among the skyscrapers and corporate offices of Abidjan. Blé Goudé's Young Patriots group had been holding weekly "parliaments" in the city, where he indoctrinated gangs of disenfranchised young men with the notion that all foreigners were enemies who were steal-ing their jobs. Following the destruction of the air force, The General turned his wrath against the French. He went on state television and called all young Ivorians to action. Following his appeal, armed gangs of youth roamed the streets hunting for French citizens. Even Ivorians were terrified.

In a week-long campaign of looting and arson, during which businesses and homes were destroyed and a number of women claimed to have been raped, the Young Patriots, along with other less well-known militias, managed to drive about half the French population of Côte d'Ivoire out of the country. French troops fought back, killing an unknown number of Ivorians.

In the midst of the melee, The General addressed his troops at one of the parliaments: "This week, the mask has fallen and we see who is the godfather of this rebellion. It is France."

Chapter Nine

CLASS ACTION **COCOA**

"Caramels are only a fad. Chocolate is a permanent thing."
— Milton Snavely Hershey

Travelling south from the Malian capital of Bamako, the road towards Côte d'Ivoire inspires a sweet feeling of optimism. Sikasso is a hub of West Africa and the halfway point between Bamako and the border. The bustling town is a sudden explosion of colour and activity, a suggestion that there is more to life than the sad and worn-out farmlands that drape the rural landscape. I can imagine that the boys who arrive here from their dreary villages are filled with a sense of adventure, even as they meet the men who would doom them to months or years of servitude. Leaving Sikasso, the drive farther south towards the frontier fills the senses: dried-up river beds and scrawny cattle give way to mango groves and lush blue-green vegetation in the south. The air smells rich and exotic, full of sensual promises.

Before the war, this route to Côte d'Ivoire teemed with activity. Great transport trucks overflowed with billowy raw cotton from the local harvest, as well as timber, cement and metal, all headed for the great Ivorian ports on the Gulf of Guinea. Buses piled with people and their meagre goods for sale—or their empty baskets, destined to hold a wealth of Ivorian merchandise—rumbled along the narrow highway, heading for the land of milk and honey.

The traffic flow dried up almost completely at the height of the war in Côte d'Ivoire. Malian rebels would allow very few vehicles to cross into the occupied northern area. And the Ivorians allow even fewer to pass over the ceasefire line that divides the country between north and south. Since the spring of 2005, the ceasefire has been holding. Restrictions are looser. Travellers and transporters willing to negotiate a thicket of road-blocks and pay the mandatory bribes can make their way even into southern Côte d'Ivoire. For Malians, whose lifeline is to the south, the possibility of peace between northern rebels and Ivorian authorities is their only source of hope for salvation.

Squatting right on the border to Côte d'Ivoire is the Malian town of Zégoua, a dusty, vulgar little place that enjoyed prosperity before the war and now awaits the return of good times. The Harlem City Hotel, just near the customs station, claims to have a tiki bar and advertises cold beer, palm wine, a jazz club and "all the comforts." These days, the comforts amount to little more than scratchy music from a ghetto blaster, warm fizzy drinks and a few glum-looking prostitutes.

A row of Chinese-made scooters lines the main drag near the customs booth, the drivers offering to carry anything or anybody over the border for a fee. After I watch the activity around the border patrol for a while (there isn't much else to do), it becomes obvious that scooters are able to cross without much hassle, no matter what they might be carrying. For a small additional payment, I'm told, the drivers will smuggle any cargo over the border at less conspicuous crossing points, following the net-work of little paths that crisscross through the backwoods. The Mali–Côte d'Ivoire frontier has always been porous, even at the height of the war and nowhere more so than in the sleepy countryside, where shepherds graze their sheep and extended families sprawl without regard to national distinctions. The rugged little bikes easily navigate the goat paths with their clandestine cargo undetected.

It's this scooter system that the Malian border police suspect has become the favourite mode of transport for the child traffickers. Alzouma Fassoum Coulibaly is a sub-lieutenant with the Gendarmerie Nationale—a hybrid force of police and military—and the chief of the border patrol in this area. He is stationed in the garrison town of Kadiolo, just a short drive from Zégoua. From this small base of operations, and with only a handful of officers, Coulibaly is the thin blue line of authority at the frontier. He's a wiry young man who speaks with a steady staccato delivery and if it is possible for an African cop to be uncorrupted, Coulibaly might be the one.

The chief is frustrated and angry—and for good reason. He has no functioning office equipment, few vehicles and no computer access. How can anyone catch smugglers in these circumstances? In his windowless office of garish green peeling paint, Coulibaly rummages through his desk drawers, looking for photos of children he has intercepted at the border. In his manic search through the mess, he comes across a stick of deodorant and discreetly dabs it just below his shirt sleeves. The police chief hadn't been expecting visitors.

The unmistakable odour of Lifebuoy fills the humid room as Coulibaly tells of his experiences. He had been a highly regarded Customs officer in his hometown of Timbuktu, in northern Mali, where he busted a sophisticated Saudi Arabian smuggling ring. "They were stealing Mali children and transporting them on planes back to Riyadh!" Coulibaly tells me, still shocked at the audacity of the crime. But he thinks the child smuggling at this border crossing is even more refined. And despite reports in Côte d'Ivoire that the problem is all but fixed, Coulibaly says the trafficking continues, albeit on a reduced scale. Coulibaly claims that he and his men still intercept dozens of children a month.

Since Coulibaly arrived here in August 2003, the border patrol has been much more vigilant. The chief figured out that the scooter drivers were transporting children one or two at time, then the smugglers were regrouping on the other side. The single advantage of the war is that he has the cooperation of the rebel Malians, who often allow border police to pursue smugglers right into northern Côte d'Ivoire. In some cases, the rebels actually send back children who are attempting to cross, though Coulibaly worries that the militias may also be keeping children to use as soldiers.

He laments the lack of cooperation with the constitutional government of Côte d'Ivoire, and, despite all the efforts to convince Malians that they should not give up their children in the first place, Coulibaly finds they are still willing to do so. "This year I caught a marabout with thirty-two children." The chief is referring to a kind of monastic Islamic teacher who traditionally takes in African Muslim children, claiming to offer them religious instruction. The marabouts rely on the piety of naive farm families, who willingly turn over their children even though there is much evidence, confirmed by Coulibaly, that many—if not all—of these religious teachers are charlatans. "We know the marabouts are just another scam. But people believe in them." Coulibaly nabbed the children, but the marabout escaped over the frontier.

The border police routinely uncover child trafficking rings, but the Kadiolo station doesn't have the resources to stay abreast of the smugglers and traffickers, who know they only have to move on to an easier part of the border and try again. "If I just had a fax machine, I could send pictures and information to the next post," says Coulibaly. Without any database, it's difficult to catch the crooks.

We take my rental car to tour the backcountry. The chief has a Japanese-made SUV, a gift from the president of Mali as a reward for busting a network of bandits in southern Mali. But the vehicle gets only six kilometres to the litre, and Coulibaly can't afford to drive it, so it sits rusting in the parking lot.

We enter a tangled grid of paths and animal trails that cut through the woods and farm fields, and it's quickly obvious why illegal cross-border transportation is often undetectable. We visit two border police outposts, strategically placed and potentially quite effective. But the farther of the little operations has been closed. The officer at that location would have to stay in the hut for a week at a time, since it was too expensive to go home at the end of the shift (the cost of petrol is prohibitive), and would have to depend on local people to bring him food. Understandably, Coulibaly had a hard time finding men who wanted the tedious assignment nor was the outpost very effective: there isn't enough budget to buy gasoline and allow for a proper patrol. The other outpost was closer to town, and the border guard could come and go at regular hours. But it was easy for the criminals to anticipate his movements. Coulibaly figures that the traffickers would just wait until lunchtime and cross the border while the guard was away for his midday meal.

The chief estimates that eighty per cent of the children who make it over the border never return to Mali. "Or they come back as delinquents and ruffians." The stolen childhood and the lack of a real social life with a family and village, Coulibaly believes, stunts development and turns young men into deviants. Many of the bandits and petty criminals they arrest in southern Mali are those who have returned from brutal years as labourers without pay. "You can see it on their faces," says the chief. "There is no human being inside anymore. That's what ten years of slave labour does to you." They have no papers, and many of them can't remember who their families are. Without kinfolk in Mali, a person is doomed.

~

The transporters union for this region of Mali has its base on the main drag of Zégoua, and, from its sprawling garage depot, drivers have a unique vantage point for monitoring the daily activities of the town. Car rental offices and minibus agencies are nearby, and they watch the boys and young men as they lurk in the corners, waiting for lifts into Côte d'Ivoire. For many years, the truckers thought nothing of it. They had, themselves, gone to Côte d'Ivoire as youngsters looking for work. But the networks of traffickers, delivering kids to farms where they will work for nothing, are relatively new in their experience.

As part of a campaign to educate Malians about the realities of bonded servitude, Save the Children Canada conducted a five-day instruction course for the truckers, paid them for the time and handed out certificates afterwards.

"We were very happy with the program," Balla Keita tells me. He's president of the transporters union here, and he calls a number of the men into the garage to explain what they learned on their course. "The instructors told us about the development of a child. How they trust adults when they are young but then turn to their friends when they are a bit older." The transporters were fascinated with this rudimentary education in child development. They realized for the first time that what they thought to be ordinary activity was, perhaps, abusive. Children seemed to go with the traffickers voluntarily, so the drivers thought nothing of it. "We didn't think it was a problem," Keita explains. "We thought the men [traffickers] were just doing their jobs. If we stopped one, he might try to sue us."

Save the Children Canada told the transporters they should challenge the traffickers—who would probably abandon the children as soon as they saw trouble—and then bring the children to Horon So, where they would be cared for and returned to their families. The transporters took up the task enthusiastically. A trucker tells me that the previous week he personally took four boys into custody. They were on foot, accompanied by a man who didn't seem to know them. Emboldened by what he had learned in his five-day course, the driver was suspicious and approached the stranger to ask what he was doing. The man was vague and excused himself on the pretence that he was going to get some cigarettes. He never came back. "I took the four children to Sikasso [a two-hour drive]," the driver explains. "I called Save the Children to come and get the children, but no one came."

The driver learned that Save the Children's Horon So operation had been shut down only weeks after they had finished their five-day course and there was no one from the agency working in the region, despite what they had said during the training program. The driver had used his own petrol to bring the boys to Sikasso. He had very little food—just his own meagre lunch—and he had no money to buy groceries. He lost a day's pay before someone finally told him that the local agency Mali Enjeu had accommodations for recovered children. He was thankful to leave his charges there, but it had been an unwelcome ordeal and he tells me he will not do it again. As they listen to their colleague's story, the other truckers finger the corners of their certificates and agree with him, grumbling that they'll hesitate before getting involved with smugglers.

Chief Coulibaly says he had the same experience. Aid agencies such as Save the Children Canada alerted him to the child-trafficking problem when he arrived here. But many of these foreign NGOs seem to have gone on to other things. He worries about who will take care of kids he might find in the future. He personally housed a group of intercepted children recently until their parents could be found. But he had to pay for their upkeep out of his own pocket. If child trafficking picks up after the war, as he suspects it will, Coulibaly isn't sure how he'll handle the volume.

Save the Children Canada says the program at Horon So was just too expensive to maintain for the number of children who needed the facility. The war years had made it more difficult and perilous for the traffickers to deliver their human cargo to the cocoa farms of Côte d'Ivoire. With the immediate crisis settled, Save the Children thought it best that local NGOs take over the task. "At the end of the day, it's a domestic issue," Save the Children's Nadine Grant says of the responsibility for taking care of the recovered children.

Coulibaly says that's all very well but he's anticipating a surge in trafficking when—or if—the war should end in Côte d'Ivoire. The country will not only be back to business but also be seeking cheap labour in order to rebuild. The chief expects the job-brokers will be even more aggressive than before and he's worried about something else. "There are a lot more weapons in the region than ever before," he says. Northern Côte d'Ivoire is now awash with small arms that will undoubtedly be available to smugglers and crime rings. "I would not encourage the truckers to stop them in the future," says Coulibaly.

Save the Children Canada is still training the transporters but now has a somewhat different program in place. A half dozen bus stations in both southern Mali and neighbouring Burkina Faso now have transporters acting as monitors who look for children in flight. The monitors register the names of any unaccompanied young people who are in transit and they also call security when they suspect a child trafficker is pursuing any of the kids. The project is sponsored by the Canadian International Development Agency but it's destined to last only until 2007. Save the Children Canada acknowledges that, should the Ivorian war come to a conclusion, the trafficking business will ignite like a brush fire. And children will be more vulnerable than ever.

~

In Sikasso, the Malian aid agency Guamina conducts a training program for teenagers from the region in an effort to discourage them from leaving the country. Since the border into Côte d'Ivoire has become easier to cross, Guamina is anxious to coach young people about the evils of the cocoa farms. Guamina has inherited the indoctrination program launched by Save the Children Canada.

Working on a little wooden stage at Guamina's community centre, teenaged boys and girls role-play various scenarios, using stories and anecdotes picked up from boys who have returned from the horrors of bonded labour. The young performers take different parts in what amounts to agitprop. Some of them play-act as traffickers who lure children with promises of wealth. Others take the roles of Ivorian farmers who beat children. Finally, we meet the heroes, representatives from Malian associations who will help them get back home. These are transparent little dramas with unambiguous messages about the evils of working in Côte d'Ivoire.

When the audience is asked for input, some of the young spectators want to see a version with a different ending, where a boy actually becomes gainfully employed. The Guamina leader steps in at this point to tell them it is not allowed. He whispers to me that they worry parents will want to send the kids, or even sell them, if they suspect there is the slightest possibility that it might yield riches. The young people sitting in the audience also whisper—they've all heard of someone who went to Côte d'Ivoire and came back with a bicycle.

The propaganda fails to dent the faint hope of the desperate.

The willingness of the children to go to Côte d'Ivoire is often cited as evidence that the children are not slaves. But "volunteering" on the remote chance that one can make a little bit of money to relieve the gnawing inevitability of a hungry belly hardly seems like a reasonable choice.

~

In Washington, months before the deadline for the elimination of the worst forms of child labour in the cocoa chain, Representative Engel and Senator Harkin felt they needed to raise a flag. On February 14, 2005, the two congressmen published an op-ed article in U.S. newspapers condemning the chocolate companies for a perceived cop-out. Billed as a valentine to Big Chocolate, the article revealed that cocoa industry officials had informed the congressmen that they were not going to meet the July 1 deadline. "Instead," the legislators wrote, "they planned to initiate a small pilot project in Ghana and, perhaps, in Ivory Coast. Although this is certainly a positive step, it falls woefully short of the robust action promised in the protocol."

The politicians wrote about the Washington certification program for precious gems, imposed on the industry a few years earlier, outlawing the sale in the United States of "blood diamonds"—African stones mined and marketed to raise funds for civil war. Harkin and Engel warned that similar coercion might be necessary for cocoa and declared, "The time for talk has passed. Children are suffering." They concluded, "This Valentine's Day, much of our chocolate will be bittersweet—tainted by the suffering of Aly Diabate and countless other cocoa slaves."

After the article was published, Eliot Engel told me over the phone that he and Harkin were willing to give the chocolate companies some wiggle room so they can get their act together, but "we're not going to cave," he warned. "They know we mean business."

The International Cocoa Initiative—the alphabet soup of NGOs, labour unions, rights activists and cocoa company umbrella organizations—admitted there hadn't been much progress. But some participants, particularly the International Labour Organization (ILO), were encouraged by the "feeling of momentum" and the fact that the chocolate companies themselves still seemed committed to the notion of "clean" chocolate. The government of Côte d'Ivoire was helpfully reminding the reformers that its country was in the middle of a war and could hardly be expected to deal with child labour while it was fighting "terrorists," the fashionable post 9–11 term the government had adopted to describe the northern rebels.

Could the low-key reaction have anything to do with money? A number of NGOs had developed partnerships with Big Chocolate since the protocol was signed. When asked about its efforts to improve conditions for farmers in West Africa, the World Cocoa Federation (WCF) says it was involved in "multi-million-dollar" projects in concert with the ILO, the World Bank, the U.S. Department of Labour and the Canadian International Development Agency. Bill Guyton of the WCF says Big Chocolate is collectively volunteering US$6 million this year, of its estimated $13 billion of profits, in "partnerships" to aid agencies. Anita Sheth, a thorn in the side of Big Chocolate, says that the WCF offered Save the Children Canada one of its partnerships—an offer the aid agency rejected, in part, because the amount of money to be provided was so appallingly small. But others have signed on.

Meanwhile, Ivorian cocoa beans flowed, uninterrupted, into the factories of Europe and North America. Canada, a leading advocate against using cocoa that might be the product of child labour, had actually doubled its cocoa imports from Côte d'Ivoire since the outbreak of the war.

~

In the spring of 2005, the war between the north and the south of Côte d'Ivoire was locked in a holding pattern that was more inconvenient than violent. Neither side had anything more to gain from fighting but the stand-off made movement from one part of the country to the other more difficult. The cocoa war in the southwest of the country, from which Kader Ouattara had fled, had not abated in the slightest. All around the villages near the border with Liberia, farm workers huddled in poorly pro-tected international displaced persons camps, unable to return to Mali and Burkina Faso. Well-armed militias and paramilitaries roamed the countryside, terrorizing people. Ange Aboa, from

Reuters News Agency, dashed off into the countryside to investigate each bloody massacre. Ange and his driver, Koffi Benoît, would not let me travel with them to many of the locations — they said it was suicidal for white foreigners to visit unless they were accompanied by the heavily armed peacekeepers. But the peacekeepers rarely intervened in the fighting, even to protect the civilian farmers and their families.

For Ivorians, the descent into war was shocking — the country had thought itself immune from the violence into which neighbours Liberia and Sierra Leone had sunk. For the outside world, the story of yet another bloodbath in an African country was a familiar drama. Foreign news agencies might not have bothered with the story at all if Côte d'Ivoire wasn't the source of such an important commodity — the world's chocolate.

Remarkably, cocoa beans continued to arrive at the main Ivorian port. The manifest for the Port Authority of San-Pédro, the cocoa- and coffee-shipping facility for Côte d'Ivoire, actually indicates a substantial spike in cocoa exports between 2002 and 2004, years of extreme violence in the cocoa belt. The first trimester of 2005 records the first dip in cocoa exports, possibly a result of the fighting, but the decrease is not as large as the gains the exports experienced during the two preceding years.

Noël Kabora is thankful that he still has work. He's the *pisteur* who introduced me to the boys in the village of Sinikosson — the ones who didn't know what people did with the cocoa beans they harvested. Kabora is a Burkinabè who doesn't want to return to Burkina Faso. Back home, there's nothing for Kabora. The war-ravaged cocoa belt of Côte d'Ivoire is a menacing place, but at least the cocoa business is still functioning. Kabora lives in Soubré, a depressing knot of shantytowns built of wood scraps, known to burn down from time to time, culling the city's population. But Soubré is a district centre for numerous cocoa traders and buyers who supply the large transnationals, and he can usually stay busy here.

Kabora agrees to take me and Ange deep into the backcountry, as close to the western war zone as possible in order to meet some farmers. When we attempt to leave Soubré, Ivorian checkpoint police detain us for hours and then demand money. The bribes we pay are perhaps inflated because I am a white foreigner, but Africans are all facing the same extortion. The *pisteurs* pay huge fees along every highway. A certain amount of baksheesh is considered normal in African enterprise, but the amount of bribery on the cocoa routes gobbles up much of the profits earned by *pisteurs* like Kabora. Cocoa middlemen, mostly Lebanese agents who work for the big cocoa companies, give the *pisteurs* sums of money to pay the farmers and to cover the bribes. By the time the *pisteurs* get to their suppliers, however, a lot of their funds have been depleted. The Arab traders I talked to speculate that one reason cocoa exports dipped in 2005 was that the highway robbery by the gendarmes had wiped out any potential profits for the *pisteurs*—consequently, a lot of them are leaving the business.

Africa is renowned for corrupt police officers, but Ivorian cocoa country sets a whole new standard for Third-World graft. The gendarmes we meet along the road poke Kalashnikov rifles through the windows of trucks and cars and demand money at gunpoint. Many of them are high on palm wine, and no one offers resistance. The few locals who have dared to challenge their authority have simply disappeared. We pass five such checkpoints in the course of ten kilometres, each one more threatening—and expensive—than the one before.

Kabora takes us to the farm of Siguino Boueima Zongo, a planter in his fifties with thirty hectares of cocoa trees, along with four wives and fifteen children to support. Zongo also has boys and young men working for him whom he recruits from his village in Burkina Faso. "When I visit home," he explains, "I let people know I am looking for workers." Boys, or their parents, volunteer. I count eleven hired hands here, ranging in age from fourteen to nineteen, and they seem as well fed as Zongo's own family, which isn't saying much.

The boys all tell me they expect to be paid for their work on Zongo's farm, but none has ever seen any money. Zongo explains, at length, how the money he earns from cocoa comes nowhere near the expense of cultivating it. I suspect this is an indirect way of saying the boys will probably not be renumerated at the end of the two years for which they have been engaged.

Zongo's enterprise was once highly lucrative, and he is respected by *pisteurs* such as Noël Kabora for the high quality of his goods. Yet even with hard work and a solid reputation, making a living in cocoa is impossible. It's not hard to see from Zongo's farm how easy it is for a producer to slip into the practice of exploiting unpaid child labour.

No one here attends school, including Zongo's own children; he says this is because there is no school to go to. The area is populated largely with *allogènes*, and the Ivorian government provides no services. Even if the schools existed, Zongo's people speak principally Bambara and don't know the official language of Côte d'Ivoire—French.

Zongo pays a flat fee for health care for his family, but Kabora tells me later that Zongo likely has no health care program for his workers.

The workers are shy. The youngest one, a slightly built, sad-looking adolescent of fourteen, tells me he is "proud to do the work of men." Zongo rarely lets them answer questions for themselves. When reporters such as Blewett and Woods first explored the labour issue in this area, farmers spoke openly about their employment practices. But everyone here now knows about the political discussions in Washington and about a possible boycott of cocoa from Côte d'Ivoire. Zongo has heard about it on the radio, and he knows there is a controversy. He says the boys are treated well and volunteers—unprompted—that there is "no slave labour here."

According to Zongo, far more menacing to the boys' welfare than anything he might ask them to do is the proximity of the drunken soldiers, who make frequent and terrifying raids. Zongo says he doesn't know how much longer he can keep his business going. When I ask him about ownership of the land, he says emphatically that the thirty hectares belong to him, though he admits he has no papers. "But everyone knows it's my land," he insists, hardly able to convince even himself.

Noël Kabora drives us even deeper into the hinterland. The road is almost non-existent, and there are potholes large enough to consume small cars. Several times I tell Kabora that the route is too washed out—we should turn back. He laughs. This is a road he takes twice a week to pick up beans, and it is never any better. The big lorry rumbles over a few planks laid down over a racing river. It's remarkable that the country's main commodity and economic staple depends on roads like this. They are one-way streets for resource wealth. The value that rolls into the ports of San-Pédro and Abidjan never bounces back in the form of profit for producers or, it seems, infrastructure for the vital trade. Desperation is the incentive to produce. Government and corporate indifference leaves primary producers virtually orphaned in the system.

Every kilometre or so there is a stack of bulging bags on the side of the road—cocoa beans ready for pickup—and the unmistakable sour odour of beans still fermenting on the racks, which will be dried and ready for transport in another week. Along the way we see dozens of children who seem to fit Anita Sheth's description of people working in "hazardous conditions." Girls carry heavy loads stacked high on their heads, while boys drag machetes as long as their arms behind them. They are stern little people who stare hard at me at first. But a smile and wave is rewarded with trusting grins.

Some of the older boys carry apparatus on their backs for spraying toxic herbicides and fungicides. They wear no protective clothing. Their feet are bare. When I stop to ask their mothers about the perils of such exposure, the women laugh and tell us the price of a protective face covering would equal the bribes they pay to get their goods to market. They can't afford to pay for both. The ironic truth is that the danger of the work is reduced by economic circumstances: Many farmers can no longer afford to buy the chemicals they need to keep their trees alive and so spraying has actually decreased.

Long after it seems there could be no more farms, Kabora edges his truck farther into the woods until we arrive at the most remote of his pickup points, a little Burkinabé commune where, Kabora tells me, there are many boys who work all day in the groves and then attend Koran school in the evenings. He looks at me warily as he tells me this as he seems to find this working arrangement bothersome. The farm sounds suspiciously like a compound for a marabout, one of the Islamic gurus who use religious faith to conceal the exploitation of young workers.

The owner is just returning from prayers. Even in this remote community, Mohamad has heard about the uproar over child labour, and he is cautious with his answers. Only the older boys work, he tells me, though I can hardly believe that the younger ones I see around me are permitted to sit idle all day. Noël Kabora begins to display anxiety when I persist in my questions about working conditions here. The farmer is indulgent. He shows me the firepit around which he conducts Koran sessions in the evening. Our conversation eventually shifts to less contentious territory—the price of beans, the cost of supplies, the inability to make ends meet. His answers echo the responses I have had from farmers everywhere: The current farm gate price for beans cannot pay even the costs of cultivation, let alone feed a family.

The sun is melting into the forest as we depart this desolate, forbidding place, conscious of the perils lurking in the darkening bush when night falls and the palm wine starts kicking in at the many checkpoints of the extortionate gendarmerie.

When we return to Soubré that evening, Kabora takes me to a warehouse where all the *pisteurs* in this region deliver their beans to be weighed on large scales and stored for pickup by the middlemen. Everyone at the facility knows about the child labour controversy in Washington, and they are reluctant to disclose what they have seen on the farms.

Alassane Traoré wants me to realize that cocoa farm work is always hazardous. He rolls up his pant leg to show me his machete scars—they all have them—and he insists that such injuries are part of the passage from boyhood to manhood. But Traoré also admits that he sees a lot of abuse on the farms these days.

Ali Sagnou, another *pisteur*, says they are all uncomfortable with the word "slavery," or in French, "*esclavage.*" It carries the weight of five hundred years of history, the burden of broken societies and their greatest grief. As the term "holocaust" is for Jews, "slavery" is a word reserved for the darkest period of Africa's collective memory. "*Pas d'esclavage,*" no slavery, says Sagnou, "but abuse, yes." What does he mean by abuse? "People don't pay the kids that they hire," he explains. As for hazardous conditions, he says everyone—hired hands and even the proprietors—take risks. It comes with the territory.

Kabora and the other *pisteurs* are crucial to the cocoa chain of Côte d'Ivoire as none of the cocoa producers have their own vehicles to transfer goods to market. Kabora is their lifeline. The *pisteurs* have regular contact with the network of 600,000 farms in Côte d'Ivoire and might be the only members of the cocoa chain who have a true overview of farm conditions throughout cocoa country. Abdoulaye Macko depended extensively on *pisteurs* when he was looking for trafficked children.

These drivers and warehouse managers could become a crucial link in the chain of enforcement should serious controls ever come into force to limit the exploitation. Activists in Washington and Geneva see them as a potential network of monitors—a front-line force to observe and report on compliance with new rules to protect child workers. Outside inspectors would be spotted quickly and, even if it were possible to create a network of cocoa cops, they would have to depend on the *pisteurs* to get them to the remote farms where the abuses are occurring.

Ali Sagnou says he would do it. He doesn't like the way children are treated. But Noël Kabora shakes his head. "You see where I go to buy the cocoa? I am alone in the bush. If I report people, they will lose their livelihoods. And they would kill me." I get his point. No one would even find the body.

But the *pisteurs* are far more worried about war than child labourers. They can hardly afford to pay the bribes to the gendarmes, whose lucrative roadblocks are becoming ever more common. And they face another threat. The authorities accuse the *pisteurs*, most of whom are immigrants, of being gunrunners for the rebels. This is a common, and vague, accusation I've heard from the authorities throughout the cocoa belt. If Noël Kabora or the others disappeared, it would more likely be at the hands of the soldiers than those of the cocoa farmers.

~

Shortly before the July 2005 deadline for the Harkin-Engel protocol, the cocoa companies, in concert with the government of Côte d'Ivoire, announced a small pilot project in a region called Oumé, near Yamoussoukro, and another in Ghana, which were to serve as experiments for how a child labour monitoring system might work. Ghana had no identifiable issue with abusive child labour on cocoa farms and Oumé, in Côte d'Ivoire, was never cited as a problem area. As the congressmen had hinted in their Valentine's Day address, Big Cocoa was offering up these small pursuits as tokens of their good intentions but little more.

I first got wind of the Oumé project in June 2005, when I attended a symposium in Abidjan for the stakeholders responsible for putting the project together. The purpose of the event was to explain to members of the cocoa *filière* or hierarchy, how Côte d'Ivoire proposed to avert any consequences of the July 1 deadline. Delegates—who were all Ivorians and members of the *filière*—told me privately that they thought the Harkin-Engel Protocol was a crock but they had long ago "learned how to play the game" the way the West wants it played. An official declaration of intent, distributed to members of the media at the end of the two-day get-together, was no less blunt than the informal message people had given me. "Faced with the threats and accusations [from the United States] that weigh heavily on our very existence," says the communiqué, the delegates to the symposium decided it was necessary to "comply with international laws against the worst forms of child labour." No mention here of protecting children because it might be the right thing to do. Instead, "We cocoa producers have to show that we are aware of this threat to our livelihood."

The Oumé project was the answer to the American critics, and it seemed everyone at the event was certain it was going to be sufficient to satisfy the congressmen in Washington. The program would cost 17 million euros for an initial duration of fifteen months, but no one at the meeting could explain who was going to pay for it or what would happen when the trial period was over.

I had recently met Malian cocoa farmers from Oumé who told me they had no trouble with either the war or the child smugglers in their region. It's an old community, and the Dioula are highly organized, with a strong association on the lookout for any badly treated workers. It's not clear why Côte d'Ivoire chose Oumé for the pilot project. Perhaps it's because it's close to the Yamoussoukro airport, an easily accessible showcase for those who might want to inspect conditions and return to the city in time for dinner in one of the many fine French restaurants in the capital.

Given the stern warning of the congressmen in their article of February 14, it didn't seem possible that these dubious little undertakings would be enough to satisfy Washington. But indeed, July 1, 2005, the much-heralded deadline for the Harkin-Engel Protocol, came and went without much ado. All those who had endorsed it mouthed platitudes about how much progress had been made, and vowed they would all "continue to dialogue." But essentially, it was a dead letter.

The congressmen had some regrets. "I am disappointed that the July 1 deadline established in the protocol was not fully met," declared Senator Harkin in a prepared statement. "But I am pleased that they [the chocolate companies] have committed to redouble their efforts to create a certification system and eliminate the worst forms of child labor and forced labor in the cocoa fields and throughout the supply chain. The farmers and children in the cocoa-growing countries deserve no less."

The "redoubled effort," seems to be a commitment on the part of the chocolate companies to meet a new deadline in 2008, three years past the original date when they promise that fifty per cent of cocoa farms will somehow be inspected for their child labour practices (the original plan was for 100 per cent). In the meantime, the cocoa companies will pursue a more achievable objective that includes "monitoring, data analysis, reporting and activities to address the worst forms of child labor as aggressively as possible."

Eliot Engel insisted again that the congressmen have not caved in. "I am assured that progress will be made and deadlines will be met," he said in his own press release. Presumably, the representative from congressional district seventeen will still be around to ensure the deadlines are met in 2008.

Privately, Pete Leon says the congressmen were extremely miffed. "It was very late in the process when the cocoa companies told us they wouldn't meet the deadline," says Leon, the legislative director for Eliot Engel's office. Leon remembers a final marathon meeting with representatives from Big Chocolate that lasted four and a half hours, but in the end, the congressmen know they'd been beat. The buzz on Capitol Hill was that the industry was mobilizing a sizable lobbying effort, preparing sympathetic politicians to take the industry's side if Harkin and Engel decided to do battle. The Democratic congressmen were no match for such a marshalling of forces. And with the Republicans in control of the Senate, there was no chance of going back to the original plan—the labelling system. Pete Leon says they realized they would be able to do nothing if the industry wasn't on side. "Do we stop working altogether and just go to war?" says Leon. "Or do we sit down and say 'let's work this out?'"

John Cadbury would have admired the modern chocolate barons who had managed to stonewall effective action for another three years. That will make it seven years altogether since Eliot Engel first read and reacted to the Knight Ridder articles, and a decade since UNICEF first flagged its concerns about the use of children in the industry. If the industry planners play their cards with skill, the impoverished cocoa groves of Africa will no longer matter by the time of the next reckoning. New cocoa producers are springing up around the world—Indonesia is now the third largest supplier of beans after Côte d'Ivoire and Ghana—and the industry could soon leave Côte d'Ivoire in the dust.

Anita Sheth was deeply disappointed by the cocoa company capitulation. "Imagine all the work we put into this to try to make something come of it. And here's what came out of it. We had an agreement and it fell on its face." But the NGOs and activists who had endorsed the deal were mollified by what seemed to be the chastened attitude and good intentions of the chocolate companies. Kevin Bales of Free the Slaves, the most gung-ho of all the activists, who had actually been a signatory of the protocol, issued a press release declaring in bold, "We failed," though he still goes on to defend the protocol as a historic first where "consumer groups, industry and government joined forces."

Bama Athreya argues there was no history made with the protocol, just more of the same old malarkey. The International

Labor Rights Fund had been the only US NGO to reject the industry partnership approach. "This whole process should be turned in to a business school case study for how to stage a public relations coup," says Athreya. "Get everyone onside with your message, come up with a big plan, make sure you have lots and lots of time for the issue to get lost, get some credible outside players like Free the Slaves in your corner and bingo! You've got yourself clear of a jam." But ILRF was determined the chocolate companies were not going to escape responsibility so easily. And it prepared to bring out the heavy guns.

~

Marx-Vilaire Aristide, the researcher for the International Labor Rights Fund (ILRF) in Washington, had made tremendous progress in ferreting out the truth about child labour in Côte d'Ivoire. Since his first visit to the region in the spring of 2002, he had been back several more times and had made key contacts with a number of informers who passed him crucial information. Aristide and the ILRF were building their case against the industry when they suffered a serious setback. In November 2004, on a freeway northwest of Washington, Aristide was killed when another driver in a stolen SUV slammed into his vehicle.

The workers at the ILRF lost a dedicated colleague and friend, but Aristide's death also meant they were cut off from his close contacts and inside knowledge of the child labour issue. It took months to recover, which they did mostly through intrepid sleuthing by another ILRF researcher, Natacha Thys, who had been with Aristide on his last trip and was able to recover many of his leads in West Africa. She conducted her own investigations over the following winter and spring and found what she was looking for: plaintiffs. People willing to sue the parties they considered to be ultimately responsible for the abuses in the cocoa business.

On July 14, 2005, the ILRF filed suit against Nestlé, Cargill and Archer Daniels Midland in a federal district court in California, charging the three U.S.–based companies with involvement in the trafficking, torture and forced labour of children who cultivate and harvest cocoa beans that the company imports from Africa. The class action claim was filed on behalf of Malian children who were trafficked into Côte d'Ivoire "and forced to work twelve to fourteen hours a day with no pay, little food or sleep and frequent beatings." Three individual plaintiffs were identified only as John Doe I, John Doe II and John Doe III. The ILRF argued in its brief that the children had to remain anonymous for their own security.

The timing of the suit was no coincidence, and the ILRF's media releases stated clearly that they were pursuing legal action on this scale because the industry had failed to meet its July 1 deadline. "A key part of the [Harkin-Engel] protocol was an obligation for companies to have in place an independent and credible system of farm monitoring, certification and verification for their suppliers, to ensure no child labour was taking place," says the ILRF statement.

Legal advocacy is new territory for aggressive activists in the United States, who use powerful tools such as the U.S. Alien Tort Claims Act (ATCA) to pursue multinational corporations. The act allows non-citizens of the United States to use federal courts to hold Americans accountable for violations of international law. There are few downtrodden labourers — especially children — who could possibly drag a transnational before a court on their own, but the ILRF frequently takes up their causes.

The organization has filed suits against Exxon Mobil, DynCorp and Coca-Cola, all under the Alien Tort Claims Act. In 2004, it sued DaimlerChrysler on behalf of the families of nine unionists at a Mercedes-Benz factory near Buenos Aires who had "disappeared" during the Argentine military dictatorship. It sued on behalf of five former Guatemalan trade union leaders who held the Del Monte food giant liable for violations of fundamental human rights.

Of course, leading U.S. business interests have filed their own petitions, asking the U.S. Supreme Court to nullify the Alien Tort Claims Act. They argue that it puts U.S. companies at an unfair competitive disadvantage, since companies in other countries don't face these kinds of suits. Considering the fact that the Act pertains only to slavery, torture, extrajudicial killings, war crimes, crimes against humanity and arbitrary detention, it's alarming that U.S. companies believe the law gets in the way of their ability to compete in the global market place.

The "Class Action Complaint for Injunctive Relief and Damages" filed against the cocoa companies on behalf of "Former Child Slave Plaintiffs" is asserting claims not only under the Alien Tort statute but also under the Torture Victim Protection Act. Among the many charges, the suit alleges that the actions of Nestlé, Cargill and Archer Daniels Midland "forced the Former Child Slave Plaintiffs against their will and under fear of harm to labour for Defendants' economic benefit and in doing so the Former Child Slave Plaintiffs were placed in great fear for their lives." The suit says the children were between the ages of twelve and fourteen when they were taken from their homes; though the brief doesn't specify, the three John Does are probably over eighteen by now.

As the class action suit was making its slow passage through the U.S. court system in 2005–2006, the status quo remained unchanged. Côte d'Ivoire still held its place as the leading producer of cocoa in the world, as Le Vieux promised it would, uninterrupted by scandal, war, Washington protocols or legal actions. But the Ivorian cocoa business was suffering its own disease, perhaps as devastating as the scourge of witch's broom that afflicts the cocoa tree. Cocoa, in Côte d'Ivoire, was becoming infested with the scourge of organized crime.

Chapter Ten

THE MAN WHO **KNEW TOO MUCH**

"Here [in Côte d'Ivoire] you can talk about politics with violent words, but the one thing that makes people mad is money. If you track money you risk the death penalty . . . Cocoa is a dark, confused world. You don't know where the money goes. And into it came Guy-André, obsessed about telling the truth."

—JACQUES HUILLERY, *Agence France-Presse, Abidjan, June 2004*

THE MEETING WAS FOR 1:30 P.M. IN THE PARKING LOT of the Prima Centre, a swank shopping mall in the upscale Marcory district of Abidjan. It was a Friday afternoon, April 16, 2004, and Guy-André Kieffer was early. He stood beside his old Hyundai Electra with its maple leaf sticker on the trunk, one of his little reminders to people that while he is French he is also Canadian, and he chain-smoked while waiting for his contact. Kieffer's two cellphones were turned on, as always. He was in constant contact with his Network: journalists, financiers, diplomats, businessmen both African and European and, most of all, the highest functionaries and money men of Côte d'Ivoire's foremost export product, cocoa.

Guy-André Kieffer, GAK, as his friends called him, knew more about the dark side of the *filière*, as the hierarchy of the cocoa trade was known, than almost anyone else alive. As a journalist, he had started investigating tropical commodities, especially cocoa, for newspapers in France even before moving to Côte d'Ivoire two and a half years earlier. In Abidjan, he eventually got a job freelancing for the Paris-based periodical *La Lettre du Continent* while contributing, sometimes anonymously, to a number of local publications.

For several weeks prior to the Prima Centre meeting, GAK's friends had noticed a change in him: he was much more agitated. He'd always been frenetic and fidgety, and he rarely stopped moving. But a colleague remarked that lately his mannerisms had become more pronounced, as if driven by a new sense of anxiety. He'd been a bundle of nerves at dinner recently, scrutinizing everyone in the restaurant suspiciously, where he would normally greet almost every diner by first name.

Kieffer told his associate over their meal that events had taken a bad turn in Côte d'Ivoire and it was now extremely unsafe for journalists, especially white ones. This was an alarming pronouncement from a reporter who seemed to be utterly fearless. Most of Kieffer's colleagues stood back in awe as he tore into government officials in public places, took on the president, and bravely published information about the cocoa *filière* and its "Mafioso" dealings. Kieffer had been charging around like a bull in an Ivorian china shop since he arrived in Abidjan. If someone like GAK was worried, things had really turned ugly.

Political conditions in the country had deteriorated rapidly after January 2004 and went into a free fall in March of that year, when a peaceful demonstration against the Gbagbo government turned into a killing spree. A coalition of opposition parties and northerners had defied the ban against public protests and marched in the streets of Abidjan. Ivorian police went on the attack, dragging people out of their homes and executing them, including some who hadn't played any role in the antigovernment demonstrations. A UN report later characterized the event as a "massacre in which summary executions, torture, disappearances, and arbitrary detention were repeatedly committed by units of the security forces and the parallel forces acting in coordination or in collusion with them."

Death squads targeted the Burkinabè and Malian immigrants who had been living in shantytowns around Abidjan since they'd been evicted from their farms, and murdered unknown numbers of them. Official records say dozens of people died; the opposition says the real number was in the hundreds. No one knows with certainty what happened during those dark days. It was suicidal for white journalists from abroad to even think about trying to cover the massacres in Abidjan. As for local reporters, at best they were attacked and harassed, at worst they were raped and beaten, or they simply disappeared. Only government-controlled media outlets could broadcast or publish. Opposition newspaper offices were torched.

What alarmed Kieffer most was that the four thousand well-armed French soldiers and three thousand African soldiers who formed the peacekeeping force in Côte d'Ivoire did so little to stop the killing. Many civilians had joined in the illegal demonstrations believing that the foreign military personnel would guarantee their safety. They didn't, and GAK told his friends at the time that if the international community failed to condemn Gbagbo for unleashing this terror, then the president would regard it as an endorsement of his power and evidence that the world would not intervene in his excesses. Memories of Rwanda haunted all the reporters who had seen the same international indifference to the killing machines of the Hutu *génocidaires* in 1994. Kieffer worried that, without a strong message from France, in particular, it would become open season on reporters in Côte d'Ivoire.

But there was little international reaction as the death squads carried on the slaughter for days. All the major news agencies withdrew their reporters—the eyes and ears of the outside world. The UN High Commission for Human Rights investigated but refused to release its report, fearing it might add fuel to the flames. When a leaked copy made its way to Radio France Internationale, it confirmed the worst fears of the foreign media.

The commission documented "the indiscriminate killing of innocent civilians, and . . . massive human rights violations." The report specified that "the march became a pretext for what turned out to be a carefully planned and executed operation by the security forces."

Other developments disturbed Kieffer as well, most notably the actions of the Young Patriots of Charles Blé Goudé and the other less visible youth militias that operated underground. The fascistic "parliaments" convened by The General attracted thousands of young angry Ivorians who were now indoctrinated with the idea that the French were responsible for all of their problems. Kieffer had a fairly good idea, from his own sleuthing, that the youth militias were well supplied with arms. The likelihood of a violent insurrection, secretly guided by Gbagbo himself, seemed inevitable in the charged Ivorian atmosphere.

As Kieffer stood in the Prima Centre parking lot on an April afternoon less than a month after those events, he had a lot to be worried about. He had just published an explosive story, claiming that Côte d'Ivoire had illegally transferred money to the dictatorial regime of Guinea-Bissau, a small troubled state next to Sénégal, and an important ally of Gbagbo. Despite the economic woes of Côte d'Ivoire, the government seemed to have enough excess cash to bankroll the salaries of civil servants and military personnel in another country. The information in Kieffer's report was extremely damaging because it strongly suggested that the Gbagbo government was diverting cocoa profits to support a dubious political agenda abroad as well as at home.

In addition to the Guinea-Bissau affair, Kieffer was investigating a high-level money-laundering scheme run out of Paris and illegal financial transactions allegedly involving the National Investment Bank of Côte d'Ivoire, a principal financial agency of the state and of the cocoa *filière*. Kieffer had been relentless in exposing corruption under the Gbagbo regime, most of it involving the cocoa industry, in *La Lettre du Continent* and other publications. He filed numerous reports making allegations about arms purchases financed from cocoa profits; shady weapons deals cooked up with Israeli and Ukrainian gun merchants; and suspicious arrangements with foreign companies to dredge sand from the cocoa-exporting port of San-Pédro.

Kieffer had received three death threats in recent weeks, more than the kind of intimidation a muckraking reporter learns to live with. What's more, these threats were coming from some of the highest offices in the land. Kieffer told friends he was confident that there were enough decent people left in powerful positions, but most suspected he was kidding himself. There was no one watching his back, especially not in the violently anti-French environment of Côte d'Ivoire. And once GAK sniffed out evidence of injustice, he became impossible to restrain.

GAK had become one of the country's leading experts in primary commodities, and he specialized in the cocoa and coffee trade. He learned the basics working as a business reporter, providing information useful to investors and traders. But his curiosity had led him deeper and deeper into the shadows of the cocoa industry and into a dark underworld occupied by the clique whose members dominate the *filière*. He took up the cause of the cocoa farmers the day he arrived in Côte d'Ivoire, and he was determined to expose their oppressors—in his mind, the regime of Laurent Gbagbo with its ties to the big multinational cocoa companies. To that end he unearthed a lot of information, perhaps too much for his own good.

Kieffer was at the Prima Centre to meet Michel Legré, a man he disliked though still called his friend. During these sinister days in Côte d'Ivoire, the word "friend" had multiple meanings, especially when your "friend" was married to the younger sister of Simone Gbagbo, wife of the president and one of the fiercest ultra-nationalists in the country. Michel Legré was the type of friend who could indeed protect Kieffer. But in the wrong circumstances, he could also help to destroy him.

Friends of all kinds were important to Kieffer. The whorl of people he contacted regularly were the sources of the energy that drove his life. And yet few could claim to know him well, or understand what motivated him. He ate too much, he smoked heavily, he thrived on stress, he obsessed over details. As he forced his way into the inner sanctums of Côte d'Ivoire's cocoa world; as he pursued the cocoa bosses and exposed their corruption; as he disseminated damning information about the most dangerous people in the country, all of his "friends" began to wonder if he had a private death wish.

Legré finally showed up, but he wasn't alone. The eight uniformed men accompanying him materialized as though from nowhere. They grabbed Kieffer, forced him into one of two four-by-four vehicles with no licence plates and fishtailed out of the parking lot at top speed. Kieffer's two mobile telephones—his lifeline—suddenly went dead. He was marooned, isolated from the protective circle of collaborators, colleagues, spies, informers, former wives, lovers, journalists and cocoa bosses who made up his complex and treacherous universe.

GAK disappeared into the haze of the hot subtropical afternoon. His phlegmy, cigarette-singed voice would never be heard again; his round fleshy face would never be seen again. The bear of a man who never stopped moving and never stopped asking questions would never exasperate his friends again. The last, best champion of the cocoa farmers of Côte d'Ivoire vanished without a trace, as completely and unexplainably absent as if he'd never been there.

~

Baudelaire Mieu was surprised when he didn't hear from GAK on Friday, and when Saturday morning rolled around without a call he became alarmed. Mieu is an Ivorian journalist, an impish-looking man in his twenties with a mouthful of conflicted teeth that he covers with his hand when he smiles. He is one moment bashful and the next aggressive, but under Kieffer's influence he had become more confident. He collaborated with his mentor on many touchy stories that Mieu wouldn't have had the courage to do alone, and they put out some damning reports together. But the partnership went deeper than just publishing: Mieu admired GAK more than anyone he had ever met. And Kieffer thought of Mieu almost as a son.

Baudelaire Mieu was twenty-two when GAK came into his life and his neighbourhood. Kieffer moved into an apartment in the Cocody district with his most recent wife, a Ghanaian princess named Lady Atta Afua, better known as Rita. She had three children whom Kieffer had adopted. GAK was a bon vivant and a bundle of contradictions. He passionately loved both fine wine and cold beer, Handel and John Lennon, contemporary politics and medieval history.

Mieu became a fixture in Kieffer's home, hanging out whenever he could. GAK would talk endlessly while he lit one Dunhill cigarette off the butt of the previous one, letting the ashes fall on the carpet. He sat on the floor, eschewing furniture as too conventional. His friends often had the impression that Kieffer considered himself more African than European or Canadian, a simple peasant and not a middle-class bourgeois. But he always had his computer on, another link with his Network, through which he shared information and challenged authority any way he could. His mobile phones were constantly ringing. Kieffer would leap to his feet and move around the room like a restless animal but would quickly end up wheezing, his weak heart pounding. Though he was only fifty-four, Kieffer's lifestyle had taken a toll on his body.

As for Mieu, his life was at a difficult crossroads. His father had just died. His wife and little girl had been caught up in the violence of western Côte d'Ivoire during a visit there, and they were forced to flee. What Kieffer was able to give Baudelaire was hope—filling his heart and soul with the idea that things in Côte d'Ivoire could change.

"A lot of journalists hated GAK because of the way he worked," Mieu says. "But I loved it."

When explosive documents materialized, Kieffer would publish quickly just to get the information before the public. He barged around the precincts of the cocoa industry, demanding answers from people known to kill for less than being asked irritating questions by nosy journalists. He went far beyond the boundaries of what other reporters considered "objective" journalism. According to Mieu, Kieffer adamantly believed that the Ivorian miracle could and should be revived. But it had to be redirected to profit the primary producers and reduce the privileges of the cocoa bosses and the multinationals. He was an idealist, and the young, impressionable Mieu loved him for it.

Mieu knew that Kieffer was meeting with Legré on Friday afternoon, and he was also aware that Kieffer planned to leave soon after to go to Ghana for the weekend. Rita returned home often, and Kieffer would occasionally join her in Ghana when he felt the need to "lay low" for a while. Mieu went around to Kieffer's house, but there was nobody home. A domestic worker knew only that he had left for work as usual on Friday morning in his car. Mieu contacted Rita in Ghana, but Kieffer wasn't there. Word of his absence spread quickly. The silence from his lifeline—the cellphones and the laptop—was uncharacteristic and ominous.

"He never went one day without calling me," says Mieu. "I knew there was something wrong." Mieu called the French Embassy.

~

Guy-André Kieffer had been a thorn in the side of French diplomats for a long time, sometimes making life miserable for bureaucrats as far away as the foreign ministry at the Quai d'Orsay in

Paris. France was trying to hold on to its influence in Côte d'Ivoire, formerly the jewel in its colonial crown. Ideas of Empire die slowly, and Côte d'Ivoire bequeathed to France some fading sense of its former grandeur. It's true that Côte d'Ivoire contributed billions of euros in profits to French businesses, but the country is also a hub of French influence in West Africa, a distant outpost of French language and culture. Recent discoveries of significant oil deposits in Côte d'Ivoire were also of great interest to international businessmen.

The Linas-Marcoussis Agreement, signed and dated in a Paris rugby arena, was supposed to heal the wounds of the warring north and south, but it had given Paris a questionable amount of sway over Ivorian affairs of state. What worried the French government more than the war was the ultra-nationalism stirred by Simone Gbagbo, given forceful expression in the racist ideology of Ivoirité, which was also turned against the French. Into these troubled waters, where everyone was accustomed to swimming cautiously, splashed Guy-André Kieffer.

In particular, Kieffer had incurred the wrath of Paul Antoine Bohoun Bouabré, the Ivorian Minister of Finance and the Economy and among the richest and most powerful people in the country. Bohoun Bouabré was one of GAK's chief targets. Kieffer exposed the minister's business deals and reported on his known—and previously unknown—diversion of cocoa funds into private interests. He often buttonholed the man in public places, mostly in the minister's own office building, where, much to the chagrin of the minister, Kieffer had many "friends." Bohoun Bouabré had threatened Kieffer in the past, and most Ivorians knew he was not a man to mess with.

But Kieffer also pursued Victor Nembellissini, the director of the National Investment Bank and the man who had his hands on Côte d'Ivoire's vast cocoa fortunes, which Kieffer believed should be in the hands of the cocoa farmers. Both of these men were tight with Kieffer's arch-enemy, Simone Gbagbo, whose persuasive powers over the president were considered the reason the head of state had abandoned his plans for reforms to limit government corruption. GAK couldn't have picked a more menacing group of people to antagonize. The French Embassy had grown accustomed to their complaints.

Now Kieffer had disappeared, which was a problem for French President Jacques Chirac and the Foreign Office. The disappearance of a French national, well known to the international media, possibly kidnapped on orders from the highest offices in the government of Côte d'Ivoire, presented delicate diplomatic challenges. And the situation was being complicated by reports from Ivorian journalists that two members of the French foreign ministry had arrived in Abidjan just hours before Kieffer was kidnapped and probably knew more about the abduction than they were prepared to admit.

The French Embassy did what embassies do when pressed for answers to awkward questions: It went silent. Kieffer's friends — his Network—were calling embassy contacts, but nobody was answering the phones. It was, after all, the weekend.

On Sunday, someone in the Kieffer Network intercepted a police radio report about the discovery of a body on a road on the outskirts of Abidjan, that of a white man. After further inquiries, the police said they had taken the corpse to the hospital at six in the evening and that a representative from either the French or the Canadian Embassy was on the way to help with formal identification.

By seven that evening, the body of the still unidentified dead white man had vanished.

~

On a late Monday afternoon, Sébastien Kieffer was finishing another in a long series of exasperating days when the phone rang in his east-end Montreal apartment. His young daughter,

Vivienne, born when Sébastien was only twenty-three and not yet ready for large responsibilities, needed a lot of time and attention. Besides being a single father, Sébastien was studying for a physiotherapy certificate. He was exhausted from daily classes and his nighttime job as a waiter. The phone call was about his father.

Guy-André Kieffer had moved to Canada in 1971 to study at McGill University in Montreal, a time of his life that few people know much about. He married a Canadian woman, presumably to get citizenship, and they divorced soon after. He left Canada after obtaining his degree—and his first divorce—to go on to Cuba and possibly China during the 1970s, always travelling on his Canadian passport, which carried less political baggage than that of his home country. He eventually resumed his studies in France, where he met Marie-André Lecompte at journalism school. Marie-André was a Québécoise-Mohawk woman from Valleyfield. It was a tumultuous relationship between two "very strong people" as their son Sébastien characterizes them.

They fell in love during heady times: France in the mid-1970s buzzed with political and social debate. The pair were both actively involved with the French Communist Party, both idealists and social crusaders. Wedding photos show a small, not terribly happy little gathering of family and friends in front of the courthouse in Strasbourg. Guy-André is a handsome but serious young fellow with shaggy black hair, an insouciant pouting mouth and an air of impatience. His bride is a fragile beauty with Renoir eyes; the slight bulge of her white wedding dress betrays her advancing pregnancy.

Sébastien remembers little of his early childhood, except that his parents yelled at each other a lot. In 1978, his mother left France, returning to Montreal with three-year-old Sébastien. Soon after, Guy-André followed them, moving to Ottawa, where he used his Canadian citizenship and a McGill law degree to get a job as an assistant to a Liberal Member of Parliament, Marcel

Prud'homme (now a senator). Sébastien thinks his father made some effort to keep the family together, but Sébastien's mother became deeply embittered towards her husband.

Sébastien says desolately, "She definitely poisoned me against him." The years with his mother, after his father left, were difficult and erratic. To compensate for the instability in his home life, Sébastien became obsessed with swimming. The discipline of high-intensity training was a creative distraction, and he was soon winning every meet he entered. Those years of endless laps paid off with an opportunity to train in France, where he became part of a competitive swimming club. But his hidden agenda in going to Paris was to find his father.

Sébastien remembers the day he called Guy-André. "It was very emotional but also full of joy." Guy-André was about to leave on a business trip to Africa—on assignment for the Paris-based daily newspaper *La Tribune*—and he would not be in France to see Sébastien. He told his son that he had married again, this time to a woman from Guadeloupe named Osange, and together they had a child, a girl named Canelle. He told Sébastien how much he had wanted to see him and be with him over the years. Sébastien was nineteen. Instead of seeing his father on that trip Sébastien was able to connect with his estranged family and he met an intoxicating crowd of fascinating relatives, including his grandparents. The next summer, Guy-André arranged for his son to come and stay with him. It became the most treasured time of Sébastien's life, helping him unlock the mysteries of his missing parent and overcome a life of anger.

Father and son met again the following summer, this time for two weeks, "but there was a lot of tension at that time." Sébastien brought with him his new girlfriend, a young woman whom Guy-André considered a bad match for his boy.

The two continued to stay in touch by telephone and email as Sébastien embarked on a troubled marriage and had a daughter of his own. But Guy-André became less communicative after he moved to Africa in 2002. As other friends and family members also noted, GAK quickly became obsessed with Côte d'Ivoire. His movements were mysterious, and he often went "underground," as he told them, for his own safety.

On Monday, April 19, 2004, the phone call came from Osange. GAK had gone missing without a trace. The family would hold on to the hope that he was alive for as long as possible, but it didn't look good.

Sébastien's life fell apart.

~

Tudor Hera had not known a moment's peace since he arrived in Côte d'Ivoire in September 2002. When the Canadian Department of Foreign Affairs and International Trade appointed him to the post of First Secretary of Public and Political Affairs in the Canadian Embassy in Abidjan, no one thought the job would be a sinecure. He knew more about how the world worked than about how diplomacy functioned. He had travelled extensively in the field, working for the International Committee for the Red Cross before arriving in Ottawa. He was young, single, without children: an ideal candidate for a mission in which the Canadian government suspected there was going to be trouble.

But no one thought it would come so soon. Hera had hardly unpacked his bags and found his desk when, three weeks after his arrival, he learned that he was in the middle of a war zone. Rebels had seized half the country and had come close to taking control of Abidjan itself. All of his plans to slowly get to know people and the country evaporated as he scrambled to find the file of contacts left by his predecessor and to figure out what was going on. Diplomatic niceties were subverted in the interests of survival, and Hera called up people out of the blue to ask for help. One of the best contacts in his Rolodex was the Canadian journalist Guy-André Kieffer.

"He was very useful and also refreshing," Hera remembers. "Kieffer was blunt and direct, not like most people in the country." Hera had a lot of contact with Kieffer over the next two years, though he never got to know him personally. "He was a deeply private man, a mystery." Also, the way GAK worked perplexed the Canadian diplomat. He knew that Kieffer met with disreputable people. He went to the hangouts of underworld types, where he would get his information. There was about him the dark, rank musk of the underworld he travelled in. "A lot of people hesitated to call him a journalist," says Tudor. "He didn't play by any rules. He didn't work for any known media group; he was a freelancer but he never signed his articles. You just knew it was he who had written something because the other newspapers would name him when they reacted to his exposés. In the government-run press he was often referred to as a spy."

It was the policy of *La Lettre du Continent* not to publish bylines, and presumably no one knew which articles were Kieffer's. But identical scoops would often turn up in opposition newspapers under a variety of names. In the close-knit world of Ivorian politics and journalism—which are often one and the same—it was presumed that Kieffer was the hand behind most of the more damning reports, even if that wasn't true. Kieffer never seemed to mind being blamed.

None of this dissuaded Hera from making use of Kieffer. He may not have acted like a journalist, but he certainly didn't appear to be profiting from his work, and he was very well informed. Many journalists in the country admitted that their primary source was Kieffer, who gave away information for nothing. "You did not get the impression that he was on the take. He had an old car, he wore simple clothes, no suits, no flashy anything. Not a person with Swiss bank accounts somewhere. It's just a gut feeling, and I certainly don't speak for the Canadian government when I tell you this," says Hera. "But my sense was that the guy was truly genuine. He wanted to expose corruption. There was no malice in what he was doing."

Other diplomats who used Kieffer's information had the same impression. "A lot of shady characters stayed behind when everyone else was leaving Côte d'Ivoire," says one man who used Kieffer's information. "They called themselves 'consultants,' but you didn't really know what profession they were in. There was a lot of money to be made, and they were after it. No one really knew what Kieffer was up to, but it wasn't in the interest of getting wealthy."

What made Hera curious was how Kieffer had managed to survive so long given how provocative his reporting was. When the Canadian diplomat arrived in Côte d'Ivoire, there were still the remnants of the kind of civility that the country had enjoyed for decades, a European patina of culture that made Ivorians snobbish. Journalists enjoyed the freedom of what appeared to be a democracy. But that genteel atmosphere was fading fast. This was not a place where you knocked over furniture and called people liars without risking consequences. This was a place to mind your p's and q's. How did Kieffer do it?

Many people in Côte d'Ivoire told me they believed that the Canadian Embassy was protecting Kieffer. Hera found that astonishing when I told him. For his part, Hera was convinced that sympathetic elements inside the Ivorian regime were watching out for the difficult reporter. Kieffer himself liked to create the impression, among both those who loved and those who hated him, that he had patrons, guardian angels of some kind. He dropped names and created around himself something of an aura of exceptional influence. A lot of people presumed he was being protected because no sane person would be as belligerent as he was in such a volatile place without some assurance of immunity. But in the days and weeks before he disappeared, Kieffer finally seemed afraid; he had lost some of the confidence that made powerful people reticent to take him on.

One diplomat suspects that the magic spell Kieffer created began to dissipate as his inside sources dried up, rendering him less useful to people. "Kieffer's intelligence became less and less reliable before he disappeared," he says. "He was obsessed with cocoa. He was trying to get at something that was quite obscure, and he ceased to have the general-interest inside knowledge he once had, especially about security issues." At the same time, Kieffer had become a major annoyance to people with power. "He was bothering the regime," says another diplomat. "It sucks to say it, but he brought disaster upon himself. There is a limit to how far you can go in a country like Côte d'Ivoire."

A foreign cocoa executive in Abidjan is not surprised that GAK disappeared. "It was inevitable. He knew too much," he says, as though kidnapping and death were as inevitable for a nosy journalist as an auto accident might be for a careless driver. Another foreigner who knew GAK went even further, suggesting he had it coming. Kieffer had a kind of post-colonial sense of superiority, not unlike other Frenchmen in Africa, the man says. "GAK thought he was a white knight. He was telling Ivorians what was wrong without being asked for his opinion. Questioning their ways. In other places he would have been asked to leave, but in Côte d'Ivoire he just disappeared."

Whatever the reason for GAK's change of circumstances, Tudor Hera was still deeply disturbed when he heard that Kieffer had vanished. One of Kieffer's friends called Hera on his mobile phone on Saturday to ask if he had seen GAK. No one knew where he was. On Sunday, the same person called to say that he thought something bad had happened to Kieffer. Hera contacted the French embassy and the Ivorian police.

From the first days of the inquiry, says Hera, the French took control of the case. They had better resources in the country than the Canadians, and also had close contact with the authorities. "French police worked with Ivorian police," says Hera. "They were training the Africans in police work." So the Canadian Embassy took a back seat. Kieffer's friends criticize the Canadian Embassy for not doing very much to find out what happened to him, but Tudor Hera said they did all that was possible. "We made a task force with the French and Canadian embassies, and we met with leading people in the Ivorian gendarmerie from the first day of the investigation," he says. "We put a lot of pressure on the police, and they genuinely seemed to be helpful."

Despite the suspicions of Kieffer's friends that the French authorities really didn't want to know the truth, Hera says that was never his impression. "There was a lot of diplomatic nudging going on at very high levels. But there is only so much you can do in someone else's country."

~

With no answers coming through official channels, the well-oiled machine that had been supplying Kieffer with information, his Network, now set out to investigate for themselves. Kieffer's friends, family and supporters, plus his associates, informers and spies, pulled out all the stops. If Kieffer had investigated his own disappearance, he probably could not have done a better job than either the police or his circle of friends.

Kieffer's Network began to assemble a picture that was as accurate as is possible in an African country where truth must be, at best, approximated from a shifting assemblage of fact, innuendo, rumour, theory and wild speculation. The first version of the story had it that agents, possibly working for the ministry of the Economy and Finance, had abducted Kieffer. The assignment was apparently to take him out of town to a military installation and rough him up: apply a bit of physical coercion try to get from him any documents he might have had in his possession concerning the files he was investigating. But the operation went wrong. Kieffer had a bad heart and needed steady doses of his medication. "He popped a raspberry" in the blunt words of one European cocoa executive who has heard some of the inside story, meaning he had a heart attack.

As local and international media dug deeper, they discovered more alarming details. The torture was probably much more aggressive. As part of the physical coercion the kidnappers beat Kieffer with clubs and iron bars for perhaps even days before he died. When the secret police realized they had killed their subject and not just terrorized him, they had to cover up the crime. The body quickly disappeared.

While using intimidation on journalists who worked for foreign agencies had become commonplace in Abidjan, killing them was still taboo. Six months earlier, police had murdered Jean Hélène—a reporter for Radio France Internationale—shooting him dead on a street in Abidjan. The sergeant who had killed the reporter was now serving a sentence of seventeen years without parole. President Gbagbo condemned the assassination, but he publicly stated that he could understand why one of his people might be driven to such a desperate act, given the Ivorian frustration with France. The message was clear: It's wrong to kill foreign reporters, but you'll get official sympathy if you are compelled to do so.

What Kieffer's Network couldn't fathom was why a white man's corpse ended up on the side of the road two days later and how it subsequently disappeared from an Abidjan hospital. Was it Kieffer's body? What happened to it? It's not easy to get rid of a white cadaver in Abidjan without someone noticing. But that seems to be what happened. One foreign diplomat says he was told that the corpse was actually an albino African man and not a white European. But Baudelaire Mieu says that the police radio chatter they intercepted distinctly said it was a white man.

What did seem clear to Kieffer's Network was that the French government wanted the GAK affair to go away even more than the Ivorian government did. The embassy withheld information that the Network knew it had regarding Kieffer's arrest, his detention and his treatment. A French foreign office representative suggested to journalists that Kieffer had been involved with nefarious activities, and that such involvement might explain his abduction. Another French official was reported to have said, "Kieffer's disappearance was best for everyone."

Another story was circulating, and it turned up in French newspapers: Kieffer had been implicated in the kidnapping of a German restaurant owner some time earlier—a business deal that went bad—and he had been killed out of revenge. Kieffer's friends concluded that this theory was not just malicious but also highly improbable, given Kieffer's nature.

Baudelaire Mieu found all of this deeply hurtful, but he didn't have time to dwell on it: A week after Kieffer disappeared, Mieu himself was the target of a death threat for his alleged role in GAK's reporting. He felt compelled to go into hiding. The authorities derided Mieu's claims of intimidation, insisting that he was just grandstanding. But the Network knew better.

Aline Richard, an old friend of GAK's from his days at *La Tribune*, was also distressed by what she believed was the French government's attempts to demonize her friend. The two had worked together in Paris when Kieffer covered commodities and she was on the oil beat, but she lost contact with Kieffer when he moved to Africa. All of the official and unofficial stories put out about her friend alleged that Kieffer was a part of disreputable activities and not really a journalist. "The embassy started to say that Guy-André was a strange guy, that he was dubious and shady. Was he a journalist? Or what? That was the tone." Aline Richard thinks if there were any questionable activities going on in Abidjan, they involved the French government, not her former colleague: "Just what is it that France is trying to accomplish in Côte d'Ivoire?"

~

A twist on the Kieffer story, and one that gave ammunition to his critics, is that he didn't initially go to Côte d'Ivoire as a journalist but rather as a consultant. In fact, he had moved to Africa at the behest of an associate, Stéphane de Vaucelles, a young idealist and a director with the HSBC Investment Bank, Africa branch, who was living in Abidjan.

In October 2001, the HSBC was asked by Côte d'Ivoire's prime minister, Seydou Diarra, to perform an audit on the cocoa *filière*, and de Vaucelles was chosen by the bank to head up the investigation. The marketing board that had kept the cocoa price stable and profitable for decades—CAISTAB—had been disbanded at the insistence of the World Bank, and some new system would have to be installed. Farmers were distrustful of attempts to launch new control systems and were attempting boycotts. World Bank leaders, who had substantial leverage in Côte d'Ivoire through their control of the state's debt, wanted some independent organization to investigate how the *filière* really functioned and to determine how it might be replaced. HSBC got the contract.

Laurent Gbagbo had come to power a year earlier, bringing with him a breath of hope that the years of instability since the death of Le Vieux had finally come to an end. Gbagbo claimed to be a socialist and professed an interest in cleaning up corruption in the cocoa industry and ensuring that the farmers got better funding. The World Bank and the IMF had made a mess of the cocoa *filière* with all of their SAPs, and Gbagbo claimed he wanted to restore its effectiveness. Indeed, the World Bank, the farmers and the government all agreed it was time for some fresh air to blow through the cocoa trade of Côte d'Ivoire. But there was one holdout. According to sources, the multinational food trader Cargill pressured the HSBC, of which it was an important client, to abandon the audit and shut down the cocoa review. It isn't clear why Cargill would want to halt the investigation, but the HSBC agreed to do so.

Stéphane de Vaucelles disagreed. He wanted to keep going, believing he was part of a fresh new beginning in Côte d'Ivoire. With some encouragement from the new Gbagbo regime, he set up a private company called Commodities Corporate Consulting (CCC) and signed a contract with the Côte d'Ivoire government to continue the investigation without the resources of the bank.

In December 2001, de Vaucelles asked Kieffer if he would move to Côte d'Ivoire and become part of the investigative team, arguing that it would be a chance for the reporter to put his knowledge of markets and commodities to work for a good cause. Kieffer was an early supporter of the regime of Laurent Gbagbo. Its idealistic rhetoric and socialist orientation fit nicely with his own ideological makeup. As he saw it, a former French colony was about to be rehabilitated and reformed by a left-wing African president who had the interests of peasants and the proletariat in mind. Here was a chance to help. He decided to take a break from journalism to assist de Vaucelles with the audit on the cocoa industry and facilitate overdue reforms in the cocoa *filière*.

Antoine Glaser, a friend and the Paris-based editor of *La Lettre du Continent*, warned Kieffer against the move. Glaser and Kieffer met often for lunch in Paris when Guy-André was working at *La Tribune* and Glaser was down the street at *La Lettre*. They would talk about life, love and commodities. When Kieffer told Glaser that he was moving to Côte d'Ivoire to work not as a journalist but as a consultant for the Ivorian government, Glaser responded that it was a very bad idea. "*Journaliste est journaliste*," Glaser told Kieffer. "If you pass to the other side of the mirror, you can't come back—it's a one-way trip." But Kieffer didn't play by the rules, says Glaser. He was "*un soixante-huitard*," according to Glaser—a sixty-eighter. "He was still thinking like it was 1968. He had no respect for power, and he had a big mouth."

~

The audit took the consultants of CCC into some very dark places, revealing a secret world of people on the take and transnational corporations who simply played the game in order to get cocoa to the seaport. Without the protection of guaranteed price stability under CAISTAB's rules, farmers were at the mercy of price swings, from either market forces or manipulation. They were, most of the time, seriously underpaid. But the two new institutions set up with the World Bank's blessing didn't seem to offer any improvement. The CCC investigators came up with a plan to restructure the cocoa *filière* and, they hoped, get a better deal for the farmers. The World Bank and IMF grudgingly supported it, conceding reluctantly that their own ideas hadn't worked very well in Côte d'Ivoire.

Initially at least, it seemed as though Gbagbo genuinely wanted to change the way Côte d'Ivoire did business. The government gave the CCC team unprecedented access to data and officials in the cocoa trade and state bureaucracy. But something changed. As the CCC went about its work, the Gbagbo regime was beginning to reveal its true colours. And they weren't the altruistic banners that Kieffer had been led to expect. Either the president was betraying his real purpose, or he'd been infected by the corruption he had promised to eradicate. Gbagbo had presented himself as a socialist. Now he was emerging as an elitist and an ultra-nationalist.

It was no secret in Côte d'Ivoire that Simone Gbagbo was a fervent evangelical Christian and had joined an American-based church that was much favoured by people close to U.S. President George W. Bush. President Gbagbo and his wife made frequent visits to the United States, where their fundamentalist religious beliefs won them access to fellow Christians in prominent positions in politics and industry. Gbagbo made friends in high places.

There were other, more ominous, changes. Gbagbo had previously denounced the policies of Ivoirité. Now he seemed enthralled by the racist sentiments of his wife, much as he suddenly shared her piety. When Muslims in the north staged their rebellion in September 2002, Gbagbo declared to his new American conservative friends that resisting the rebels was his contribution to the war against Islamic extremism. He was as committed to "the war on terror" as were the Americans.

Watching this metamorphosis from a distance, Kieffer and his idealistic friends were appalled. This was not the regime, or the country, that Guy-André Kieffer had adopted as his own.

Within a year of his arrival in Abidjan, Kieffer and about twenty others who were part of CCC found themselves caught in a crossfire of competing interests. When the dust settled, there was an entirely new political configuration in Côte d'Ivoire. Paul Antoine Bohoun Bouabré became minister of finance. He was a wealthy ultra-nationalist who didn't have a lot of time for enthusiastic white boys from France, especially socialists, telling Africans how to run their affairs. The CCC's role in reforming the *filière* was suddenly terminated. The regime devised a solution of its own: four new cocoa agencies, accountable to the government.

The new bureaus were neither completely public nor completely private; they had the authority to tax cocoa profits and to spend the revenue as they saw fit, but they were not obliged to account for where the money went. To the astonishment of those watching these developments, the World Bank and the IMF approved the proposed new system. Within months, Kieffer and his colleagues were on the outside, flabbergasted at the audacity of a scheme that seemed designed to institutionalize larceny.

The erstwhile reformers became the targets of attack from powerful politicians. Many of the idealists in the CCC packed up quickly and left the country, hounded by physical harassment and death threats. As the others fled, GAK decided to stay, to pass back through the mirror to a place he knew well, a place to transform his idealism into activism: journalism. He remained enough of an idealist to think that he could get away with it. He believed he could put to good use all the inside knowledge he had gleaned in the months he had spent with his Euro-Canadian nose buried deep in the system that cultivated the corruption that had infected the cocoa *filière*.

Despite his earlier pronouncement that, once outside the vocation, the journalist mutates into something else, Antoine Glaser commissioned Kieffer to write for *La Lettre du Continent* from Côte d'Ivoire. GAK had been not just a friend but also a very good reporter. And Glaser would discover that Kieffer had never fully left the world of journalism; according to those who knew him, he had passed back and forth through the mirror so often that he never really knew which side he was on. Even as a consultant, GAK had been feeding stories to the outside, "working as a consultant by day and a journalist by night," says a colleague who knew him well.

Kieffer, as a born-again reporter, was even more contemptuous of rules. Though contributors to *La Lettre* are supposed to be anonymous—they often publish information that could put people's lives in danger if the source was known—Kieffer introduced himself to people as a freelancer for the paper, much to Glaser's unease. "GAK was writing under pseudonyms for the local press as well," says Glaser with exasperation. "Things would turn up in the Ivorian press that were word for word what he had submitted to *La Lettre*."

As Côte d'Ivoire descended into xenophobia, war and the tyranny of death squads in 2002, GAK took up his old job with a crusader's zeal. He became the front man for the Network, most of whose members were active behind the scenes and even in government offices. They would give him information; he would get it into print while protecting his sources, including

Ivorian journalists who were too afraid to publish it themselves. Sometimes, the Network would disseminate information informally to a broad circle of diplomats, politicians, aid workers and foreign journalists, in the hope that it would eventually reach someone with the power and inclination to do something about it. It was a deadly game, but Kieffer pursued it fearlessly. "People said that GAK didn't care about his safety. That for some reason he no longer cared to live and that's why he was so cavalier," says Baudelaire Mieu. "But he loved life. He just hated the corruption."

One way or another, Kieffer exposed schemes for diverting cocoa money to myriad enterprises with little or no benefit for the poor Ivorians who produced the country's best cash crop. Money that properly belonged in funds to support the market price for the farmers was being collected by the new regulatory agencies and used for weapons purchases. The new agencies were taxing the life out of the cocoa producers. They were sinking deeper into poverty even when prices were strong.

The information collected by the Network and reported by Kieffer gradually revealed a tangled conspiracy involving extortion, the diversion of cocoa and coffee shipments to offshore companies (some with ties to companies registered on the Canadian stock exchange), and financing for French and Kosovo-Albanian mercenaries who were brought to Côte d'Ivoire by the Americans to fight Islamic militants in rebel-held territories. Many of the stories involved Pastor Moïse Koré, a mysterious Rasputin-like character said to be Gbagbo's spiritual advisor and a man with strong connections to right-wing American politicians.

One report led to an international police investigation into a complex money-laundering scheme, known as the Comstar affair, run through a mobile phone company. A network of foreign companies, registered in the Virgin Islands and Belgium, with close ties to the Gbagbo regime, imported prepaid phone cards, which they declared to Ivorian customs at a highly inflated value. Real money from cocoa profits was then funnelled through the company books to various secret destinations—including Liberia, where the laundered funds found their way to opponents of the Charles Taylor regime.

Then there was the equally opaque Magnific A Services operation, a financial group ostensibly based in Los Angeles that collaborated with Lebanese import/export companies and the Italian Mafia to launder money through a phony tomato-processing factory in Côte d'Ivoire.

The most intriguing investigation linked an Israeli financial company called the Lev Mendel Group to Simone Gbagbo, who was a company director in Côte d'Ivoire. With the patronage of the first lady, Lev CI became a private partner with the National Investment Bank of Côte d'Ivoire in managing the finances of the cocoa *filière*. The partnership enabled the bank to divert cocoa money to the president's wife. The bank president, Victor Nembellissini, is a close associate of both the Gbagbo family and the powerful minister Bohoun Bouabré.

In July 2002, Kieffer published details of a European Union investigation that exposed the shady management of ANAPROCI, the big cocoa farmer's cooperative that was notorious among the farmers for diverting profits into other enterprises. The head of ANAPROCI, Henry Amouzou, publicly challenged the Gbagbo regime "to get rid of" Kieffer or he would do it himself. But those who wanted to get rid of Kieffer were forming a long queue.

Before he disappeared, GAK told Antoine Glaser that he was on to something even bigger but he didn't yet have the proof he needed. Glaser has no idea what it was.

~

A cloak of silence and secrecy enveloped the investigation in the following weeks after the journalist's disappearance, with the

French and Ivorian governments seemingly in collaboration to cover up the Kieffer Affair. Aline Richard at *La Tribune* in Paris, working with others in Abidjan, pushed for answers at the Elysée and the Quai d'Orsay in Paris, where she was sure that people knew more about the case than they were letting on. "I just wanted my government to do its work," she says. Richard organized the "Truth for Guy-André Kieffer Association," a group of concerned friends and journalists who staged rallies in Paris. The international group Reporters Without Borders put out numerous media releases about the failure of authorities both in France and Côte d'Ivoire to pursue an investigation of Kieffer's disappearance.

Osange Silou-Kieffer, GAK's second ex-wife and mother to his daughter, became one of his most vocal champions. She took up the cause of his disappearance with a vengeance. Silou-Kieffer is a skilled agitator from the same political school as her former husband. She's short and stocky with a round face and large black eyes that flash fire when she talks passionately—and when she speaks of the disappearance of Guy-André, she is the embodiment of passion. Her public statements in Paris were calculated to embarrass the French government, but she also flew to Abidjan and met Laurent Gbagbo, who, she says, put his hand on his heart and swore that he was sure her husband was still alive. An Ivorian newspaper that is the voice of Gbagbo's Front Populaire Ivoirien party reported that Kieffer was living in Ghana, where he had fled for his own safety. An anonymous caller told Osange that rebels had kidnapped Kieffer and he was secretly being held in a stronghold close to the Malian border. "I listened politely," Osange told reporters, "but I resented it as an insult to my intelligence."

She deftly dispelled rumours and innuendo about her ex-husband while making it clear that she felt it was the Ivorian government's behaviour that needed investigating, not GAK's. She told the French media that her husband (no mention was ever made that they were not still married) had many enemies, but one name came up repeatedly in their frequent communications—that of Paul Antoine Bohoun Bouabré. "I don't know if he is mixed up with this affair," she told reporters carefully but deliberately.

As Silou-Kieffer took up the crusade from Paris, Rita, his Ghanaian-born wife, faded into the background, fearing for her own life and descending into poverty. Kieffer's friends and associates found themselves under constant threat. Guy-André's brother Bernard emerged as another pleading voice, issuing press releases asking for information about his brother's fate. The extended family, spread out over three continents, kept up the pressure, young Sébastien doing all he could to push the Canadian government in Ottawa for help.

Eventually, this ad hoc coalition of crusading women, foreign journalists, well-informed insiders from the Network, family members and worried friends had an impact at the Quai d'Orsay. The French government suddenly abandoned its strategy of demonizing Kieffer and turned to damage control. President Jacques Chirac had called Laurent Gbagbo shortly after the kidnapping to inquire what Côte d'Ivoire was doing about it. (There has never been a similar inquiry from the Canadian government.) But there had been nothing more. In mid-May, a month after the aborted meeting at the Prima Centre, the Ministry of Justice in Paris appointed a judge, Patrick Ramaël, to investigate Kieffer's disappearance.

Judge Ramaël was no stranger to Ivorian politics. France had sent him to investigate the murder of Jean Hélène, the Radio France reporter shot dead by police six months before the kidnapping of Kieffer. Ramaël's unsubtle nickname among policemen was "Le Bulldog."

The judge made his way to Abidjan in May 2004, bringing with him an entourage of police, forensic investigators and detectives who pushed the Ivorian police into the background. Tudor

Hera, the front man for the Canadian Embassy on the Kieffer file, was astonished at the size and strength of the French police probe: "Whatever people were saying about France not caring about this operation, it certainly didn't appear that way when Ramaël arrived."

One of the first orders of business for Ramaël was to get telephone records. With a team of French experts and the most modern technology available, the investigators sorted through a million calls a day for a month in order to trace people's movements. From this, the French police got their first leads.

The Ivorians gave Judge Ramaël permission to question Michel Legré, the last person known to have seen GAK alive. Legré denied any responsibility, but his mobile phone records suggested otherwise, as investigators tracked his movements through indisputable satellite footprints. The records indicated that, on April 16 at 1:30 p.m., Legré was in the Prima shopping centre zone, where he presumably met Guy-André Kieffer; at 4:00, he was in the area of the ministry offices, including the office of Minister of Finance Bohoun Bouabré; at 7:00, he was back at the Prima Centre shopping plaza; and at 9:00, he was at Houphouët-Boigny International Airport, where Guy-André Kieffer's little Japanese-made car with the Canadian-flag logo was later discovered, abandoned in the parking lot. Legré's phone records also showed he was in continuous contact with people close to the minister of finance, including on the day that Kieffer disappeared.

With so much incriminating evidence, Ramaël was able to break Legré, who gave the French magistrate the names of eight people he claimed were involved in Kieffer's abduction. The eight were all part of the inner circle of Bohoun Bouabré. The list included the finance minister's cabinet director, Aubert Zohoré; Victor Nembellissini, head of the National Investment Bank (the one with Simone Gbagbo's company Lev CI as its partner); Pastor Moïse Koré, Gbagbo's advisor and chargé d'affaires for Defence; Patrice Bailly, head of security; and two senior military officers. Under questioning, Legré told Ramaël that at 4:00 he had indeed been in the zone of government ministries, as his phone record indicates, and had gone to the office of Aubert Zohoré, where Bohoun Bouabré himself gave Legré an envelope full of West African francs (amounting to 1,500 euros), calling them "professional fees."

The case was definitely pointing towards a high-level murder by agents of the state, rather than a revenge killing for a bad business deal. Kieffer's computer was found in the apartment of an associate of Legré's. GAK's friends knew that he was never far from his precious laptop, the electronic hub of his Network, and he would never entrust it to any third party, replete as it was with damning documents. Ramaël discovered that someone had opened the computer and attempted to access its files half an hour after Kieffer was bundled into the four-by-four in the Prima parking lot. Whoever abducted the journalist did so because of the man's work, not his personal business affairs, concluded the investigators, who also discovered that Kieffer's hard drive had been wiped clean. No matter what the rumour mill was spitting out, Kieffer's disappearance had all the hallmarks of a political assassination.

~

The pressure was now on the Côte d'Ivoire government to do something. Predictably, they found a conspicuous scapegoat. Prosecutors charged Michel Legré with complicity in kidnapping, illegal detention and murder, even though no body had been found. Reporters Without Borders called it an effort to focus attention on one person instead of pursuing all those Legré had named as being complicit. It was revealing that the Ivorian police also charged Legré with criminal defamation of character for giving up the names of eight influential Ivorian men—an act that blocked any further efforts by the French magistrate to get Legré to tell him more about the roles played by those individuals.

Legré went to jail, but this was probably a blessing; life behind bars was safer for Legré than life on the street. During the November riots following the French destruction of Ivorian military aircraft, demonstrators tore down the doors of the Maison d'Arrêt et de Correction d'Abidjan (MACA prison). The prisoners seized the opportunity presented by this unofficial amnesty and fled—all except for one. Legré didn't want to go.

Ramaël, for one, wanted him out. Interviews in prison were controlled by the presence of guards and government minders. But when Ramaël attempted to have Legré transferred to Paris for questioning, his request was blocked both by Ivorian authorities and those of France.

Despite his famous tenacity, "Le Bulldog" Ramaël would have nothing but trouble in his pursuit of the truth, and not only because of obstructions in Côte d'Ivoire. The French government found just as many ways to delay his work. Requests for information that had to go through the Quai d'Orsay were never transferred to Abidjan. As the judge narrowed his investigation to focus on the Bohoun Bouabré circle, the Quai d'Orsay vetoed his next visit to Côte d'Ivoire, citing security concerns. His bosses later relented under pressure.

Ramaël kept going back, tackling the obstacles, only to find that his targets were constantly moving farther away. He wanted, most of all, to interview the two military personnel on Legré's list of eight, who may have led the abduction. One of them was the head of security for the first lady, Simone Gbagbo. and the other was Bertin Kadet, counsellor to the president for defence affairs. Neither would agree to a meeting, and the Ivorian government would do nothing to help. As far as the regime was concerned, they had their man—Michel Legré.

The French investigators, like countless Europeans before

them, were also up against nature itself. "The heat and humidity destroy everything," says one person who was on the inside of the investigation. "Fingerprints, for instance. They literally melt in the heat." When police found Kieffer's car at the Abidjan airport, it was obvious that whoever had driven it there was much smaller than Kieffer, as the front seat was pulled up close to the steering wheel. But the old car had been in the sun for two weeks and was effectively sanitized. Investigators could learn nothing more from it.

Ramaël used every weapon in his arsenal to try to get to the targets of his investigation, and he also had some lucky breaks. When Bohoun Bouabré's communications minister was passing through Paris on business in early August, Ramaël had him arrested. Under questioning, Léonard Guédé confirmed the involvement of the eight collaborators on Legré's list. Guédé also admitted that he had personally and publicly threatened Kieffer's life, in the company of Victor Nembellissini, shortly before the kidnapping. Police searched Guédé's Paris apartment, where they found a substantial computer file on Kieffer. Guédé couldn't be charged under French law and was soon released from custody. In any case, Guédé and Legré were not the people Ramaël was after: His sights were set on people much higher up the political food chain.

With new momentum, Ramaël returned to Abidjan in October when he was finally able to interview the special advisor to the president, Bertin Kadet, as well as the shadowy spiritual advisor, Pastor Moïse Koré; Victor Nembellissini of the National Investment Bank; and Aubert Zohoré, the chef du cabinet to Bohoun Bouabré. People close to the investigation say Ramaël achieved amazing results. He was pushy, aggressive and very effective. "But at some point," says one insider, "the momentum just stopped. It became blocked. There was just no further he could go. Why? He speculates that maybe the judge was just getting too close to the top.

Ramaël had also become concerned for his own life. He had received several death threats. They might have been discounted as a crude kind of obstruction but for what had recently happened to a fellow Frenchman on an investigative mission in Côte d'Ivoire.

Xavier Ghelber was a lawyer who had been sent to Abidjan by the European Union (EU) to perform an audit on the cocoa *filière*. Hundreds of millions of euros were disappearing into an African void, and the EU had been trying to get to the bottom of what clearly seemed to be systemic corruption.

In November 2004, a group of armed soldiers stormed into Ghelber's hotel room during the night and took the lawyer into custody. When they attempted to put a sack over Ghelber's head in the hotel hallway, he resisted. During the struggle a rifle went off and a bullet ricocheted off a hotel wall and severely wounded a soldier. In a kind of Keystone Kops panic, the soldiers took Ghelber's cellphone and called someone to ask for instructions. The Ivorian soldiers then took Ghelber to military headquarters, where he was threatened with execution but was finally released. When French investigators examined the phone record later, it revealed that the call was placed to the president's office, specifically, to the bodyguards of Laurent Gbagbo.

Xavier Ghelber survived, and French soldiers whisked him out of the country for his own safety. But it was a lurid illustration of how this world worked—this world of cocoa into which Ramaël was poking his European nose and into which Guy-André Kieffer had vanished, leaving no trace.

Judge Ramaël returned to Côte d'Ivoire four times, reassuring the Kieffer family that he would not stop until he found the truth, even if it took him the rest of his days. Bernard Kieffer's plea for information about his brother's murder eventually yielded some results, as a number of secret informers risked their lives to feed the investigators information—all of it leading, according to Bernard Kieffer, to the highest offices in Côte d'Ivoire. More arrests are imminent, according to the family, but members of the Network have their doubts that the truth will ever come out. "Not until Gbagbo is gone," they say of the man who once seemed as full of promise for a new Côte d'Ivoire as Le Vieux himself.

Chapter Eleven

STOLEN **FRUIT**

Developing countries have been forced into a horse race with
the rest of the world in which the thoroughbreds have already
churned up the turf before their heavily handicapped horse has
left the starting gate. The rules of the Global Trade Handicap
Race were, of course, designed by the owners of the best horses."
— PETER ROBBINS, *Stolen Fruit*, 2003

IF ABIDJAN COULD BE SEEN ONLY FROM A DISTANCE,
or through rose-coloured lenses, one might have the idea that it
is a truly modern African city. It cuts a smart, contemporary sky-
line of skyscrapers and office buildings, with foreign boutiques
and a buzzing neon nightlife of bars and casinos. The massive
Hôtel Ivoire, with its tennis courts, swimming pools and skating
rink, sits on a charming blue lagoon, where long wooden fishing
boats bob all day long. But a closer look reveals a fashionable city
gone to seed: broken pavement, buildings crumbling in the thick
humidity. The lagoons are garbage-strewn and much in need of
dredging. The Hôtel Ivoire is shabby, the swimming pools are
drained, and the skating rink, once kept smooth and glossy even
in soaring heat, is only a distant memory.

When Félix Houphouët-Boigny built modern Abidjan, the
city offered the promise of an African future as prosperous and
as culturally alive as any in Europe. Now it's just another
unhappy place with a sharp divide between the very rich and the
desperately impoverished. The elite neighbourhoods with their

patisseries and fine restaurants are guarded against petty thieves; the downtown streets are clogged with the expensive cars of organized crime bosses; white people never go out alone, and some don't venture out at all; refugees who have flooded in from the countryside to escape poverty and death squads try to shield themselves against more poverty and death squads.

At the fortified Canadian embassy office in central Abidjan, a team of mostly Québécois diplomats divides its time between documenting Côte d'Ivoire's breathtaking free fall into the world of failed states, watching out for Canadians, and wondering at what point they should join the other foreigners who have fled the country. Being Canadian helps them, but only if they have time to explain to a potential attacker that they are not from France. And at some point, if the violence gets out of control, being Canadian won't be much of a safeguard either.

This is probably the most sympathetic Canadian embassy I have encountered in my travels. They are obliged to tell me, they say, that I should not travel around the countryside asking a lot of questions about the cocoa *filière*. But since I insist that this is what I must do, we exchange all the numbers we have, including those of their homes, their mobiles and even satellite phones.

I first learn here that Guy-André Kieffer had been an important contact for this office for the few years before his disappearance. He was always willing to share information with his fellow citizens, though embassy staff knew that GAK's facts might be a bit undigested. Benoît Gauthier, the embassy's first secretary for political and cultural affairs, who replaced Tudor Hera in the summer of 2004, warns me that if I really must go around the country asking a lot of questions, I should take special care not to mention Kieffer. It's not a safe topic.

This good advice proves not very useful, since everywhere I go it's others who raise Kieffer's name, usually by way of veiled threats.

~

Just as in the days of Le Vieux, cocoa producers play key roles in government and bureaucracy. But Laurent Gbagbo and his cronies have essentially turned the country's lucrative cocoa sector into a source of funds for pet projects and personal enrichment. The corruption is widespread and systemic. But even the blatant abuses are brushed aside in bland denials and allegations of external conspiracies.

Michel Yehoun is a large, blustering man, educated at the University of Dallas. I met him at the Atelier on the Responsibility of Producers in the Battle Against Dangerous Child Labour in the Cocoa Culture, the grandly titled conference where I first learned about the Oumé pilot project. The parking lot is chockablock with expensive SUVs. Cocoa bosses, who blame foreign influences for all their problems, dominate the event, chowing down on the luscious buffets that are replenished every few hours. Yehoun is especially dismissive of allegations regarding the exploitation of children. The issue of child labour is a fiction, he says, a tactic in a perverse campaign by powerful NGOs trying to raise money from gullible Europeans and North Americans.

Yehoun is overdressed for the occasion. In an effort to emulate the American business people he admires, he's wearing a long-sleeved herringbone shirt with a dark tie and a sports jacket, plus his trademark felt hat. The outside temperature at Grand-Bassam, the seaside resort area where the lavish conference takes place, soars into the forties.

"I love Americans," he declares. "Especially Texans. It's every man for himself in Texas. No laws. Land of liberty. Do you know, there are no beggars anywhere in that state?" he tells the Africans sitting with us at a patio table near the Gulf of Guinea. "That's because everyone is hustling. Everyone's working." Yehoun hasn't met the Bush family yet, but he can't wait. He owns a house in Texas and an apartment in Washington, so he expects that one day he is destined to cross paths with the great George W. Yehoun travels often to the United States, where he's involved in a number of deals he won't discuss with me.

Yehoun has profited handsomely from Gbagbo's restructuring of the cocoa *filière*. He is vice-president of the FDPCC—Fonds de Développement et de Promotion des Activités des Producteurs de Café et de Cacao—one of the key para-public organizations with authority to collect money from the cocoa and coffee growers but with no responsibility to account for the spending. The money is to be used at the discretion of the cocoa producers for public projects such as roads, wells and schools and for short-term loans to help farmers through rough economic periods. But it's difficult to find any evidence of the benefits of this money in the poverty-ridden cocoa groves of Côte d'Ivoire.

The funds are supposed to be distributed through the small farmer's cooperatives in the regions, but the cocoa producers are poorly organized and powerless to face the FDPCC to use the money for those public projects. One of Kieffer's most shocking allegations was that FDPCC funds were being systematically diverted through a series of fictitious cooperatives into the direct control of Laurent Gbagbo's circle. A lot of it ends up in the hands of arms dealers. Gbagbo justifies spending the farmers' money on guns by claiming it's for their own security.

Yehoun is a master of the Ivorian blame game, holding others responsible for the appalling prices the farmers get for their cocoa beans. Yehoun says it's the multinational corporations who are responsible for the corruption in Côte d'Ivoire, ignoring the fact that his own cooperative supplies beans to Cargill. When I ask him to explain how the multinationals are to blame for the plight of the farmers, he quickly shifts his criticism to the media. The press is a large part of the problem, he says, turning to Ange Aboa, the Reuters reporter who is with me.

Aboa is well known among Côte d'Ivoire's cocoa bosses for his coverage, and Yehoun accuses him of a hidden agenda. Negative reporting on corruption in cocoa cuts into his profits, he snaps at Aboa. "Who are you really working for?" he demands. Then, apropos of nothing, he raises the forbidden subject: "Where is Guy-André Kieffer now? Is he under here?" Yehoun pulls up the tablecloth and peeks under, then looks up, laughing. "Kieffer was a spy," he says, chillingly. "And you know what happens to spies."

The cocoa *filière* forms a complex organigram of agencies. Kieffer's Network has produced a chart that tries to simplify the money trail from the primary producers into the void of corruption, much of which has been confirmed by a series of audit reports authorized by the European Union. Kieffer's associates provided me with a copy of this document to help me understand the mechanics of the process. The Dead Sea scrolls would be easier to decipher. A series of arrows represents a money flow from the hands of the farmers into three principal entities: the FDPCC, for which Michel Yehoun works, the Bourse du Café et du Cocoa (BCC) and the Fonds de Régulation et de Contrôle Café-Cacao (FRC). More arrows lead away from these agencies into a maze of private interests and then consolidate into a thicker arrow pointing towards the National Investment Bank. From there a very large arrow leads to a discretionary fund that is under the control of Gbagbo. Some of it then goes to international financial institutions, thus keeping the World Bank at bay. Most of the balance ends up in private hands or the various enterprises of the political elite.

It's important to remember that this is money extracted from farmers in the form of taxes and fees, which are supposed to be redirected back into projects that will improve the lives of people and communities already impoverished by exploitation and pitiful prices. They are told that the funds will be used to stabilize the price of cocoa beans and help them through inevitable sags in the market. But as much as two-thirds of their potential income from cocoa farming vanishes, in the form of "special"

levies, into the coffers of government and the elite para-public
agencies for purposes about which the farmers know little or
nothing. No matter how much liberalization affects the cocoa
prices, the tariffs imposed by Gbagbo's regime are a major cause
of the chronic poverty in the countryside.

~

As head of the Coffee and Cocao Bourse (BCC), Lucien Tapé
Doh is one of the most formidable members of the *filière*. The
waiting room in his office is full of people with needs who all
jump to their feet nervously when he enters the room. Tapé Doh
ushers Ange and me into his inner sanctum, along with another
very anxious-looking couple. "Just a moment," he tells us and ges-
tures to chairs. He makes a call on his mobile phone and barks an
order: "*Il faut que tu payes tout de suite!*" (You must pay immediately!) He clicks off the phone and tells the couple that their
money will be in their bank account the next day. They are
hugely grateful.

Tapé Doh is a squat round man who wears traditional attire:
loosely fitted colourful shirt and pants. But his clothing is much
too big even for his extensive girth, and he seems to be lost in its
floral fabric. I detect a familiar sweet smell in the office as we
wait for him to adjust papers on his desk, and I notice a large slab
of chocolate cake, melting in the heat. It's decorated with a bul-
bous sugary orange object that looks like a miniature pumpkin
but, on closer examination, is supposed to represent a cocoa pod.
The inscription on the cake reads "Côte d'Ivoire—Land of
Cocoa." It's odd to see and smell real chocolate here, since
almost no one eats the stuff in Africa, in part because it's too
expensive, but also because it turns to liquid much too quickly.
(In an effort to find chocolate that could be sent with U.S. troops
into the deserts of Kuwait in 1991—a highly lucrative contract—
the Mars Corporation tried to develop a bar that could take the

heat. The people most famous for the confection that "melts in your mouth and not in your hand" found it was difficult not to compromise the taste and texture when you changed the fundamental chemistry of chocolate. As the Marquis de Sade knew from his suppositories, solid chocolate liquefies quickly in warm places.)

Tapé Doh is another very wealthy man who has profited from the reorganization of the *filière*. The BCC is one of the most impenetrable of the agencies that supposedly manage Côte d'Ivoire's most important exports. Local people describe him as an uneducated "bushman," but one who is nonetheless a shrewd and cagey operator. What he does best is to show how the passion of African nationalism can be manipulated to serve any purpose.

The BCC is neither private nor public, he explains, but a unique African mix of the two. These unaccountable agencies that control cocoa are simply "Africa's solution to Africa's problems," a phrase expressing a sentiment that has galvanized nationalist feeling all over Africa since the end of colonialism. Though all of the BCC's money comes from obligatory taxes and fees, the agency is not a public service, he says. "Transparency is an idea of the foreigners that simply gives an advantage to our competitors," he explains. "The European Union just wants to get control of us." Tapé Doh gives the same nationalist line one hears from the *filière* everywhere, including the mayor of Gagnoa, Roger Gnohite, as well as the Young Patriots who justify the expulsion of immigrants from the farmlands of the region as an act of "masters in our own house."

The Bourse is in charge of coordinating cocoa and coffee exports and establishing the floor price for beans sold in Côte d'Ivoire. It's supposed to guarantee a decent income from the exports and to help farmers benefit from higher world cocoa prices. But even at the height of the civil war, when prices were at their best, the farmers didn't profit. Tapé Doh says the high taxes and fees are necessary to pay for the war effort. Farmers need security, and the weapons are for their own good. If the violence is sometimes directed at the immigrants, well, it's possibly because they are supporting the rebels.

Billions of West African francs flow into the coffers of the BCC with no public record of where the money goes from there. Ivorian farmers have started to smuggle their beans into Ghana to take advantage of the price that farmers in the Gold Coast enjoy. Tapé Doh chuckles as he dismisses this: "When our price is higher, the Ghanaians smuggle beans into Côte d'Ivoire. This has been happening for decades." But the recent trade in contraband cocao has cut deep into Côte d'Ivoire's profits, and the farmers have started to expand their pirating activies. "The important thing is that Ivorians take back the power, that we not be controlled by outsiders," he says repeatedly. Tapé Doh supports liberalization, claiming it just needs time to take effect. "We had the CAISTAB for forty years. The BCC has existed only for four years," he says. "Give us time."

But time is running out for Côte d'Ivoire, and the overwhelming sense one gets from reading the EU audit reports is that the opportunists who run the *filière* are killing the goose that lays the golden egg. Nowhere is that more apparent than at the third most important cocoa agency, the Regulation and Control Fund (FRC). This is the biggest kitty of money and one that is frequently called "*la caisse noire*," the black deposit box of the ruling party of Laurent Gbagbo. The FRC is in charge of all financial regulations regarding cocoa and coffee, and it has absolute control over the cocoa and coffee treasury.

The president of the FRC is a woman named Angeline Zilahou Killi, who is tightly tied to the first family and is the godmother of a movement called Two Million Girls for Gbagbo, a campaign that uses children to mythologize the president as the father of the nation. Killi has few if any ties to cocoa production and little expertise in the area. According to Kieffer's Network and suggested by the EU reports, billions of West African francs have left the fund to pay for arms, to finance a new agricultural bank and to provide "loans" to Gbagbo and his circle. The EU audit reports conclude that the awarding of grants and loans from the FRC is done with "manifest irregularity."

Madame Killi was not available for an interview when we visited the offices of the FRC, as she was travelling in the United States.

"Where in the U.S.?" I ask her secretary, who had earlier that day confirmed our appointment.

"New York," she answers. "Madame Killi has just left."

I ask, "Has she, by any chance, gone to Fulton, New York?"

The reception area at the FRC suddenly falls into an ice-cold silence.

Dropping the name Fulton has much the same effect as mentioning Guy-André Kieffer. Fulton is a subject no one wants to talk about, a word that can clear a room or shut doors. Michel Yehoun, who babbles away about anything, simply snapped, "It's none of your damn business," when I asked if we could discuss Fulton. It turns out, he had good reason to be defensive. Fulton has become a code word for scam.

Fulton is actually a small town in upstate New York that all but shut down in 2003, when Nestlé, one of Fulton's principal employers at the time, closed its century-old chocolate factory, moving some of its production to other locations, including Brazil, and putting five hundred Fultonians on the street. Nestlé said at the time that the plant wasn't viable, but apparently the experts at Côte d'Ivoire's cocoa *filière* felt differently. Soon after, the FRC bought the plant and declared it was about to put Fulton, New York, back to work.

Americans cheered the Africans when they arrived. New York Senator Charles Schumer helped to broker the deal (Michel Yehoun was apparently a major player in arranging American support), and the senator's picture appears in a number of promotional photos featuring the plant, now called the New York Chocolate and Confection Company (NY3C). Federal agencies provided $850, 000 in loans and much more in tax breaks to help the Ivorians revive the operation. Then things got complicated.

Months and then a year passed with not a whiff of the familiar cocoa smell in the air of Oswego County. The economic development agency for the county told the *New York Times* that the company had funds "in the high seven digits" in its bank account and was paying its taxes. But the people of Fulton and the chocolate company creditors were getting nervous.

So what was the holdup? The Ivorians initially claimed they were having trouble getting cocoa beans out of Côte d'Ivoire because of the civil war. This seemed like a plausible explanation. Except that other cocoa corporations importing from Côte d'Ivoire weren't having any supply problems. According to the records of the San-Pédro Port Authority, exports of cocoa surged in 2003 and 2004.

Accountability has never been a strength of the Ivorian cocoa *filière*, and when U.S. politicians and financial agencies started to ask questions, the FRC had few answers. Lion Capital Management, a San Francisco–based investment company, is listed as the Ivorian chocolate company's U.S. partner with twenty per cent ownership. Lion Capital's creditors were making it clear that they were unhappy with what appeared to be unorthodox business practices and a conflict of interest involving two Ivorian advisors to NY3C. The African treasurer appointed by the FRC, Yalle Agbre, wasn't following the established rules governing American business and the company was slow in paying its bills. The African legal advisor to the company, Kemakolam Comas, had been practising law in the United States since 1997 but his licence was indefinitely suspended, according to the New York Law Journal, after clients complained about him.

Over time, the truth about the Fulton chocolate factory would begin to emerge. After Nestlé had closed the plant in 2003, it had stripped and auctioned off the equipment. After much arm-twisting, local politicians convinced the Swiss chocolate company to at least leave the county the building, in case investors wanted to get the operation rolling again. Nestlé subsequently sold the sprawling red brick factory to Oswego County for a nominal $100. Lion Capital Management bought it from the state for the same price and transferred it to the New York Chocolate and Confection Company. Soon, the owners were retrieving the chocolate-making equipment and hiring employees, filling Fulton with optimism, if not the smell of baking chocolate. The African purchasers, for their part, made the altruistic claim that the factory was for the benefit of Ivorian cocoa farmers. The whole arrangement had a kind of story-book gloss to it.

In principle, African ownership of a chocolate company made sense. Côte d'Ivoire's president said they were just trying to get some added benefit from the country's primary commodity. Financing for the factory came from taxes and levies that farmers had to pay, but profits would be returned to them. Revenue from the New York plant would allow the FRC to open schools, build water wells and improve the lives of the farmers. Meanwhile, Fulton would get exclusive access to a farm-gate price for beans, much cheaper than cocoa purchased on the open market. What could be wrong with any of this? Plenty, as Jerry Lamphere discovered.

Lamphere is a native of Fulton, who worked at the Nestlé plant for twenty-six years before it closed. He was retained by the new owners of the chocolate plant to be the manager. Lamphere was happy to get the job but even keener to start hiring back the people he had been obliged to fire for Nestlé. His happiness was short-lived.

Lamphere had seen a lot of strange things over his nearly three decades of making chocolate in upstate New York, but as the manager of New York Chocolate and Confection Company, he came up against things he couldn't quite fathom. "These were definitely not businesspeople," says Lamphere of the directors from Côte d'Ivoire. Or at least they were not engaged in any kind of business the fifty-two-year-old Fultonian could understand. Lamphere says that the board of NY3C was dominated by people who also served on the board of the FRC. There were only two members of Lion Capital among the directors but Lamphere says eventually the Ivorians found a way to have them removed.

In the spring of 2004, the Ivorian managers announced that money would soon start to flow into the factory. But Jerry Lamphere was struggling to keep the wolf from the door and his employees paid. He later learned that funds were coming from Côte d'Ivoire but going directly into another account — that of a company called IC Management which was owned and operated by Yalle Agbre, who just happened to be the treasurer for New York Chocolate and Confectionary Company, and one of the directors of the FRC.

Lamphere sent the bills to Lion Capital Management, who sent them to Agbre, who paid them out of his company's account (if they were paid at all). Lamphere has no idea how much money rolled through the operation in this fashion; he heard that the Ivorian media had reported tens of millions of dollars had been doled out to the Fulton plant. If that was the case, Lamphere says, he never saw any of it. "It was just rotten," says Lamphere. "Something stunk."

What was even more peculiar for Lamphere was how the company purchased the beans. Contrary to the claim that they would get cocoa directly from the Ivorian farm gate, NY3C was obliged to buy its beans from U.S. brokers at a premium prices. And the man who was doing the buying was none other than Yalle Agbre. Lamphere wasn't sure the company could really make a go of it without cheaper beans but what was even more vexing was that the beans were of such poor quality. Lamphere couldn't figure it out. Even though his technicians inspected the lots of beans they were buying and tested them, the product that would eventually arrive at the factory was inferior to what they thought they had purchased. Lamphere had contracts to sell cocoa butter to companies such as Hershey, but he was often stuck with bad beans. Who was making money from all of this? Lamphere often asked himself.

Lamphere had managed to hire as many as seventy people and he was actually producing bulk chocolate powder and butter. His profits were just enough to pay the staff. But in March 2006, the employees found their cheques were bouncing. Soon after, the city shut off the factory's water. The company's unpaid tax bills amounted to US$450,000. By the spring of 2006, NY3C was seven million dollars in arrears. A high-level delegation of Ivorians arrived for a tour of the plant at the end of March, and then retreated to Côte d'Ivoire, promising to review the situation. Embarrassed politicians, who had taken part in ribbon-cutting ceremonies and had helped to finance loans and grants to the African company, urged the Ivorians to get their collective act together and at least reimburse the employees for their wages.

Another European Union audit report on the Ivorian *filière* was released in the spring of 2006. It paints a damning picture of the FRC and its cavalier attitude towards even the notion of accountability. The European auditors got hold of Côte d'Ivoire government records revealing that the FRC directors voted to purchase the old Nestlé plant for nine billion West African francs (about US$10 million) without even investigating the plant's viability. The FRC controllers along with their friends in the banks, Bouhoun Bouabré and Victor Nembellisini, went ahead anyway and bought the Fulton plant, investing as much as US$26 million in the doomed chocolate company over the next year (though the Ivorian press claims several times that amount flowed to the chocolate company).

For Kieffer's Network, the purpose of the plant was obvious. The American company, with its veneer of legitimacy, provided a way to transfer money to other concerns, including financing "the war effort." The chocolate makers of Fulton, New York were just hapless pawns.

Now hanging around his home in Fulton, Jerry Lamphere is looking for a new job, or hoping that some serious investors will come to put the plant back on its feet, something he's is convinced is possible. But he shakes his head and wonders about the encounter with the FRC. "I don't know what went on behind the scenes or what they did with the money," says Lamphere. "I don't think the plant was ever supposed to come on line, personally. I think we did things in spite of them and got it operational . . . . I guess they got the wrong people involved in their project. Because all of the staff was just simply dedicated to making chocolate."

~

One day in Abidjan, Ange Aboa takes me to see the boss of one of the most successful, and legitimate, cocoa cooperatives in the country. The man will not let me use his name or refer to anything that might identify him. We'll call him Mr. X.

Mr. X meets us in his garden, a walled and fortified compound that is protected by his security specialists. Even here, in his own yard, he whispers as we talk and he glances over his shoulder from time to time. The fear is palpable. Mr. X was a farmer before he became a successful businessman; he has little education, and despite his fashionable suit he comes across as a bit of a country bumpkin. But he is also one of the most knowledgeable, and reputably honest, people in the business. I ask him to explain how the *filière* really works. Where does the money go? His jaw drops and he emits a little sound, like a squeal. "You want me to tell you how these guys run cocoa? Where is Guy-André Kieffer right now?" he asks wide-eyed, his whispered voice barely audible. "Where is Jean Hélène? [the reporter from Radio France who was shot]. That's what they do to people who ask questions. Can you imagine what they do to those who answer them?"

Ange is able to persuade Mr. X that we are on the level, and the cocoa manager finally agrees to describe the *filière* as he sees it. He explains the evolution of the cocoa hierarchy through the ancient clan system of Côte d'Ivoire. The former president, Houphouët-Boigny, he says, put control of cocoa into the hands of farmers he knew and trusted. These farmers cultivated the land and developed their cocoa expertise while working in the countryside. Other clans, principally the Cru people, functioned as bureaucrats, while still others became experts in commerce. All of this worked, and for many decades there was a system of checks and balances; opportunities for corruption were limited by a widely dispersed control system. It was the genius of Le Vieux, but he is gone and times have changed. "Now the Cru have all the power," says Mr. X. "They invent phony co-ops, they have all the connections to the minister of finance, but they produce nothing. We [the producers] are afraid. We have no power. But we grow all the cocoa."

Money appropriated from the producers in levies is supposed to help them by providing infrastructure and soft loans. But once that money disappears into the network of fictitious agencies, they lose track of it. They no longer have access to subsidies or loans, as they did in the old days. There is no money for basic maintenance of their resource, not even for chemicals and new trees.

"Why don't the farmers refuse to pay the fees?" I ask.

"They try to do that. But they have no choice."

"What would happen to you if you reported all of this?"

"They would kill me," he says. The words are hardly audible. Sweat beads on his forehead.

It's hard to understand the extent to which the state machinery has been undermined by opportunists. A French NGO worker who has lived in Côte d'Ivoire for many years but who also wants to remain anonymous confirms the bitter, frightened analysis of Mr. X. The NGO worker has been all through the country, taking care of migrant workers and trying to shield them from the excesses of the Gbagbo regime. "Think Mafia," he says, simply. "Think Sicily."

Going from one office tower to the next in Abidjan and in the cocoa district, setting up appointments for interviews with secretaries and exchanging official business cards, you get the impression that you are moving within conventionally legitimate state machinery. But outward appearances are misleading. "These are Bushmen who have taken over the levers of power and authority," my NGO friend explains, betraying some of his French chauvinism. He says their veneer of credibility, with all of their rhetoric and official trappings, is false. A foreign businessman who has been in the country for just as long says much the same thing: "There is corruption all over this continent, but here it goes beyond even what is normal in Africa. This is criminal."

GAK became convinced that Côte d'Ivoire's cocoa business had been systematically criminalized. Other foreign observers have been reluctant to embrace his grim analysis. The World Bank and the IMF have suspended funding to Côte d'Ivoire in the past, but as long as the Gbagbo regime keeps up to date on its obligations to international lenders—and allows the cocoa companies to export their precious goods—these bodies seem intent on ignoring evidence of government corruption. Diplomats say privately that there is another reason for international tolerance of obvious corruption in Côte d'Ivoire: As bad as the situation seems to be, it is at least politically stable. Overt criticism might alter that, and West Africa can ill afford another Liberia or Sierra Leone.

And there is another factor. Côte d'Ivoire, according to diplomatic sources, is easy to control from the outside. "It never really stopped being a colony," says one diplomat who studied France's influence in the country. "No matter what Ivorians tell you, they are still in the thrall of Paris."

The European Union has tried to penetrate the murky activities in the cocoa *filière*. The EU began to closely audit the comings and goings of cocoa money in 2002. Kieffer got hold of many of their preliminary reports and circulated the documents widely, while he worked for CCC and after. In those reports, the EU auditors are increasingly frustrated with the lack of transparency and their inability to get access to significant—public—documents. Managers of the *filière* tell the auditors the internal workings of the cocoa trade are none of their business. The cocoa trade is private enterprise, they say. The language of the audits gets more critical in each edition and finally condemns the Ivorian system in the strongest terms the EU can muster, stopping just short of calling the *filière* criminal.

The EU reports reveal a shell game in which the money passes through a maze of agencies and gradually disappears and regards the FRC, the group that subsidizes the Fulton chocolate factory, as the worst of the lot, since it has control of the treasury. The money that is supposed to support a base price for the farmers is diverted first of all for war funds and then to the president's office. The auditors describe a tragic cycle: crushing taxes and fees and arbitrary pricing force farmers to sell their beans illegally in other countries; the government of Côte d'Ivoire recovers the money it is losing in this manner by increasing fees and taxes and by raiding reserve funds that are supposed to improve the lives of farmers and stabilize the prices they get for their product. Farmers increasingly seek their own solutions to escape the exploitation. The resource withers and eventually will die.

The greed of those who are within the circle of political power and influence seems inexhaustible. According to the preliminary investigation by the EU, billions of West African francs are loaned to the president and the defence ministry, loans that are organized by Côte d'Ivoire's finance department and facilitated by the National Investment Bank. Other unusual money transfers include a payment to the Washington World Group of (a public relations firm whose client list included Idi Amin and Saddam Hussein among many tyrants and despots) to lobby for the Ivorian government in the United States. The FRC would tell the auditors nothing about these endeavours, not even agreeing to explain how the agency managed to start up yet another financial institution without ever registering it. The Agricultural Finance Bank (BFA), appears to be the agency that manages the cocoa and coffee treasuries, though no one is clear on who actually owns it or where the money goes.

The EU targets the cocoa *filière* and the Ivorian regime, but Kieffer's reporting went to the heart of the political system. GAK was deeply concerned about the activities of the transnational corporations that had managed to get a stranglehold on the cocoa industry of West Africa. Fifteen foreign corporations control ninety per cent of all the cocoa trade in the country, and a few at the top share a virtual monopoly.

Cargill and Archer Daniels Midland are supreme in both cocoa and coffee and, according to documents Kieffer distributed, they are fiercely competitive for domination in the Ivorian cocoa trade. Cargill's warehouses and cocoa-grinding facilities are prominent throughout Côte d'Ivoire, but nowhere was there a single company representative who would talk to Ange and me. We would make appointments, only to have them cancelled before we arrived. The cocoa industry as a whole is highly competitive and notoriously secretive. Few journalists gain access to its managers.

Based in the farm fields of Minneapolis, Cargill is a massive international corporation and at the same time a family concern, possibly the largest privately owned corporation in the world. Cargill's influence over the food we eat—where it comes from and how it's produced—is staggering. Brewster Kneen, a Canadian agribusiness expert, is one of the few people to penetrate the mysterious conglomerate. In his book *Invisible Giant: Cargill and its Transnational Strategies*, Kneen describes a company whose influence over people's lives is pervasive, but basically unknown. There is hardly a mouthful of food consumed in North America that did not pass through part of its corporate empire.

Cargill has said in the past that its corporate goal is to double in size every five to seven years. Its multi-billion-dollar annual turnover rivals the GDP of all of the poorest sub-Saharan countries put together. Like all transnationals in agriculture, Cargill has helped to persuade countries to abandon food production in favour of export crops, with help from World Bank liberalization schemes that strong-arm developing countries into importing food, principally from transnationals. Cargill's trade in coffee alone is greater than the aggregate GDP of the countries where it buys the coffee. It's one of the world's biggest players in genetically modified foods, and it is fighting strenuously to open African farmland to its scientifically produced seed stock.

Archer Daniels Midland (ADM) is the other dominatrix in international agriculture, and is second only to Cargill in Ivorian cocoa trading. ADM is the largest processor of cocoa beans in the world, manufacturing much of the raw material that becomes the brand name chocolate confections we eat. What ADM does best, though, is play politics. This publicly traded company has been one of the largest recipients of corporate welfare in the United States, much of it through personal suasion in the corridors of power. *Fortune* magazine once called agribusiness "the most manipulated industry on the planet," and few play the game better than ADM.

In his book *Rats in the Grain: The Dirty Tricks and Trials of Archer Daniels Midland, the Supermarket to the World*, American author James Lieber describes the extraordinary influence ADM has had: "Probably no one since the trust chieftains of the late nineteenth and early twentieth centuries has drawn more on the

connection between business and politics or done more to cultivate government officials." Former Canadian prime minister
Brian Mulroney, whose Canada–U.S. Free Trade Agreement
profited U.S. corporations such as ADM, sits on the company's
prestigious board of directors. When Senator Tom Harkin (of the
Harkin-Engel Protocol) was being sued for libel in the early
1990s, the head of ADM put $10,000 into his defence fund.
Harkin is from Iowa, a leading U.S. producer of ethanol, a controversial fuel additive that ADM manufactures. Ethanol kept
ADM "drunk on tax dollars" as one think tank expert noted.
James Lieber discovered that, by the late 1990s, ADM had
become the number one recipient in the United States of all government subsidies to corporations.

While the Washington-based international financial institutions forced Côte d'Ivoire to suspend government subsidies to its
agricultural sector and to dismantle its marketing boards, heavily
subsidized American corporations were able to move in and take
control of the country's cocoa trade. The monopoly over cocoa
and coffee in Côte d'Ivoire means that no indigenous company
can get even a toehold in the business. The transnational corporations encourage overproduction of their commodities throughout the world as a way of keeping the price as low as possible and
discouraging other players. With so little functioning state
machinery in Côte d'Ivoire, and with the small parts that still
exist after liberalization under the sway of corrupt leaders,
Ivorian companies cannot compete. Credit is essential to create
and to run businesses but the giant conglomerates have international guarantees that allow them to borrow at much more competitive rates.

Côte d'Ivoire exports most of its beans raw, since European and
U.S. tariffs on processed foods are so much higher than those on
raw commodities (tariffs that the "liberalized" countries such as
Côte d'Ivoire are not allowed to apply on imports). But even the
little bit of cocoa grinding that is done in Côte d'Ivoire, providing

manufacturing jobs, is shutting down as the giant cocoa companies monopolize the industry and move it to other countries.

How much of Côte d'Ivoire's corruption is because of international meddling and transnational monopolies, and how much is
because of the devious activities of the Ivorian elites? A lot of
people are on the take in Côte d'Ivoire, though global law and
international institutions protect the corporations. The goose
that lays the golden egg is being eviscerated by the greedy.

~

The hotel staff is aghast that a white woman would leave the
premises after dark, but just after midnight, I take a taxi to an
address in one of Abidjan's upscale neighbourhoods, where I am
to meet with a few members of the Network. I know their names
well, since they are in constant contact with each other and I've
been talking with them, in France and Côte d'Ivoire, for some
time. There is no front man anymore, as GAK was, to publicize
their research, but that hasn't deterred them from continuing the
work he started.

The members of the Network are black and white, African
and European. But these days, all members feel equally threatened in Côte d'Ivoire, especially since so little has been done to
find GAK's killers. The official investigation into Kieffer's disappearance is painfully slow, and possibly pointless, according to
those who follow it closely. "Ramaël wants to know, but France
does not," says one man in reference to the French judge conducting the investigation. Ramaël is good, they all agree, but
Côte d'Ivoire is not France, and it's doubtful he will ever get to
the bottom of things.

Kieffer's friends are very disappointed in Canada as well,
believing there was more the Canadian officials could have done
to put pressure on the Ivorian government. France carries a lot
of baggage as the former colonial power, but Canada has unique

abilities in Africa—if its diplomats knew how to use them. (Canadian officials insist they have done all within their power.)

"Guy-André was a fool," one friend in the Network says abruptly. "He was drugged by his need to know everything. He would go to the bars where the *filière* hung out. He knew all their names and their addresses." He hated capitalists, they tell me, which isn't surprising, given his personal politics. "But most of all," one friend declares flatly, "he hated the power of money."

The Network is trying to pick up where Kieffer left off, tracing all the swindles and suspicious deals. A lot of people wonder why they bother. "So what if they can find another person who's lined his pocket with $10,000!" a foreign businessman said to me one day. "They're not going to change anything. No one cares. Guy-André Kieffer lost his life for nothing." But some kind of spell has been cast by Kieffer's obsession, perhaps not unlike the force field Henry Nevinson created more than a hundred years earlier. Maybe the cocoa *filière* will be exposed in Côte d'Ivoire as it was in São Tomé. Of course, then the big international cocoa companies will just move on to other countries, where they will start again.

Yet in this nocturnal conversation with the Network, I feel more and more drawn in to the circle, a reticent member of the secret sect. They pass me documents and feed me names and information, much of which is obscure. A swirl of intrigue envelops us, like the steamy, oppressive tropical air. The Network constantly reminds me about discretion, to be careful what I say and to whom, something Kieffer was incapable of doing.

"But how do I know when I've crossed the line?" I ask.

"You crossed it when you came to Côte d'Ivoire."

Chapter Twelve

BITTERSWEET **VICTORY**

"I have heard that people may become dependent on us for
food . . . If you are looking for a way to get people to lean on you
and to be dependent on you, in terms of their cooperation with
you, it seems to me that food dependence would be terrific."
— U.S. Senator Hubert Humphrey, 1957

"Foreign aid is a method by which the United States maintains
a position of influence and control around the world."
— U.S. President John F. Kennedy, 1961

"Let us remember that the main purpose of aid is not to
help other nations but to help ourselves."
— U.S. President Richard Nixon, 1968

Leaving the chaos of Belize City's airport, with
its crush of tourists and ubiquitous billboards for Nestlé products,
the tiny fifteen-seat twin-prop plane lifts off into the hazy tropical
sunshine and turns south. The verdant jade green jungle clings to
the slopes of the Mayan Mountains below, while on the far side of
the plane the sparkling aquamarine of the Caribbean vanishes over
a distant horizon. The shallow coastal waters of Belize, with the
hemisphere's longest barrier reef, nourish an extraordinary universe
of marine life: tropical fish, sea anemones, manatees. A scattering of
limestone *cayes* and tiny islands are today a refuge for fishermen, as
they once sheltered the ships of a more predatory breed long ago.

English buccaneers and pirates once hid out in these flashing bays and tropical lagoons, waiting to plunder the Spanish galleons departing the New World, their holds filled to overflowing with wealth stolen by conquistadors from the land and the people they discovered here. With no empire particularly interested in the swampy, forested territory from southern Yucatán to the "Mosquito Coast" of Nicaragua, it eventually became British Honduras. The region has been fully independent, and named Belize, since 1981.

Pirates ruled for years, but gradually British merchants discovered the potential in the area's natural resources: the logwood tree, used in making dyes for fabrics; mahogany for furniture; sugar; citrus fruit. British colonists moved over from Jamaica and set up thriving business enterprises.

In time, the Baymen, as they came to be known, lost the market for logwood—artificial dyes provided cheap alternatives to the rainforest product—so they pushed further into the interior in search of new sources of wealth, eventually settling the area and becoming the colonial overlords of an English-speaking outpost in a world dominated by Hispanics. National and linguistic differences notwithstanding, English overlords or Spanish, there was one common feature that defined the mercantile adventures in the New World: forced labour.

Africans, not Baymen, did the hard work in the most horrendous conditions imaginable. Much of low-lying Belize's jungles are insect-infested swamp; the lumber camps where the slaves lived were built on bogs. There was often not enough to eat. Countless thousands of Africans died of hunger and disease. Many committed suicide.

While Africans lost their lives providing mahogany for chairs and tables in Britain, the native Maya of Belize managed to avoid the British slave-drivers. For centuries they had successfully dodged the outsiders or, when confronted, managed to fight them off. Their knowledge of the difficult terrain, and of bush-fighting tactics, served them well, and to this day they remain relatively independent people.

Since the time of Montezuma, this region has yielded some of the best cocoa beans in the Americas. Yet neither the Spanish nor the British seemed particularly interested in developing the potential for cocoa agriculture—lumbering was more lucrative. For hundreds of years, the Maya of Belize cultivated cocoa for trade only among themselves and for their own use. Women still prepare the traditional foaming hot-chili-and-spice cocoa drink that the Olmec passed on to them two thousand years ago, though they now create the bubbly top with the aid of the Spanish-style *molinillo* and not by pouring the liquid back and forth between jugs. The lush forests still produce a number of wild cocoa trees, just as they did before the conquistadors. But outsiders never seemed to notice the cocoa. Until recently.

After a few brief stops, the plane lands on the tar and gravel patchwork airstrip of Punta Gorda, the largest "city" in the south. It likely took Hernán Cortés many days to pass through these dense jungles when he was chasing his imperial dream, plunging through the alligator swamps and poisonous thickets, overcoming snakes and scorpions, not to mention the resistance of the proud and hostile Maya people, who would bow their heads to no intruder. Now there's air service and a (mostly) paved highway that extends all the way from Belize City, ending abruptly here, twenty kilometres from the Guatemalan border.

Punta Gorda, or PG, as local people affectionately call the sleepy settlement, is little more than a post office, a pier, a park with a clock tower that stopped keeping time long ago, a hospital and a smattering of small cafés and hotels for the few tourists who manage to penetrate this far. The tourist beaches and world-famous snorkelling destinations are in northern Belize. Visitors tend to avoid the swampy jungles of the south. The hardy few who come are interested in trekking into the bush to see Mayan culture as it was, or to experience one of the last relatively pristine places on the planet. Many visitors are simply waiting for the next water taxi that will transport them to Guatemala.

Gregor Hargrove is a bit of an anomaly here. He lives and works in Punta Gorda but has no connection to tourism and not much to do with the other foreigners. His office is on the main drag of PG, in an L-shaped concrete building designed simply to keep the sun, wind and rain out. A few small windows and the door are always left open for ventilation, except during hurricane season, but this also means that the noise from the street overwhelms conversations on market days, when people from outlying villages pour in to the town in brightly coloured buses.

Hargrove's office is a hub of activity: farmers and farm bureaucrats drop in to chat with the man who runs the region's cocoa trade; peddlers sell him everything from warm buns to fresh fish; children come to ask if Hargrove has any chewing gum (he usually does). The phone rings constantly, but often the calls are from a woman whose husband runs the shop next door, where there is no phone. Behind Hargrove's makeshift desk are shelves piled with notes and books about agriculture in general and cocoa in particular, the recorded wisdom of regional farming gleaned by foreign agronomists over time. An American Peace Corps volunteer in the office is diligently attempting to record an inventory of all the cocoa farms in what's known as the Toledo district, the area surrounding Punta Gorda.

Hargrove seems familiar to a visitor from Canada. There's something in his demeanour and his accent—something decidedly Maritime-Canadian. And sure enough, he reveals that he hails from the Saint John River area of New Brunswick. Then there's the question of his name: one that's familiar to Canadians who follow the affairs of the Canadian Auto Workers Union and its high-profile president, Buzz Hargrove. Gregor is Buzz's cousin. The name and the birthplace might suggest a disposition towards social activism and Gregor Hargrove doesn't disagree, but he has a clear-eyed view of the potential for social development in a well-run business.

"I watched the area where I grew up go from poor to prosperity because of the McCains," Hargrove says. The McCains are a powerful East Coast family that is often criticized for its economic dominance in New Brunswick's agriculture and for a chemically dependant potato monoculture in the northwest of the province. But Hargrove argues that the province of his birth has done well by the McCains. They never tried to own the land but just to buy its bounty from the farmers. They processed the produce in the region, transforming millions of tons of potatoes into precut frozen french fries right next to the fields from which they came. "It's better to manufacture than to export raw goods," Hargrove explains. "We shipped out coal, we shipped out logs, we shipped out unprocessed fish, we shipped out people," he says of the Maritimes. But not the spuds. The McCains' approach to business, he says, allowed people to stay on their land and share in the prosperity.

Hargrove ran his own successful timber business in New Brunswick. The work was hard. His wife died of cancer when his children were young, and he struggled with the burdens of single parenthood. He promised himself that once he'd weathered all the storms, fulfilled his responsibilities, he would leave—find something meaningful to do with the rest of his life. Time passed, his children grew, and life settled down and, in fact, became quite dull. One day he saw a job posting on a bulletin board from CUSO (Canadian University Service Overseas), offering work in Belize to mature people with business expertise. It sounded like the opportunity he'd dreamed of: a chance to make a difference in the world.

"I thought I had died and gone to heaven," Hargrove says of the day he arrived in Belize. He was paid only a pittance, but it was enough for food and a car. When that job ended, he went to work on a UNESCO contract studying the barrier reef. Then there was a stint with the Audubon Society, examining the tourist potential of bird sanctuaries. In 2001, Hargrove's work sent him to the outback of Belize, where he met the elusive natives of the region. He spent a lot of time in the remote and relatively undeveloped Toledo district around Punta Gorda, where the majority of people are Mayan farmers. One topic dominated conversation. "All the people were talking about was cocoa and the cocoa market," says Hargrove. He knew nothing about the industry or the long Mayan history with the beans, but he was intrigued by what they were saying. The farmers were convinced there was a ready and growing market for whatever amount of cocoa they could grow. But they were nervous about investing any further. The Toledo farmers had been burned before.

In the early 1990s, Mayan farmers in the region had started to grow premium cocoa for a British company called Green & Black's. The company, however, was getting more than a bit frustrated with what they perceived as a lack of business acumen on the part of the Belizeans. The Toledo growers were coping with too many problems, not least of which was a lack of organization. They had a fledgling co-operative, the Toledo Cacao Growers Association (TCGA), to represent them in their dealings with the outside world, but it was no match for the dealers in the volatile cocoa industry.

Hargrove realized that, if the farmers didn't get some real help, they would probably lose the contract they had signed with Green & Black's. He had been planning to move on from Belize after the Audubon job, but there was something about the Maya that reminded him of the people he had grown up with back home in the Maritimes. The communities were tightly knit and reluctant to challenge accepted wisdom. "Mayan families are very large," observes Hargrove, who was the oldest of eleven children. "Well, they're no bigger than at home, but the connections are like the Saint John River Valley and how Cape Breton used to be. And whether you believe what your extended family member is saying or not, they're your family." The farmers needed to take control of their affairs, and they needed a hard-nosed business type with knowledge of how things are done in the "white" world. Hargrove took over the management of TCGA.

The Toledo farmers were mostly Maya from the tribes of Mopan and Kekchi, descendants of the clans that the Dominican friars of the sixteenth century had sent back to Spain along with the first samples of *cacahuatl* to show Prince Philip. Bartolomé de Las Casas had found the Kekchi difficult four hundred years ago, and Hargrove found them no less obstreperous when he started working with them in 2003. Some of the farmers welcomed him, but he also made enemies as he began to fire incompetents and hire people he thought might regard the organization as a business and not a social club. It was a harsh blow, coming from a foreigner who had never seen a cocoa tree before he arrived in Belize.

In the backwoods of Toledo, progress is spotty. The road to San Pedro Columbia, at the foot of the Mayan Mountains, is a potholed lane that meanders through many villages. Houses are built of thatch and wood and occasionally the more expensive stucco. Some have electricity; others are lit by lamps. Most evening activity is around the small cookhouses, where wives and daughters prepare meals of rice and beans, much as they have since before the conquistadors came.

Cocoa is still a large part of the Mayan culture in the villages, and people cultivate some of it for their own consumption. When the beans are harvested, the children suck the sweet pulp when they get a chance, while men stroll around with pockets full of dried beans, shelling and eating them like peanuts. Armando Choco, an administrator of the TGCA, still looks forward to the chili-spiked chocolate drink his mother prepares for the family once a week. A native woman hauls out a bar of solid chocolate from Guatemala. She drops pieces of the hard confection into boiling water to make a drink, just as Cortés had seen women like her do centuries ago. But the little general store in San Miguel also sells Kit Kats, Nestlé's Crunch and Mr. Big, while the Punta Gorda supermarket is awash with foreign cocoa products, including Hershey's. If you want cocoa prepared the ancient Mayan way, you have to make it yourself.

At the first annual meeting of the TCGA after Hargrove took over, nearly five times as many farmers turned out as were in attendance at previous gatherings. "We had 350 people," recalls Hargrove. "They were in the streets and everywhere. It was a hard meeting, and they were asking hard questions."

Nothing was going to happen unless everybody pulled together, he told them, with Justino Peck, a local farmer and chairman of the TCGA board, at his side. The office would be open every day, unlike in the past, when most of the time there was no one running the shop. All transactions would be done fairly. Nobody would work for nothing, Hargrove promised. "So we opened her up and kept it going, and they started coming in. It just kept growing."

Hostility towards outsiders runs deep, originating with the Maya's first contact with Europeans centuries ago. From marauding conquistadors to British merchants, their memories are of exploitation and abuse that moderated only slightly after the British outlawed slavery in the 1830s.

Belize turned to American markets for its trade relationships and, by the 1950s, the entire region was a patchwork of mostly U.S. transnational businesses stitched on the tattered blanket of colonialism. As was the case in Africa, the national borders in Central America were arbitrary, configured by the needs of empires, with little bearing on historical and tribal realities. The term "banana republic," coined for neighbouring Honduras, came into general usage in the region.

Following years of logging as the prime industry, agriculture finally emerged as an important source of exports for Belize: citrus fruit, bananas, sugar and, slowly but surely, cocoa. In the 1970s,

U.S. food companies moved in to exploit the British colony's resources. One of them was the Hershey Chocolate Company of Pennsylvania.

American chocolate-makers, who had been importing cocoa beans from Ghana, wanted supplies of cocoa closer to home, in countries under the direct sway of American foreign policy, principally those subjected to the regional hegemony of the Monroe doctrine. Hershey's managers inherited their founder's obsession with having secure sources of raw material, and they began to look seriously at the original source of *Theobroma*, the area south of the Yucatán Peninsula. Streets in Hershey, Pennsylvania, bear the names of old-time cocoa-producing regions: Aruba, Caracas and Granada—locations where much of the cocoa production had been struck down by overproduction and disease. If Hershey could develop a hybrid tree that was impervious to witches' broom, capsid and pod rot, then it would not only guarantee supply but also gain an important advantage in a growing field of competitors.

Belize excited American corporations such as Hershey for many reasons: it was near the United States; it was underpopulated and undeveloped; there was virgin land and good soil; people spoke English; the natives were docile; and Belize was politically stable, unlike the dictatorships of the other countries in Central America. Cocoa production in Belize was small, limited to local production. It was wide open for corporations that wanted to build on the homegrown operations. The Belizean government allowed for a hundred per cent foreign ownership of any business enterprise in the country, and offered an exemption from import duties and extended tax holidays. It was exactly the sort of place the Hershey Chocolate Company was looking for.

Hummingbird Hershey Limited became a Belize-based enterprise dedicated to developing hybrid cocoa trees and providing them to the farms of producers interested in growing for Hershey. The tree nursery and plantation soon stretched for hundreds of acres along the Sibun River, near the principal artery, the

Hummingbird Highway. Hershey would not only produce cocoa from the hybrid stock but also conduct research and train local producers.

One might have expected that Mayan farmers who had cultivated *Theobroma* for thousands of years would know a thing or two about growing cocoa. But Hershey was not interested in the slowpoke farming methods of yore. The old-fashioned Criollo tree stock that grew naturally would be dug up in favour of cultivars that would yield many times as many beans as the native species. Hummingbird specialists said they could plant the new trees close together in order to increase productivity per acre. The scientists told the farmers that the horticultural assumption that cocoa trees needed shade was not entirely true. *Theobroma* could actually grow in full sun, without a canopy of other trees, although such growing conditions were possible only with much larger amounts of chemical fertilizers and pesticides. Industrial farming of this nature and scale would cost money, of course, but loans would be provided.

The 1970s saw some of the highest prices for cocoa beans in the history of the international market, up to US$5,300 per ton, and the Belizean government was anxious to get its share of the pie. Of course, there was the problem of land ownership— Mayan Indians had reservations and had never owned their own property—but over time the government could resolve that. The important thing was to take advantage of this opportunity that Hershey was offering. Given the spike in cocoa prices, the farmers had few qualms about the Hummingbird Cocoa project, and many of them soon became involved.

The Maya of Toledo, in particular, wanted a piece of the action. To circumvent land ownership issues, they came together as a collective—the TCGA. The farmers were shocked, a few years after they planted their trees in the early 1980s, when the price for cocoa tumbled to a low of $1,530 a ton. But the World Bank issued an influential report in 1986 anticipating that cocoa prices would soon reverse the downward trend. The farmers of Toledo had no idea that Félix Houphouët-Boigny's Ivorian miracle was at this point falling apart as the international market flooded with cocoa, much to the delight of the transnationals. All the industry players reassured the farmers that this was a small black spot on an otherwise rosy outlook.

Part of the optimism came from the knowledge that U.S. government policies and programs were offering influential incentives for Belizean cocoa. A driving force behind cocoa production in Belize was the United States Agency for International Development (USAID), an important tool of U.S. foreign policy. For all the material benefits available to needy clients, USAID has never been in doubt about its priorities, unsubtly described in 1961 by John F. Kennedy as being to "advance the political and economic interests of the United States."

The USAID bureaucracy has also had controversial links to the Central Intelligence Agency and, though regularly denied, a history of links to subterfuge in Southeast Asia during the Vietnam War, in Central America during unrest in Nicaragua and El Salvador, and in Afghanistan during the occupation by the Soviet Union. Whatever else it might be, USAID is an instrument of political and economic influence wherever U.S. interests lie.

In the late 1980s, USAID and the conservative Pan American Development Foundation (PADF), a sub-agency of USAID, joined forces with Hershey and the Belizean Department of Agriculture to launch the Accelerated Cocoa Project, a program to push more farmers into hybrid tree production faster. Documents and transcripts from an extensive three-day conference in Belize in 1988 reveal the degree to which the big players were sugar-coating the commercial possibilities in the cocoa industry. The event was billed as the first Belize National Cocoa Forum, and it was convened in the capital, Belmopan, to discuss "the problems and opportunities" in the cocoa industry. All the players were there: Hershey; the foreign aid agencies (the event was funded by USAID); the government, including the prime minister; and the farmers. Given the promises and commitments offered at the forum, the Toledo Cacao Growers, who were present, must have come away feeling quite hopeful.

The highlight of the event was an apparent corporate and government commitment to Belizean farmers. The record shows that, throughout the conference, Hummingbird Hershey made it clear it would purchase "all cocoa produced in Belize" and would pay $1.70 a pound for properly fermented and dried beans. Attempts to secure a commitment from Hershey that this was a guaranteed price were brushed aside. The company promised it would always pay the market price for all the beans and since worldwide demand for cocoa was increasing and Hershey's demand for cocoa was not about to decrease, there was nothing to worry about. At least, not in the sunny atmosphere of the cocoa forum.

The Belizean minister of agriculture took the podium at one point to reassure farmers that, while prices for cocoa may have been in a slump at the time, there was "no need for despair." With Hershey's guarantee, and the quality of Belizean cocoa, what could go wrong? The only hope for success for the time being, said the minister, was to change local farming practices and implement the accelerated cocoa project Hershey and its financial backers recommended. The farmers "must plant the improved hybrid varieties and apply the recommended cultural practices," he told them. Father knows best.

A Belizean government representative eventually took the stage to announce the most tantalizing tid-bit: Belize was negotiating a US$20 million loan with the World Bank in order to transform the rainforests of the country into productive cocoa farms. With two of the most influential agencies in the world onside and convinced of the wisdom of the cocoa project, no Toledo farmer was in a position to argue.

Of course, the dream could be realized only if the farmers did their part, and that meant they would have to borrow—a lot. The

Development Finance Corporation (DFC), a Belizean government agency that provides credit to entrepreneurs, was standing
by to provide the financing but only under certain conditions:
every farmer would have to spend at least three days at Hummingbird Hershey being trained in the new farming methods; the
farmers would have to offer their land and all their assets as collateral for loans; they would have to use the new hybrid stock, with
its dependence on expensive chemicals (for the purchase of
which they could borrow more money); and they would have to
use crop husbandry policies that the international agencies recommended.

The problem for the Toledo Maya was that they had no collateral for loans because they didn't own their land as individuals.
So the lending agencies provided "crop loans," using other commodities from their collective farming operations, such as rice, as
security, and they encouraged the Maya to acquire additional
land outside their reserves so they would have new collateral for
their loans (even though the farmers would have to borrow in
order to buy this land). Interest rates were twelve per cent, a staggering figure for a government lending agency that was promoting economic development. But, according to the DFC, it was
consistent with international lending rates.

For the accelerated cocoa production, the farmers would
require chemicals such as the herbicide paraquat—dubbed
by environmentalists as one of the "dirty dozen" of toxic
agrochemicals—and U.S.–produced Roundup. Conference delegates questioned the environmental consequences of these
advanced farming methods. One delegate, Erasmo Franklin,
provided one of the few dissenting voices when he blurted out:
"The Hummingbird landscape is being raped . . . the waterways
are being polluted by pesticide and nitrates (fertilizers). It ends
up being a risk/benefit thing. Do we die of hunger or put nitrites
in our water?"

There was no answer.

Gordon Patterson, listed in the program as a Hershey scientist, urged the farmers to cultivate new markets for their cocoa—possibly a rhetorical device: "We encourage you to seek other buyers, to encourage a competitive market. It's the only way that you can convince yourself that you are getting a good deal from us."

A government agriculture spokesman reassured the farmers they had nothing to worry about. "Cherish the guaranteed market with Hummingbird Hershey!" said Albert Williams. "If the projections made by the World Bank prove to be true, Belize has a good future in cocoa."

~

The Toledo farmers were hugely in debt by the time their Hershey hybrid *Theobroma* was ready for harvest in the early 1990s. U.S. government agencies were long gone by then, leaving the farmers to work out the details of their relationship with their corporate customer. It's possible that some of the people who created Hummingbird Hershey genuinely thought they were offering an economic gift to southern Belize. Plant scientists and agronomists had worked closely with the farmers to grow new trees and to increase the yields. But there is no one left today to explain what they were trying to accomplish, or if any of them knew that predictions of an upturn in cocoa profits were absurd.

Hummingbird Hershey was willing to fulfill its commitment to buy all the beans Belize could produce for "market prices." In 1988, when the company made its promises to a room full of producers in Belmopan, it was offering $1.70 a pound. The price soon dropped to $1.25 in the early 1990s, then to $0.90, then to $0.70. When Hershey was willing to pay no more than $0.55 a pound in 1993, the farmers realized they were sunk. "It no longer made sense even to harvest the crop," says Mayan farmer Justino Chiac of the TCGA. The farmers simply left the cocoa in the fields to rot.

Their obligations weren't so easy to dispose of. All the loans were coming due now that the trees had reached maturity, but with the collapse in prices no one had money to repay their debts. The Maya left home in search of work, picking citrus or sugar cane, in order to finance their payments. They lost land, savings and whatever was left of their faith in international agencies and cocoa companies. By 1993, the TCGA was bankrupt. And the dream of escaping poverty through the miracle crop that their ancestors had farmed two thousand years before was shattered.

Enter Green & Black's.

~

Craig Sams is a leader in the fastest-growing sector of packaged foods in the world—organics. Riding the wave of consumers obsessed with an antiglobalization, small-is-beautiful ethos, Sams scours the world from his home base of Hastings in southeastern England, looking for new products to sell to the "green"-minded consumer. In 1987 while travelling in southern Belize, he had come across small numbers of indigenous farmers who still cultivated native-grown Criollo cocoa trees with the methods they inherited from the Olmec three millennia ago—no fertilizers or pesticides, a cover of rainforest trees overhead and organic mulch around the base. All of this tradition was consistent with what the developed world now calls organic, for which consumers are willing to pay a premium price. Sams made some notes in his diary for later consideration. Mayan cocoa was not only ecologically encouraging, but also had enormous commercial potential. Rainforest products, in particular, have a special cachet for the ethical consumer.

Craig Sams is a sixty-something American-born Englishman and a pioneer of the macrobiotic food industry. He opened one of the first organic foods restaurants in London and started one of the earliest natural food stores, selling ginseng, miso and aduki beans to a growing market of health food addicts. In the 1970s, Sams and his brother launched their Whole Earth brand, starting with simple brown rice and eventually extending to a line of sugar-free organic cola, peanut butter, tomato-free spaghetti sauce, baked beans and bread.

Most of the food revolutionaries of the flower-power generation had grown up on a diet of canned vegetables, cheese slices, white bread sandwiches and marshmallow jelly moulds, all made from products processed in the factories of big agribusiness. Their revolt was against industrialized corporate agriculture and the pesticide-laden nutrient-depleted diet that most people consumed in the post-war years.

Sams had been an advocate of the counterculture since his youth, but he was also a shrewd businessman with a flair for publicity and an uncanny knack for marketing to the food obsessed. Soon he had his organic brand in the major grocery store chains of Great Britain, where many traditional customers hadn't quite fathomed oregano and chili powder, let alone sea salt and kelp. Sams was often ahead of the latest food trend, baking whole wheat bread and making fruit juice–sweetened jams just as the mainstream medical world began to warn that a diet of white flour and refined sugar could give you stomach cancer, heart disease or, at the very least, chronic constipation.

Getting chocolate into the shopping baskets of nutrition-obsessed Birkenstock-wearers, however, took special skill.

It was Craig Sams's wife, Josephine Fairley, who pushed the idea of moving into the lucrative chocolate trade with an organic alternative. Her husband was reticent, since a large part of the Whole Earth marketing strategy was that their food was all sugar-free, except for the natural sweetness of fruit juices. "All our packaging boasted 'no sugar added,'" says Sams, "so there was no way we could use this well-respected non-sugar brand for a product that was thirty per cent sugar." But Fairley was convinced that they would be fools not to find a way to sell specialty organic cocoa, given that chocolate was an obsession with so many people, particularly women, who are also the most likely to buy ethical products.

Fairley had sold her house when she married Sams in 1991. Now she invested her money in producing a new label under which they could market organic chocolate. Choosing a name was a challenge. "We dismissed the obvious 'green' names such as Ecochoc, Biochoc, Nature's Choc or Chocorganico," says Sams. They settled for one that resonated with establishment connections: Green & Black's. "It sounded like something that had been around for a long time and was resolutely English." The name had green in it for the ecologically minded, and black connoted the seventy per cent cocoa content the organic chocolate would have.

Finding a source of organic chocolate was much more difficult. Throughout the world, the hyper-productivity of mass-market cocoa meant there was hardly a tree standing that had not been raised on a diet of synthetic fertilizers and protected from disease by regular showers of toxic pesticides. To have a product certified organic requires adherence to very strict criteria for cultivation— basically, zero synthetic chemical input in the production process.

Green & Black's lucked out in Togo, where the French government was funding a pilot project for chemical-free cocoa trees in its former colony. Togo is a narrow slice of a country, sandwiched between Ghana and Benin on the Bay of Guinea. It had been the fiefdom of assorted military dictators since the days when Craig Sams was first selling tofu to London's hippies. The French eco-project was a guilt-ridden effort to try to reverse some of the environmental degradation from colonization, and the project was run well enough for Green & Black's to win it the blessing of the rigorous British Soil Association (the agency that verifies organic standards in the United Kingdom).

In 1991, Green & Black's organic seventy-per-cent-cocoa chocolate bar started rolling off the assembly line at a factory in

France, where high-end chocolate is a specialty. The product was an instant hit, and Sams soon had his bars in major supermarket chains as well as at the high-end gourmet chocolate counters at Harvey Nichols and Harrods. Green & Black's played the ethical card to the hilt, putting out the message that it was paying a premium price for the cocoa beans while allowing African farmers a chemical-free environment. The company won the Ethical Consumers Award and got support from the Women's Environmental Network by claiming that Togolese matriarchs were the main beneficiaries. A headline in the *Independent* stated: "Right On!—And It Tastes Good, Too."

But the volatile world of African politics soon caught up with the makers of eco-chocolate. Fraudulent elections in 1993 led to violence in and around Togo's capital city, Lomé. France froze its aid to the country as opposition leaders mobilized a national strike that crippled commerce and shut down Togo's exports. On a West African scale, it was a minor dust-up, but it seriously affected Green & Black's operation. The company had contracts with clients who didn't accept revolution as an excuse for delayed shipments. "We had to fly a container of cocoa beans out to our co-packer in France and then fly the freshly made chocolate to Gatwick Airport, where a van was waiting to rush it to make our two-thirty delivery slot at Sainsbury's [one of the major grocery chains in the U.K.]," recalls Sams.

Green & Black's began to ease out of its contract with the Togolese while looking around for a more peaceful cocoa country, where the natives might be less restless. Sams remembered his encounter with the Maya in the 1980s, Could the Maya grow enough organic chocolate for Sams' U.K. market?

Sams and Fairley learned that the farmers of Toledo had taken on a contract to grow commercial cocoa for Hershey, but the deal had gone bust at just about the same time as the Togolese were fighting in the streets. So things were wide open in the Belizean cocoa industry. There was only one problem.

The Mayan farmers had accepted Hershey's advice and planted the chemically sodden hybrid trees. To grow organic Criollo beans for Green & Black's, they would have to change their ways—in fact, return to the practices of their ancestors but on a commercial scale. Craig Sams rang up Justino Peck, president of the TCGA, to ask if this was feasible.

Peck gave Sams a sense of just how bad things had become since Hummingbird Hershey pulled out. "This was a disaster. People were abandoning their plantations, and the jungle was taking over." Sams says. So he offered the TCGA a deal. Green & Black's would make the Toledo farmers a principal supplier with a rolling five-year contract for organically grown cocoa, and they would get $1.75 a pound (a little more than the amount Hershey initially offered and a long way from the disastrous $0.55 it was willing to pay at the end). Green & Black's would get organic certification for the TCGA so that even if the U.K. firm pulled out they could still take advantage of Europe's premium cocoa market, and Sams would give the association $20,000 in start-up cash. The TCGA was understandably skeptical, and at first its members resisted. But Toledo was not a place with a lot of options, especially for the Maya, and many of the farmers eventually agreed to the deal.

Green & Black's decided to go one step further and produce a brand-name chocolate bar called Maya Gold. Of course, the Maya would not make the chocolate or even grind the beans— those high-paying jobs would go to manufacturers in Europe. But Sams and Fairley declared that the new Maya Gold label would have another exclusive property: It would not be just a certified organic chocolate bar, it would also be declared a "fair trade" product.

The nascent fair trade initiative was the most recent development in the growing consumer consciousness movement of Europe and North America. Backed by Oxfam, Christian Aid and the Women's Institute in the United Kingdom, it provides a stamp of approval—a fair trade logo—for goods that are bought from manufacturers in the developing world for what is considered (by the fair trade foundation) to be a fair price. For a product to be certified as "fair" requires an even more rigorous screening process than the organic certification. It must be made with no abusive labour practices, in particular no child or slave labour. Chemicals can be used in the growing or manufacturing of a product so long as workers are provided with adequate protective clothing and air quality (though chemicals are disallowed by the organic certifiers). An additional fair trade premium is paid to the cooperative or company, which is supposed to be used communally, to build clean water systems or provide schooling for the children of workers. But the most important aspect of the fair trade system is that it gives people in the developing world some advantage in the amoral jungle of supply and demand where the profit motive reigns supreme.

Maya Gold was launched in March 1994. In addition to being organic, it was the first product to be stamped by the Fairtrade Foundation's logo in the U.K. Food reviewers declared that the bar had an exceptional flavour, a wisp of orange and spice accents in a complex dark chocolate.

High quality is a small part of the battle for the fickle consumer in the ruthless world of product placement. The fair trade label was far more important in many respects than the superior taste of the chocolate. Green & Black's held a press conference to announce its major development in ethical luxury, while the BBC sent a news crew to Belize to produce a documentary on the Mayan farmers who were producing the beans. Among the plethora of choices available to the U.K. consumer, there was now a chocolate they could eat with the satisfying confidence that it was, in the judgment of Oxfam, principled. The name Maya Gold had cachet, evoking images of a mysterious tribe that once governed with an advanced culture and sensibility in the lush tropics of the New World. The fact that the British Empire had reduced the natives of Belize to bare-knuckled subsistence after several centuries of looting, killing and subjugation was more information than anyone would care to read on a cleverly branded product.

The Belizean farmers receive roughly six pence for every bar sold at £1.60 in retail stores in the United Kingdom. It's not much, though it is several times what non–fair trade cocoa pays. The farmers' income is not the real reason for fair trade's success and Craig Sams is among the first to admit that the popularity of ethical purchasing is more about the consumer than the producer: "Consumers don't want to be part of a problem. They want manufacturers to help them be part of the solution to these problems and to relieve their feelings of despair, pessimism and helplessness over the disappearance of rainforests and indigenous cultures and global warming."

Even if the whole operation was geared more to assuaging First-World guilt than benefiting developing-world farmers, Sams did not let the farmers down. He bought every one of their beans over the coming years and paid his set price no matter what happened to cocoa beans on the open market, plus the fair trade premium of ten per cent. The British Department for International Development intially warned the Toledo farmers not to get involved in yet another (probably) ill-fated cocoa growing project, but with a few years of success, the DFIF heartily approved of it, giving the Toledo venture a grant of nearly US$500,000. The farmers of TCGA slowly returned to traditional farming, nurturing their old tree stock back into existence and growing Criollo varieties without chemicals.

Other international agencies such as the UN had also initially tried to discourage the Maya from going along with the Green & Black's venture, dismissing the project as doomed. The market for premium beans was too small, they argued. If the farmers wanted to grow cocoa, they should return to the high-volume mass market; it was hoped that the price would increase in a few years. But by 2001, naysayers were hard to find. The World Bank produced a report about cocoa-growing in Central America, a document that was never released, admitting that Craig Sams had done wonders for the Toledo area. The farmers were producing the highest-quality cocoa in the region, mostly because the guaranteed price allowed them to develop proper fermenting and drying techniques. Elsewhere in Central America, said the report, farmers didn't bother with quality since it made no difference to the price. The Maya of Belize now had an edge on the whole region.

With their added income, most of the Toledo farmers began sending their children to school again in such numbers that Punta Gorda had to provide a regular bus service. High school enrolment has increased from ten per cent of the community's children to seventy per cent today. But no matter how much life improves, the Maya will never do more than grow the beans that others make into chocolate. Tariff barriers in Europe prohibit finished food products from entering the country: Only raw materials are imported, ensuring that consumers get the products they want and European workers get the manufacturing jobs they need. Until that changes and the Maya can export more than just their beans, they will never be wealthy enough to buy the expensive chocolate bar that bears their name.

~

Green & Blacks was a runaway success by the early 2000s, but Craig Sams knew he needed capital if the company was to keep expanding. "I had pretty well gone as far as I could with our limited financial resources, and we needed to become increasingly professional," says Sams. The counterculture maverick of the food industry now needed establishment types to keep his products in the market. Enter William Kendall.

Kendall was not part of the mod scene in London during the 1960s as Sams had been, but instead part of a savvy new generation who have become major players in the organic food industry in the United Kingdom. Kendall is a London-based businessman who entered the highly competitive prefabricated organic soup market when he took over management of a product called New Covent Garden Soup. He was only in his late twenties when he transformed the loss-making enterprise into a corporation with an annual turnover of US$20 million. Kendall and his partner made a hefty profit when they sold the soup firm in 1997, allowing them to purchase one of the fastest-growing organic lines in the U.K., a chocolate company called Green & Black's.

By then, Green & Black's was doing well in the U.S. market. It was even providing stiff competition to America's bestselling organic chocolate bar, Newman's Own, a product line founded by the legendary Hollywood actor Paul Newman and managed by his daughter. Newman's Own, like other products he has launched, has additional moral clout because Newman gives all of his profits to charity. Another major American competitor, Endangered Species Chocolate, funds wildlife protection. In this tough struggle for guilt-based consumer loyalty, Green & Black's Maya Gold, branded as both organic and fair trade, increased its market penetration in the United States thanks to the flint-eyed business acumen of the new majority shareholder.

Kendall is in all respects the new face of the organic world, swapping Birkenstocks for brogues and counterculture hangouts for corporate boardrooms. He owns a three-hundred-acre organic farm in Suffolk but declares that he is a businessman—a venture capitalist—who just happens to be interested in organic and fair trade products. He doesn't see any contradiction between the values of the antiglobalization movement and the ethos of the corporate world. Business is always a tricky balance between morality and acquisition—some would say an impossible one— and many have faltered in the past. Surely the Cadbury family believed themselves to be ethical traders looking to offer people improved working conditions in Bournville while providing a

cup of hot cocoa as an alternative to gin? Yet the Cadburys were
ultimately roasted on the same spit as all the other slave traders of
the British Empire.

In 2002, William Kendall wanted more capital to run Green
& Black's, so he made a deal with a new shareholder. Cadbury
Schweppes bought five per cent of the company in its bid to
move into the lucrative market of the conscientious consumer.
The idealists who invented organics and fair trade accused
Kendall of selling out, but he argues it was just good business.
Craig Sams defended the deal as well: "We are learning a lot
from them about the cacao market . . . and they are learning a
lot from us about organics, fair trade and corporate responsibility.
I suppose, indeed I hope, it's inevitable that their involvement
will deepen and lead to control, but in that process we will have
engineered a sort of reverse takeover, on a cultural level, of the
world's largest confection company."

It was part of a trend. The consumer wouldn't know by looking at the labels that some of the most popular brands of organics
in the alternative food stores are now owned by transnationals.
Mars, Inc. has acquired Seeds of Change, which first came on
the U.S. market in the late 1980s with the stated objective "to
restore biodiversity and revolutionize the way we think about
food." Seeds of Change owners said much the same thing as
Craig Sams when they were questioned about "selling out":
They needed the cash. The alternative press buzzed with talk of
the merger—a company that built its reputation on the importance of providing proper nutrition to American families is now
the property of a junk food purveyor.

But Seeds of Change is hardly alone. Heinz Corporation owns
a long list of organic products with names that evoke the "small is
beautiful" mantra of the movement: Imagine Rice Dream,
Health Valley, Walnut Acres, ShariAnn's and Mountain Sun—
all companies bought in a sweep when Heinz acquired Arrow-
head Mills. Unilever owns the counterculture ice cream line

Ben & Jerry's; Coca-Cola owns the fruit juice and granola bar company Odwalla; Tyson Foods, the controversial U.S. meat-packing enterprise with a reputation for having the worst working conditions in the slaughterhouse business, owns Nature's Farm Organic, the marketers of chickens that apparently enjoyed life before they became dinner.

Craig Sams's dreamy idea that selling to agribusiness constitutes a "reverse takeover" that will teach the big folks about corporate responsibility is difficult to substantiate in view of the robust effort by the transnational food industry to dilute the rules and regulations for determining what should be called "organic." The United States Department of Agriculture (USDA) is the agency that sets the standards for the organic label (most of Canada's organic food lines come from the United States). The original regulations for organic certification were established in the 1970s by the grassroots consumer organizations that had launched the food lines. At the time, the food corporations ignored the process, even when those regulations became enshrined in law.

None of them could have imagined that so many consumers would demand alternatives to their mass-produced products. Now they know: Green sells. Organic is good. The big food companies began to pressure the U.S. government to reverse some of the stringent conditions that assure the integrity of the food that claims to be different and healthier. They want to lift the prohibitions on genetic modification and irradiation and the use of questionable types of fertilizer. Since the rash of corporate takeovers in the organic food movement, the USDA has several times attempted to change the laws to allow hormones and antibiotics in dairy cattle, pesticides on produce and questionable fishmeal as feed for livestock. The Organic Trade Association (OTA) does much of the lobbying for change. Once dominated by back-to-the-land types, the OTA now includes Dole, Kraft, the Grocery Manufacturers of America, General Mills and Tyson. The primary funding for the OTA's policy research and advocacy comes from the biggest corporations.

The supermarkets that now sell Odwalla and Kashi right next to Chips Ahoy and Sugar Pops argue that consumers are the biggest force behind watering down the rules. People want organic food, but they want it to be cheaper. The big corporations with their marketing potential can do that, while at the same time finding more inexpensive sources of the raw ingredients that make up organic foods, mostly by paying farmers less money. The organic movement has now been almost entirely co-opted by the same market forces that compel agribusiness and that have driven farmers into poverty around the world: pushing costs down, pushing profits up.

The corporate analysts are not entirely wrong: The real motivating force in the trend comes from consumers, who don't really care who or what produces their food so long as it's safe to eat, convenient to prepare and inexpensive. William Kendall, for one, believes he can find the middle line. The new custodians of Green & Black's are all blue-chip business types with instincts for hard promotion and competitive selling, but they also claim to be firmly committed to the principals of the counterculture. Prominent among those goals should be the commitment to give farmers a better deal. It was Kendall's people who met with the new manager of the TCGA in Toledo, the New Brunswick wood-supplier cum CUSO volunteer who had promised to turn the TCGA into a proper business.

~

Gregor Hargrove arrived on the scene in 2003, ten years after Craig Sams had first talked to Justino Peck and they decided to make a deal. Hargrove, in retrospect, believes the problems he encountered on his arrival were those of a company that became a victim of its own success. When Hummingbird Hershey pulled out (it's called "the exodus" in Toledo circles), only twenty thousand pounds of cocoa were harvested in the region that season. The first shiploads for Green & Black's in 1993 were in the neighbourhood of sixty thousand pounds. The U.K. company proved to be insatiable and, five years later, farmers sold Green & Black's a half-million pounds. "And now we've had inquiries for 700,000," says Hargrove. "If we'd ever dreamed of it, we could have provided it. We just never dreamed." Hargrove commissioned two buffer nurseries to start producing more trees and installed an additional fifty thousand plants, but they still couldn't keep up with the demand. And that's when the men from Green & Black's started to put the heat on the farmers.

Soon after he arrived, Hargrove met with the executives from Green & Black's, who announced they were tired of the TCGA and accused the farmers of being deadbeats: "Man, these guys [the Toledo cocoa growers] think the sun rises and sets on your ass!" Hargrove replied, "That's rough talk." But Kendall's agents said there would be no more breaks: It was time for the Toledo growers to get their act together.

There were, by now, many different kinds of Green & Black's organic bars, including milk chocolate, almond and hazelnut, but Maya Gold was the only fair trade organic product. The new executives had ambitious plans. But what the corporation could not get around wasn't the organic label but the other little logo on every bar of Maya Gold—that of the Fairtrade Foundation.

The fair trade movement began in 1988 in the Netherlands with Max Havelaar, a forward-looking activist who concluded that commodities from the developing world would always be sold for the cheapest price possible unless companies were forced to pay a premium. The uncompromising fair trade movement is touted as the last best hope for cocoa farmers worldwide—the only chance they have to shrink that growing gap between the hand that picks the bean and the hand that unwraps the candy bar. Activists in the movement have aggressively lobbied Big Chocolate to join fair trade, arguing that the stringent rules of the foundation would be the answer to many of the cocoa companies' problems. The fair trade premiums, they insist, would pay the farmers of Africa enough that they would not be obliged to seek the cheap, or even slave, labour of children in order to meet their expenses. And it would be a great public relations coup for the companies.

The activists have also sought out opportunities to shame Big Chocolate for its record on child labour. Global Exchange, the most visible and insistent of the fair trade advocates in the United States, has a very effective program in the school system, warning young Americans that their consumption of mainstream chocolate brands means that children in other countries cannot go to school. The message is oversimplified and stark, but it has the desired effect on impressionable young minds. The *Fair Trade Chocolate Activity Book* for grades three to six is all about injustice in the production of a chocolate bar. The message couldn't be simpler nor more accurate: "Cocoa farmers are poor because they do not get paid very much for their cocoa." Children are instructed to circle the coins that add up to twenty-five cents, the amount paid for a pound of cocoa beans. On another page, they can circle the coins that add up to eighty cents, the amount a farmer gets for a pound of beans under the fair trade system.

Global Exchange and its sister organization in Canada stage rallies and campaigns at Halloween, warning kids of the slave labour that went into their goodie bag and lobbying schools to stop selling questionable chocolate products to raise money for gym equipment. They held protest rallies outside screenings of the recently released *Charlie and the Chocolate Factory* and got favourable coverage even in the conservative magazine *Forbes*.

Global Exchange has also joined the class action suit filed by the International Labor Rights Fund against Nestlé, Archer Daniels Midland and Cargill. The fair trade advocates allege that Big Chocolate has an unfair competitive advantage over fair trade chocolate sellers since the companies are willing to use "forced child labour" to harvest their raw ingredients. The suit claims that the three transnationals have enjoyed "unjust enrichment" at the cost of fair trade chocolate manufacturers, who must spend extra money to ensure forced labour is not a part of their product.

So far, there's little chance of Big Chocolate jumping on the bandwagon of fair trade as they have for organics. Given the pressure they are exerting in the organic foods industry to decrease standards, perhaps it's just as well. Susan Smith, of the powerful Chocolate Manufacturers Association, says plainly that "fair trade is not for us."

Gregor Hargrove isn't sure that fair trade is for him, either. While fair trade is, in theory, one of the most ethical movements of our time, in practice it generates a cumbersome bureaucracy. "I spend my life in this crap," he declares in his Punta Gorda office, gesturing towards the mountain of paperwork necessary to satisfy the fair trade headquarters in Bonn, Germany, where international standards for fair trade are enshrined in a series of rules. Most of the fair trade agencies, especially those in Europe and the United Kingdom, register in Bonn. But for so many operations in the developing world, the fair trade administration has become just another burdensome chore.

Hargrove mocks the Bonn fair traders as pencil pushers with no roots in the real world, in particular the one in which he lives. "The administration has taken over," says Hargrove of the technocrats. What comes out of the German offices is a mishmash that "looks excellent on their desk in the First World and looks like a Frankenstein monster by the time it hits my desk in the Third World. So what I say is that it's becoming a hell of a good deal for First-World bureaucrats and it's becoming less of a good deal for producers, and we have to pay for it."

The fair trade levies are staggering for small operations like the TCGA. Hargrove estimates the TCGA pays twenty to twenty-five per cent of its income in fees, including all the expenses of the apparatchiks who come over periodically to conduct inspections. "I don't know how long the list of prosperous fair trade cooperatives and associations would be, but I'm thinking it's not very long," he says. What Hargrove worries about most is that the farmers would be incapable of completing the complex—despite being in English it is often incomprehensible—paperwork on their own. Yet the fair trade organization insists it be done. It's not that the farmers can't read, it's that no one unfamiliar with the workings of a European bureaucracy could make any sense of the documents. Hargrove hasn't identified a single member of the co-op who could manage it, should he leave.

A tour of the cocoa fields around Toledo bears out what Hargrove is saying. Few of the farmers have the literacy skills required for full documentary compliance. An American Peace Corps worker spent half a day trying to explain to the farmers what "alphabetical order" means, an obsession with the hard-heads in Bonn, who like information submitted to them in highly organized lists.

But mostly, according to Hargrove, the Maya don't seem amenable to change. The farmers know what they must know about farming cocoa—about the soil, the plants, the weather conditions—but their collective wisdom comes to them naturally, through instinct and practical experience. They have no knowledge of the science of organics or of the fair trade A-B-C labelling requirements, nor are they much interested in learning systems they don't really understand. All the farmers understand is that there is a market for their beans if they grow them a certain way. But there was also once a market for their beans if they grew them an entirely different way. Markets are funny like that. Growing beans without pesticides and being able to send your children to school is, of course, superior to what the farmers experienced earlier. But how long before the bubble bursts, and the fickle consumer wants something else?

Justino Peck is frustrated by the skepticism of his fellow farmers. "They need to sacrifice the time to get started, and you have to stick out the lean years," he says. He thinks the farmers often give up too soon, or they don't tend their cocoa trees well enough to get the high yields necessary for prosperity.

Peck's face appeared in newspapers around the world a few years ago when the fair trade people presented him as a kind of ambassador of fair trade chocolate. It was reminiscent of when the missionaries and conquistadors brought Mayan natives to the Spanish court to show the monarchy what interesting human specimens the New World could produce. But Justino didn't feel used. "That's just the way of the world," he says with a sigh.

~

In early 2005, the multinational corporation Cadbury Schweppes bought controlling interest of Green & Blacks. William Kendall told the London's Financial Times that the company "stands to make a lot of money for our shareholder and plant a fertile seed in a larger company to carry on fair trade." But he was quickly put on the defensive when customers bombarded Green & Blacks with complaints that the organization was selling out. Kendall issued a statement on the company's website: "We do not have time for prejudice at Green & Blacks and this includes a prejudice that all big companies are bad."

For Gregor Hargrove, the jury is still out. When he heard the news of the take-over, the New Brunswicker thought of home, where the McCains were also very acquisitive, and Hargrove remembered "what happens when big companies take over little ones." But his first experience of working for a large multinational is that he feels he has more room to manoeuvre. "There's a certain comfort in having a big company behind us," says Hargrove, warily. But then again, he adds, maybe Cadbury has learned a few things over the past hundred years.

Epilogue

IN ALL FAIRNESS

We want a five cent chocolate bar;
Eight cents is going too darn far;
We want a five cent chocolate bar,
We want a five cent bar.

—SONG COMPOSED BY THE CHILDREN OF THE
CHOCOLATE PROTEST OF 1947

THE CHOCOLATE "CRUSADE" IN THE SPRING OF 1947 WAS one of the strangest strikes of the twentieth century in Canada—or anywhere, really. It began as a proud outburst of youthful assertion, emblematic of new freedoms recently won on the battlefield, a call for justice and fairness. The enthusiasm of a handful of children on Vancouver Island quickly spread from one end of the country to the other. Parades of young people snaked their way through city streets in Regina, Ottawa and Quebec City; crowds of youngsters carried homemade placards throughout the Maritimes; and a large, noisy mob stormed the provincial legislature in Victoria.

The campaign was a demand that the world be a fairer place for children—at least for those privileged enough to enjoy chocolate. The big chocolate bar companies had jacked up their prices to eight cents for a bar of candy. Young people throughout Canada thought it should remain at five cents, as Milton Hershey in the United States and the Ganong Brothers of New Brunswick had done in Canada. The kids took to the streets to protest what they regarded as unfair.

Crispy Crunch, Jersey Milk, Aero Bar, Coffee Crisp, O Henry!, Sweet Marie, Burnt Almond and Malted Milk were among the delights one could buy for a nickel in Canada and the United States during the 1930s and early '40s. But according to manufacturers, the price was artificially low. The end of wartime wage and price controls meant chocolate bar companies would have to pay more than twice the price for their cocoa beans and substantially more for labour—wages had almost doubled since the 1930s. Those added expenses would have to be passed on to the customer. Everything was now increasing in price and—with the exception of a very few outspoken housewives' consumer groups—people grudgingly accepted inflation as the side effect of a normalizing economy. But the children didn't see it that way.

The crusade started in sleepy Ladysmith and neighbouring Chemainus on Vancouver Island where young Bruce Saunders, Parker Williams, Bert Gisborne and Gerald Williams rallied their friends to picket a local ice cream parlour called the Wigwam, their common source of penny candy and chocolate bars. News of the protest inspired other children on the island to launch their own campaign, and within days dozens of them swarmed the British Columbia Legislature, shouting "Bring Back Our Nickel Bar" and shutting down House business for part of the day.

The movement soon caught on in Regina and Weyburn, Saskatchewan; then on to Winnipeg, St. John and Halifax. More than three thousand young people marched down Toronto's Bloor Street after school and picketed a candy store on Lippincott Avenue. In Ottawa, they mobbed Parliament Hill and chanted that they would rather eat worms than eight-cent bars.

A forest of homemade protest signs sprouted up across the country. "Don't be a Sucker! Don't Buy 8-Cent Bars!" "Eight-Cent Chocolate Bars—Phooey," "Candy's Dandy but Eight Cents Isn't Handy," "Knuckle Down for Nickel Bars," and the most emblematic of them all, "What This Country Needs Is a Good Five-Cent Candy Bar."

The crusade quickly captured the imaginations of adults, who resented the price increases on all consumer goods but had thought it unpatriotic to complain. Now the movement had enormous support from the media and even politicians, all of whom were fed up with the rising cost of living.

Initially, the candy manufacturers tried to reason with the children. As Canadian chocolate bar sales dived by eighty per cent in a period of weeks, Rowntree, now a large multinational corporation with production in Canada, published open letters to its consumers, explaining things from its point of view. The open letters lamented the increased cost of cocoa beans purchased from faraway lands in equatorial Africa and Central America. There was also the ballooning price of cane sugar imported from the Caribbean, and finally the problem that post-war full employment meant the company needed to compete for labourers, unlike in the days of the Great Depression.

Rowntree published newspaper appeals that ended with its advertising slogan: "Rowntree's Chocolate Bars Are a Nourishing and Pleasurable Form of Supplementary Food: Buy Some Today." Chocolate company spin doctors hit the radio waves to talk to the boys and girls about the hard reality of market forces and the global pressures on commodity prices. But the children would have none of it. They had Big Chocolate on the ropes, and they weren't going to relent.

But a confluence of interests suddenly turned against the strikers, effectively shutting the protest down and blackballing its juvenile leaders. Following several weeks of effective protest, the right-wing *Toronto Evening Telegram* wagged a paternalistic finger at the kids and their supporters, warning ominously that "candy [was] a dandy weapon." Almost instantly priests, police officers, youth clubs, school principals and parents mobilized to stop what had suddenly been characterized as a threat to national security.

According to the community leaders, principally led by the Royal Canadian Mounted Police, who feared the children were

delinquents threatening civic order, the protest was not so inno-
cent. The boycott was a part of the Red Menace, cooked up in
Moscow under Stalin's direction. And it could not be tolerated.
The strike was rebranded in the *Telegraph* the "Communist
Crusade," along with charges that subversives lurked in the shadows, manipulating the country's youth. "Chocolate bars and
world revolution may seem poles apart but to the devious
Communist mind there's a close relationship," wrote the
Telegram. "The indignant students parading their placards and
demanding the five-cent candy bar have become another instru-
ment in the grand strategy of the creation of chaos.

Winston Churchill had just declared that an "iron curtain"
had descended over Europe. Cold War jitters would soon become
hysteria around the world. Senator Joe McCarthy was revving up
a potent conspiracy theory that would darken discourse in the
United States for much of the 1950s. Ottawa had been the epicentre of an international uproar in 1945 with the sensational
disclosures of the existence of a Soviet defector named Igor
Gouzenko and also that the Soviets had an active network of
espionage here and in the U.S.; the Communists were everywhere, stirring up dissent, even it seemed over eight-cent chocolate bars.

It didn't help when it was discovered that there was, in fact, an
active socialist influence in the "Communist Crusade" for candy
justice. The National Federation of Labour Youth, affiliated with
the Canadian Communist Party, helped organize many of the
larger rallies while socialist youth groups were among the more
vociferous protesters. But any objective reading of the contemporary newspaper accounts and CBC interviews of the time reveals
the essential spontaneity of the movement. It was an honest
expression of a childish desire to have some control in their small
part of a complex chocolate universe.

Gradually, the hysteria subsided. The tone of the response to
the children moderated but was no less stern.

In May 1947 the *Telegram* wrote, "No one is more anxious than this newspaper to see the return of the five cent chocolate bar; in fact, the return of the five-cent soft drink and the nickel cigar. They are all eminently typical symbols of that strange way of life we call democracy. There is, in fact, little evidence that such commodities are available for the equivalent price in Moscow." But the item concludes that there are more important values at stake. Children in a democracy just have to understand the real cost of candy, which presumably is to support capitalism.

In 1947, Canadian children were told that the democracy their fathers and grandfathers had just fought to secure included the privilege of paying the market price for their chocolate. The children lost what, from the start was probably a hopeless battle. The price went up in spite of their actions. It wasn't fair, but they went on buying chocolate bars.

~

The story of chocolate has a lot to do with what is fair. Bartolomé de las Casas, Henry Woodd Nevinson, Guy-André Kieffer, Marx Aristide, and many others, were driven by an intuitive sense of fairness. Each man in his time was offended by what he saw in the cocoa groves of equatorial colonies and post-colonies. They provoked the disapproval of the powerful to make their controversial points. Fairness or its grown-up sibling, justice, demanded a better deal for the people who produced the raw material for luxuries like chocolate. But they were ignored or vanquished by powers greater than their moral rectitude. They were up against elites and the ethical insensitivity of the marketplace. The greatest impediment of all was the moral ambiguity of a consuming public that has always been quick to decry injustice, but also determined to enjoy the fruits of the earth at the lowest prices possible. The right to do so is still considered, by many consumers, to be only fair.

After the candy crusade, prices rose steadily to where they are today. An eight-cent chocolate bar is now as unimaginable as gasoline at forty cents a gallon. And yet, with a few exceptions, the people who toil to produce the raw material for chocolate bars remain excluded from the benefits of higher prices and unprecedented demand.

~

In the spring, when the snow melts and the detritus of an entire winter is left clinging to the fences and shrubs of my Toronto neighbourhood, the most ubiquitous garbage is the chocolate bar wrapper. Hundreds of the brightly coloured paper and foil packages tangle themselves in bare bushes, looking like tinsel clinging to dead Christmas trees thrown out with the January trash. Mars Bars, Snickers, Mr. Big, Kit Kat, Almond Joy, Mounds, Reese's Peanut Butter Cups, and Caramilk decorate the dull spring cityscape with their cheerful promises of sensory delight.

I watch the young people as they leave a nearby 7-Eleven convenience store clutching bars of chocolate, soon to be devoured in seconds. Each one costs a dollar, a small sum for most teenagers in our world of privilege. In supermarkets, mothers hand candy bars to restless children to buy their silence during shopping expeditions. Chocolate milk, chocolate cake, ice cream, Halloween treats and cocoa cookies are all abundant and cheap. Teams of youth canvass city neighbourhoods selling boxes of chocolate-covered almonds to raise funds for school trips and sports equipment. All of this seems fair and reasonable. Chocolate has become a universal luxury, blindly crossing ethnic, religious and national divisions—a reasonably priced frivolity for everyone, except those who've never heard of it or can't afford to buy it. Ironically, that unenviable group includes the people who produce its most essential ingredient.

The young Malian boys I met who went off to find work and adventure in Côte d'Ivoire and spent a part of their lives in forced labour growing cocoa, learned the hard way about the true price of a chocolate bar, even though they've never seen one. Now they know it was a price that included the incalculable cost of the enslavement of hundreds of children like themselves, kids who would have never known and will never know what chocolate tastes like; now they know that the true history of chocolate was written in blood and sweat of countless generations of people more or less like them. For as far as anyone can see into the future, there is little likelihood that this ancient and enduring injustice will be corrected.

SOURCE NOTES

Introduction: In the Garden of Good and Evil

The interviews here were conducted in May and June 2005 in the centre and southwest of Côte d'Ivoire. There is ample information on the Internet about the chemical benefits of chocolate, though we should be aware that many of the research findings that extol the virtues of chocolate, true or not, are funded by the chocolate companies. See the *New York Times Magazine* article "Eat Chocolate, Live Longer?" by Jon Gertner from October 10, 2004, for a good debunking of some chocolate health claims.

Chapter One: Death by Chocolate

The most authoritative history of chocolate is *The True History of Chocolate* by Sophie and Michael Coe, the source of much of the history in this section. Additional material came from the research of Boston University scholars Patricia A. McAnany and Satoru Murata, *From Chocolate Pots to Maya Gold: Belizean Cacao Farmers through the Ages,* of which I was generously given a working copy; Henry Kamen's book *Philip of Spain;* Jim Tuck's *History of Mexico: Affirmative Action and Hernán Cortés;* Anthony Pagden's translation of Hernán Cortés's *Letters from Mexico;* C.A. Burland's *Montezuma: Lord of the Aztecs;* and Richard Lee Marks's *Cortés: The Great Adventurer and the Fate of Aztec Mexico.*

Chapter Two: Liquid Gold

The sources cited for Chapter One were used again here, as well as the authoritative *A History of the Modern World* by R.R. Palmer and Joel Colton. Adam Hochschild's book *Bury the Chains: Prophets and Rebels in the Fight to Free an Empire's Slaves* was a source of information on the slave trade, as was Peter Macinnis's book *Bittersweet: The Story of Sugar.*

Chapter Three: Cocoa on Trial

Material for this chapter came from *Honderd Jaar (Hundred Years)*, a centennial book published in 1928 on the hundredth anniversary of the firm J.C. Van Houten and Son, parts of which were superbly translated for me by my CBC colleague Jet Belgraver. The *Anti-Slavery Reporter* is available at the University of Birmingham Special Collections, along with the Cadbury Brothers archive, from which much material came. More material on the Rowntree family and its company came from the Borthwick Institute for Archives at the University of York, U.K. Lowell J. Satre's book *Chocolate on Trial: Slavery, Politics and the Ethics of Business* was an important source for this chapter, especially for the dramatic trial anecdotes and for information about Henry Woodd Nevinson, of whom little is written. Adam Hochschild's book *King Leopold's Ghost: A Story of Greed, Terror, and Heroism in Colonial Africa* has the extraordinary story of Edmund Dene Morel and his battle with the monarch of Belgium.

Chapter Four: The Geopolitics of a Hershey's Kiss

Material about Milton Snavely Hershey and his company came from the Hershey archive and from oral history in Hershey, Pennsylvania, as well as from residents of Hershey who had personal knowledge of the history. More material about both Hershey and the Mars empire came from Joel Glenn Brenner's book *The Emperors of Chocolate: Inside the Secret World of Hershey and Mars; Crisis in Candyland: Melting the Chocolate Shell of the Mars Family Empire* by Jan Pottker; *Hershey: Milton S. Hershey's Extraordinary Life of Wealth, Empire and Utopian Dreams* by Michael D'Antonio; *Milton Hershey:*

Chocolate King, Town Builder by Charnan Simon; and *Chocolate by Hershey: A Story about Milton S. Hershey* by Betty Burford.

Chapter Five: No Sweetness Here

In addition to travel and research in Côte d'Ivoire, I consulted Peter Schwab's book *Africa: A Continent Self-Destructs*; Joseph E. Stiglitz's *Globalization and Its Discontents*; *Africans and Their History* by Joseph E. Harris; *Hungry for Trade: How the Poor Pay for Free Trade* by John Madeley; and *La guerre du cacao: Histoire secrète d'un embargo* by Jean-Louis Gombeaud, Corinne Moutout and Stephen Smith. Additional material came from *Africa Report* articles from the 1970s about problems with the African Miracle; *The Economist* articles on Côte d'Ivoire from the 1960s and 1970s; United Nations Conference on Trade and Development reports; World Bank reports from the 1980s: *Structural Readjustment for Côte d'Ivoire*; "Employment Problems and Policies in the Ivory Coast" from the *International Labor Review* of December 1971; the 1961 edition of *Political Africa: A Who's Who of Personalities and Parties*; and the 1961 review *Political Parties and National Integration in Tropical Africa*, edited by James S. Coleman and Carl G. Rosberg, Jr. For material about Ghana (Gold Coast) and its beginnings in cocoa, I consulted the 1966 *Journal of Economic History*.

Chapter Six: The Disposables

Most of the material for this chapter came from first-person interviews with Abdoulaye Macko and Salia Kante; with people working at Save the Children Canada and the Malian NGOs Mali Enjeu and Guamina; with the BBC's Humphrey Hawksley; and with representatives of the government of Côte d'Ivoire. Additional material came from newspaper accounts, BBC reports, UNICEF reports and U.S. State Department reports.

Chapter Seven: Dirty Chocolate

Material for this chapter came from travel in West Africa and interviews with the principal players in Canada, the United States and Europe, including the NGOs; the labour organizations; politicians; the chocolate companies by way of their umbrella organization, the Chocolate Manufacturers Association; and the confectionery Manufacturers Association of Canada and their public relations people. Other sources used for this chapter include reports by Anti-Slavery International, in particular the exhaustive 2004 study called *The Cocoa Industry in West Africa: A History of Exploitation*, which has much useful field study information; a series of detailed reports by Anita Sheth of Save the Children Canada; reports by the International Institute of Tropical agriculture, which performed the survey; and the Harkin-Engel Protocol.

Chapter Eight: Chocolate Soldiers

This chapter was developed almost entirely from interviews with cocoa farmers and their workers, both in Côte d'Ivoire and in Mali, plus interviews with political players in Côte d'Ivoire, including Roger Gnohite and Charles Blé Goudé, and with NGOs, both on and off the record. Additional secondary source material came from reports of Amnesty International, Human Rights Watch and the International Crisis Group.

Chapter Nine: Class Action Cocoa

Material for this chapter came from travel and interviews in Côte d'Ivoire and Mali, and from interviews with principal players in the Protocol, including the NGOs, labour leaders, Winrock International, the World Cocoa Foundation and the International Labor Rights Fund, supplemented with material from all of their websites.

Chapter Ten: The Man Who Knew Too Much

This chapter was built almost entirely from interviews conducted in Côte d'Ivoire, Canada and France with the friends, family, colleagues and enemies of Guy-André Kieffer, most of whom are named in the text. A number of them chose to be interviewed anonymously because they feared for their safety.

Chapter Eleven: Stolen Fruit

This chapter was crafted from interviews in Côte d'Ivoire with the principal players of the cocoa *filière*, plus members of the cocoa cooperatives and farmers. Many of them cannot be named for their safety. On-the-ground research was also done in Fulton, New York.

Chapter Twelve: Bittersweet Victory

Material for this chapter came from on-the-ground travels in Belize, interviews with farmers and their association, and interviews with Green & Black's, Global Exchange and other experts on fair trade, plus extensive archival documents on Hummingbird Hershey and its operations in the Toledo district.

Epilogue: In All Fairness

Travesty Productions' film *The Five Cent War* is the best source of the story of the children's chocolate strike. Additional material for this chapter came from archives at the Toronto Reference Library.

ACKNOWLEDGEMENTS

THIS BOOK COULD NOT HAVE BEEN WRITTEN, OR HAVE BEEN as informed as I believe it is, without the efforts of Maggie MacIntyre, my researcher and editorial assistant. Maggie travelled to Great Britain, France, the United States and Belize for this project, using her extraordinary range of talents to suss out the stories and facts, whether they were to be found with a reluctant interview subject or in a labyrinthine library archive. My first debt of gratitude is to her.

Ange Aboa was a tireless, amusing and very informed escort for my travels in Côte d'Ivoire, Mali, Burkina Faso and Ghana. Koffi Benoît did all the driving for many hard weeks over deplorable roads, but he still had the energy and wit to negotiate lower "fees" with the police and soldiers who extorted money from us almost on an hourly basis. Ange and Koffi made a difficult, often-dangerous trip enjoyable.

I was also happy to have the reassurance of Benoît Gauthier, first secretary of political and cultural affairs for the Canadian Embassy in Abidjan, who kept a bead on me during all my movements in the country, and then kept me informed about the changing landscape of Côte d'Ivoire.

I will never forget the company of Youchaou Traoré, who travelled with me in Mali, translating and explaining things patiently. His breadth of knowledge and depth of personal experience is only exceeded by his warmth and charm. Youchaou's family took me in, fed me and entertained me graciously. Special thanks to Salia Kante for his honesty and integrity and for his endless struggle to help children.

Jean-François Bélanger, Radio Canada's reporter in West Africa, was extremely helpful, finding me contacts, numbers and background. I am in his debt. Humphrey Hawksley of the BBC gave me the insights and advantage of his extensive experience both in Africa and on the cocoa file; Bernard Taylor of Partnership Africa Canada and David Lord of the Canadian Peacebuilding Coordinating Committee shared with me their extensive contacts in West Africa.

In France, the friends, colleagues and family members of Guy-André Kieffer were especially generous. Of those who can be named, I would like to thank Aline Richard, Léonard Vincent of Reporters Without Borders, Thomas Hoffnung of Libération and Antoine Glaser of *La Lettre du Continent*. The others, who remain anonymous, know that I would like to thank them as well, and one day I will be able to do it more publicly.

In Belize, many thanks must go to everyone at the Toledo Cacao Growers Association—Gregor Hargrove, in true Maritime style, was frank, welcoming and passionate about his work; Armando Choco, Annamarie Cho and Oscar Canelo shared their first-hand knowledge of cocoa culture; and the farmers shared their stories of struggle, sweat and success.

Anita Sheth was the first person to bring to my attention the issue of child labour exploitation in cocoa, and I admire her for her tireless pursuit of children's rights. Richard Swift of the *New Internationalist* shared with me his cocoa research in West Africa; Professor Patricia McAnany of Boston University gave me generous access to her research as well.

Libraries and archives are essential for any book like this. I am indebted to the Toronto Reference Library, York University Library in York, England, the Cadbury papers in the University of Birmingham Special Collections, the Hershey archive in Hershey, Pennsylvania, and the ICCO library in London.

Jet Belgraver, my colleague at CBC TV, provided reliable information on the Dutch cocoa industry, blowing through a fair bit of folklore, and she also translated much material, even after she knew that this book might damage her ability to enjoy chocolate in the future. Other colleagues who routinely fed my craving for news about the cocoa industry, while knowingly affecting their future indulgence of chocolate, include Harry Schachter, Dan Schwartz and Jay Bertagnolli. Special thanks to Alex Shprintsen for his moral support and for procuring for me the best chocolate I sampled in the course of writing this book. It's made in Russia!

Don Sedgwick and Shaun Bradley are my agents but that doesn't come close to explaining what they do for me, both personally and professionally. In addition to careful and helpful reading of this manuscript and many fine suggestions for how to make the book better, they have been much moral support throughout the project.

Anne Collins, publisher of Random House Canada is, of course, the person who made this book possible. Her encouragement to me as an editor along with her rigour as a journalist made this book much stronger than it deserved to be with my talents. I also had the great pleasure of working for the first time with Pamela Murray, managing editor at Random House Canada, who performed some hard slogs through every version of the manuscript (which will be happily relegated to the recycling bin) and helped me make huge improvements, while encouraging me to continue. Scott Sellers, Random House of Canada's director of marketing strategy, gave me much encouragement for this book and I know he'll get me through the hard sell as well. Kevin Kelly, who did the publicity photos for this book, must be mentioned. He not only made me look reasonably good—an almost impossible task—but also was a joy to work with.

My husband, Linden MacIntyre, knows what he did to help me write this work and if I spelled out my entire acknowledgement to him it would be longer than the book itself. Suffice it to say, you wouldn't be reading these pages today if not for him.

INDEX

Toblerone, 87
Tocqueville, Alexis de, 111
Togo, 280–1
Toledo Cacao Growers Association
        (TCGA). *See* TCGA (Toledo
        Cacao Growers Association)
Toledo district, Belize, 267, 269
Toronto Evening Telegram, 297, 298, 299
Torture Victim Protection Act, 207
transnational corporations, 259
        and organic foods, 287–8
        See also multinational corporations
transporters, 188–90, 200–1
Transvaal, 65, 66
Traoré, Alassane, 200
Traoré, Madou, 127–9, 132, 137, 138, 158
triangular trade, 42, 56
La Tribune, 219, 226, 228
Trinidad, 81–2
True Story (Finkel), 159
Truth for Guy-André Kieffer Association,
        234
Two Million Girls for Gbagbo, 249–50
Tyson Foods, 288

Uhrich, Richard, 99
Ukraine, gun merchants in, 212
UNESCO, 268
UNICEF, 130–1, 168, 182, 204
Unilever, 287–8
United Kingdom
        African colonies, 88, 97–8
        and cocoa trade, 53–4
        colonies, 81
        Department for International
                Development, 284
        Foreign Office, 65, 66, 67, 68, 70
        holdings in Africa, 65
        and introduction of cocoa to Gold
                Coast, 96–7
        Mars in, 87–8
        in Nigeria, 104
        organic chocolate in, 281
        and Portugese, 65–6
        Portuguese cocoa in, 58
        press, 68–9
        tariffs on cocoa beans, 82
United Nations
        child domestic workers in New York
                City, 134
        on demonstration in Abidjan, 209

        on Green & Black's, 284
        High Commission for Human
                Rights, 210–11
        peacekeepers, 172, 174, 178, 195
United Nations Conference on Trade and
        Development (UNCTAD), 117
United States
        Agency for International
                Development (USAID), 274
        agricultural appropriations bill,
                139–40
        Belize and, 271, 272
        blood diamonds and, 193
        business interests, and ATCA, 207
        on child trafficking, 151
        and chocolate for troops, 247–8
        civil war, 84
        on cocoa as product of slave labour,
                84
        cocoa supply sources, 272
        and Cuba, 84–5
        Customs Department, 149, 150
        Department of Agriculture (USDA),
                288
        Department of Labour, 194
        and labour practices in Americas, 84
        on Malian children in Ivorian planta-
                tions, 133
        organic chocolate in, 286
        Portuguese cocoa in, 58
        Senate Agricultural Committee, 144
        slavery and, 84
        State Department, 133, 151
        and unrest in Côte d'Ivoire, 180
        Ways and Means Committee, 83–4

Van Houten, Coenraad, 46–7, 49
Van Houten press, 49, 50, 58
Vaucelles, Stéphane de, 227, 228
Velasquez, Diego, 19–20, 26, 27
Venezuela, 44
        Criollo beans from, 48
Vera Cruz, 17, 19–20, 21, 22, 23, 26
Le Vieux. *See* Houphouët-Boigny, Félix
Voltaire, 41

wages, 59
        for child workers, 121, 122, 143
        Congo labourers and, 57
Walter Baker Company. *See* Baker
        (Walter) Company

CAROL OFF has witnessed and reported on many of the world's conflicts, from the fall of Yugoslavia to the U.S.-led "war on terror." She is presently the co-host of CBC radio's current affairs program *As It Happens* and has won numerous awards for her documentaries. She lives in Toronto.